HOME/SCHOOL/COMMUNITY INTERACTION

What We Know and Why We Don't Know More

Cynthia Wallat

Kent State University

Richard Goldman

Nova University

Charles E. Merrill Publishing Company
A Bell & Howell Company
Columbus   Toronto   London   Sydney

Published by
Charles E. Merrill Publishing Company
A Bell & Howell Company
Columbus, Ohio 43216

This book was set in Optima.

The production editor was Dawna Ramage Ayers.

The cover was prepared by Will Chenoweth.

Library of Congress Catalog Card Number: 78-71156

International Standard Book Number: 0-675-08281-1

1 2 3 4 5 6 7 8 9 10—85 84 83 82 81 80 79

Printed in the United States of America

Preface

This book is intended as a guide, a manual of reference, or a set of working tools for parents, educators, and students who intend to contribute their services to educational concerns. It provides a summation of what we know about the development of school/community communication and a guide to future ventures which recognize the school's capacity for positive contributions to society. Although we have delineated the issues of context and of influences on building school/community communication into specific chapters, you should keep in mind that all these areas are related.

The organization of the book is broad in scope and therefore offers alternatives for use in undergraduate and graduate classes, in-service meetings, parent-teacher meeting topics, administrative seminars, as well as shared reading between parent and teacher. The written text provides a summary of what we know and what is going on. This can be read continuously or can be discussed by specific topic, for example, community development in practice, parents as educators, or teachers as social technologists. Throughout the book you will also find descriptions of successful home/school programs, parent education programs, advice articles, and references to inexpensive information sources. These, too, may serve as the focus of class or group discussions. We will also point out data from research studies to help you convince others of the importance of school community communication. In addition, we will help put you in touch with the organizations that are available to help you implement your goals.

When you are familiar with the content, you will be able to relate how parts of the whole picture promote or deflect from effective home/school communication in your community. For example, based on past activity in community development, role expectations, and development of attitudes towards political activity: Have I taken into consideration how change will be perceived? How long do I expect the people involved to remain interested? Will change appear threatening to community members, teachers, and administrators? What are the present priorities in the community that are competing for people's time and money? What value will be attached to my friends' and/or colleagues' concerns? Have I attended to developing the expectations of individual community members, school board members, administrators, parents, and teachers? Have I attended to developing support systems by gathering up-to-date information on what areas of agreement have been reached in the past in order to remind parents and/or colleagues that progress is possible? Have I arranged for keeping up-to-date on publication and discussion of inexpensive source books? Have I kept my own optimism by calling the Network toll-free number when I am stuck on a problem?

In addition to serving as a checklist for helping to answer the questions presented above, the activities mentioned throughout the book may serve as a means of clarifying the content in the written text. Many of the activities would be completed more efficiently and effectively if parents and educators (presently employed and in training) completed them together.

Richard: Cynthia, should we introduce ourselves to the readers?

Cynthia: We better. The readers may want to know where "we are coming from"—our values, experiences, prejudices as they relate to issues of school/community relationships. Why don't you begin?

Richard: OK. I'm one of those people with multiple roles—parent, teacher, teacher educator, child advocate, parent advocate, teacher advocate, union member, political party member, department member.

Cynthia: I bet you find yourself in some interesting dilemmas!

Richard: You're right! I'll discuss them in the book. Who are you?

Cynthia: I have the same multiple roles that you have. In addition, I'm interested in school/community relations in the Soviet Union, China, and Europe.

Richard: They don't know much about us yet—they'll learn more as they progress through the book. Should I tell the readers you can't stand to be called "Cindy"?

Cynthia: OK, "Richie."

Richard: All right! You made your point. I do want to inform the readers that our dialogues will continue throughout the book. These dialogues will enable us to share our viewpoints and confusion. A second purpose for the dialogues will be to suggest learning activities for the readers.
What should the reader do now?

Cynthia: Turn to page 3 and begin to become involved with the complex and critical issues of school/community relationships.

Contents

v

Contents

Groundwork PART I

Introduction to the School and the Community

The concept of cooperation and responsibility between American families and their educational institutions is not a question of whether or not there should be a working relationship. "The idea that people who are affected by public agency decisions should play an active role in the decision-making process"[1] is, after all, a vital part of our democracy. The translation of the ideal into practice has been given a push by recent evidence from early childhood program evaluations that have concluded that parental involvement is associated with program success (Butler 1970; Gray 1970; King 1970; Adkins 1971; Roby 1971; Lille 1975; Stevens 1976). Studies concerned with student achievement at elementary and secondary levels also have suggested that parental attitudes toward education and their "direct" involvement in education is associated with academic success (Pomfret 1972; Mattox and Rich 1977).

Whether parental involvement in decision making will be translated from the ideal to the practical at all levels of our education system is not insured. An analysis of recent attempts to widen the scope of community participation in policy formation included the following description:

A distinguishing characteristic of recent decades has been the recognition that the social upheaval we have witnessed is in part a reflection of two different factors: the different community systems are interactive; they need

---

[1]Seymour Sarason, *The Community at the Bargaining Table, A Report on the Community's Role in Collective Bargaining in the Schools* (Boston: Institute for Responsive Education, 1975), p. 54.

each other, but their individual modes of governance and decision-making do not facilitate effective and productive conflict resolution.[2]

One could spend a great deal of time adding fuel to the latter description. It is a far easier task to print admonitions that we "need each other" or to find criticisms of parents, teachers, administrators, and school board members, than to locate reports of members of the educational community working toward effective and productive conflict resolution.

As a practical problem and as a theoretical problem, the management of relationships between schools and their families and neighborhoods has not heretofore received much systematic attention. Practitioners usually offer examples from their practices but provide few guiding principles.[3]

The remaining chapters of this book are concerned with approaching the question of your involvement in building future effective communication among members of the educational community by synthesizing what is known and what's going on. We cannot begin to solve the major problems in school/community relations unless we have some understanding of what forms of involvement are considered appropriate by different sectors of the educational community. Without awareness of what type of involvement is considered appropriate, it appears premature to criticize the entire educational system for not building mechanisms to accommodate involvement. Our review of the situation to date is intended as a focus for you for the activities that follow. Without a focus, assertions and arguments will continue to end on as fruitless a note as the following argument between theorists and program developers:

I know you believe you understand what you think I said, but I'm not sure you realize that what you heard is not precisely what I meant to say.[4]

Richard: Are you saying that despite evidence that parent involvement adds to student achievement, there are still schools that aren't going to implement parent involvement? That is going to upset many of our readers! Let's take it out.
Cynthia: You can't be serious! This is the theme for the entire book.
Richard: I know, but we're going to have many professionals upset

[2]Ibid.

[3]Eugene Litwak and H. J. Meyer, *School, Family and Neighborhood: The Theory and Practice of School-Community Relations* (New York: Columbia University Press, 1974), p. vii.

[4]D. Bruce Gardner, *The Influence of Theoretical Conceptions of Human Development on the Practice of Early Childhood Education.* ERIC File ED 033 766, 1970.

with us. Let's change the theme slightly or maybe we
shouldn't. . . .

Cynthia: Let's put the question to our readers. We'll ask them to write
their reactions to your statements above and return to the
reactions after they finish the book.

Richard: A means of self-assessment?

What We "Know" and Why We Don't "Know" More

The Victims

Much time, money, and energy have been directed toward describing the lack of communication, trust, and interest and the role conflicts between members of the educational community. The vicious cycles have included: (1) everyone's blaming everyone else, (2) passing the buck, (3) attempting to entrench one group as the sole decision maker, and (4) neglecting implementation of legal statutes that are aimed at insuring "a public school system which is genuinely public, (and) open to participation by a broad cross-section of the local populace."[1]

With this much attention having been directed at locating the "villains," it is possible to lose sight of the "victims" of the power struggle —the children.

It is possible for the U.S. Department of Agriculture to count the nation's cows. The Department of Commerce knows how much we spend on beans, barley, booze, books, and bananas—or so they say. And we know how many board feet of lumber we can cut from vast forests scattered across the continent.

But it is far more difficult to determine how many delinquents there are in a city like Chicago, or how many children can't read at grade level in New Jersey. Nor do we know the number of creative youngsters in America who see their creative sparks extinguished before they reach the age of ten, or how

---

[1]Robert J. Braun, *Teachers and Power* (New York: Simon and Schuster, 1972), p. 11.

many children run away from home each year, or how much child neglect or abuse exists.

The problems of children are hidden. But it is important to know that few people ask for such figures.* If there were more requests, it is quite possible we would work harder to get answers.[2]

Howard James's suggestion that we know more about consumable items in this country than we know about children is an interesting point. The question remains, however, whether collections of figures alone can contribute to advocacy of citizen participation in school concerns. Past experience, such as the veto of the Child Development Act (despite extensive collection of data to support the fact that children need more services), suggests that turning around recent backing-off in federal policy from implementation of citizen participation[3] will require more than requests for figures.

> *Richard:* Oops! The comment that "citizen participation will require more than a request for figures": Is that statement suggesting political action on the part of parents or teachers (or both together)?
>
> *Cynthia:* Why not? Don't we train most teachers to be neutral or apolitical even if the issues relate to the needs of children?
>
> *Richard:* We sure do—even though I don't agree with this aspect of our teacher training.
>
> *Cynthia:* I have an idea. Why don't we recommend to our readers that they interview faculty in education departments in neighboring colleges, teachers, public school administrators about the issue of teachers' involvement/noninvolvement in political issues related to children?
>
> *Richard:* I agree—if we add parents to the list. Don't forget that we're talking about their kids!

The answer to whether parents and educators can work together in implementing policies that are aimed at helping the "victims" has, until quite recently, leaned toward the negative. Rather than being described as professionals involved in educational policy implementation, teachers

---

*The first time all available statistical information on children was collected in one volume was 1970 (*Profiles of Children*, U.S. Government Printing Office).

[2]Howard James, *The Little Victims: How America Treats Its Children* (New York: David McKay, 1975), p. 38. Reprinted by permission of David McKay Co., Inc.

[3]David Safran, *State Education Agencies and Parent Involvement* (Oakland, Calif.: Center for the Study of Parent Involvement, 1974), p. 4.

have been accused of "timidity—or lack of competence—in the face of controversy."[4] Rather than being seen as members of a vocation in which a professed body of knowledge in some department of learning or science is used in its application to the affairs of others, "the teacher is not expected to display outstanding competence."[5] Public expectations for teachers have been based on their roles of "technicians, record keepers, clerks, and supply-doler-outers."[6]

> Cynthia: After 128 university credits, four years of sweat, and many thousands of dollars, the public views teachers as "supply-doler-outers"! When students read this they might rethink their career choice—how do we prevent them from getting depressed?
>
> Richard: I have a suggestion for our readers. If a reader is a professional educator, s/he writes a list of competencies a teacher has (10-15 competencies). S/he then asks a small sample of parents (3-10) to state the competencies that they feel a teacher has. The educator's next task is to compare the similarities and differences between the lists. For the final task, s/he suggests ways in which teachers can better inform parents of their competencies.
>
> Our readers who are parents should reverse the above task—list competencies that you feel teachers have; ask a small sample of teachers to state the competencies that they feel they have; compare the similarities and differences between the lists; suggest ways in which the teacher can better inform parents of their competencies.

When one searches through educational research on teacher's roles, one finds that the direction of research has not been toward teachers working within the educational community but toward what goes on when the classroom door is closed. Some indication of the complexity of this approach is presented in Adams's (1972) report of 4,500 tasks performed in thirty-two elementary lessons, Gump's (1971) description of 1,300 tasks performed by a teacher in a "typical day," Simon and Boyer's (1970) fourteen volumes of procedures for analyzing teachers' behavior

---

[4]Frederick M. Wirt and Michael W. Kirst, The Political Web of American Schools (Boston: Little, Brown, 1972), p. 32.

[5]M. Chester Nolte, "And How Hard Is It to Oust a Bad Professional?" American School Board Journal 159 (1972): 21–22.

[6]F. J. Seymour, "What is Professionalism?" in Professionalization, ed. H. M. Vollmer and D. L. Mills (Englewood Cliffs, N. J.: 1966), p. 179.

in the classroom, and Ryan's (1960) extensive study of teachers' characteristics.

> *Richard:* I can't believe it. Simon and Boyer have written 14 volumes on procedures for analyzing teachers. I'll bet not one page includes a description of an observation instrument on parent-teacher interaction.
>
> *Cynthia:* Perhaps this could be a useful task for our readers. Skim through Simon and Boyer's anthology and list the instruments that focus on parent-teacher interaction. If any exist, critique them. Perhaps you will want to design your own instrument. If so, you might check out Earl S. Schaefer's report The Development of Inventories for Assessing Parent and Teacher Interaction and Involvement (ERIC File ED 105 980, 1974).

In addition to designing instruments for classroom observation, educational research has attempted to determine teacher's role perceptions by soliciting the opinion of teachers about what their role should be. The magnitude of this approach is exemplified by cross-cultural studies of the teacher's role in sixteen major cities (Edman 1968; Biddle 1970).

Attempts to determine teacher's role perceptions have depended heavily on frequency counts presented in tabular percentages. On the whole, the results have been presented in piecemeal fashion with few significant results. Most authors present an impressionistic interpretation of the data they have collected. For example,

> raising the self image of teachers is one of the most challenging problems facing both East and West. . . . Nations have not convinced their teachers that their roles are of vital importance to the national welfare. . . . teachers in both East and West are, for the most part, not actively engaged in the professional and political life of their countries. They seem more like a group of onlookers than molders of the kind of society that they are endeavoring to create through education.[7]

It is at the same time both fascinating and infuriating that teachers, as a group, have been accused of passing the buck by not becoming involved. Statistics regarding membership in professional organizations,[8] participa-

---

[7]Marion Edman, *A Self-Image of Primary School Teachers* (Detroit: Wayne University Press, 1968), pp. 60, 71.

[8]James Guthrie and Patricia Craig, *Teachers and Politics* (Bloomington, Ind.: Phi Delta Kappan Educational Foundation, 1973), p. 10.

9

tion in national elections,[9] and the findings that point out that teachers are working daily with over forty-five million children between the ages of three and eighteen,[10] stand in direct contrast to the verdict that teachers are a group of onlookers. But as we mentioned earlier, the question of whether the collection of figures alone can contribute to solving the problem of lack of trust is doubtful.

> For example, parents, teachers, and school officials are seriously at odds with one another over matters of attendance and performance at PTA and other similar meetings. Parents see teachers as desiring to avoid PTA, while teachers, in fact, wish to attend and do so. School officials see teachers as wanting to speak out (so do parents), while teachers attribute to these small groups a desire for teachers to keep quiet. In fact, teachers say they do not speak out—this is in violation of their own norms. Other major areas of contention are matters of discipline, techniques for instruction, teacher self-indulgence, and relations with others in the school system.[11]

The observations presented above offer little hope of breaking the vicious cycle of "blame the parents—blame the schools." Information is typically inconclusive and provides no basis for understanding processes of interaction within and between the ecological context* of the home and school. Typically no attention is paid to developing a framework for the exploration of particular processes in parent-teacher-child interactions. Without a theoretical framework that attends to the interaction of the school and community, the implementation of public laws and state mandates for parental involvement are restricted.

Three recent *exploratory* studies have suggested that parents and educators have positive directions that offer a means of lifting criticism out of its present pedantic trap.

The first positive direction stands as a contrast to past studies which have shown that school boards are the servants of administrators and do not represent the public (Kerr 1973). Goodrich (1976) interviewed school board members concerning particular educational issues facing one community. He then asked community members and school personnel for their opinions on the same issues. Rather than reporting his results as

---

[9]*New York Times,* 22 August 1976.

[10]National Center for Educational Statistics, *The Condition of Education, 1976 Edition* (Washington, D.C.: U.S. Government Printing Office, 1976).

[11]H. A. Rosencranz and B. J. Biddle, "The Role Approach to Teacher Competence," *Contemporary Research on Teacher Effectiveness,* ed. B. J. Biddle and W. J. Ellena (New York: Holt, 1964).

*We discuss the concept of ecology in chapter 5. In brief, the concept of *human ecology* includes people's beliefs about the appropriate means to foster human development and how the environment reflects those beliefs.

conflict, Goodrich went one step further and showed the school board the summary of community and school personnel responses. He then asked the same questions concerning the board's opinion of educational issues facing the community. Goodrich found that the school board members changed their original opinion in favor of the community and school personnel results.

> *Cynthia:* Isn't Goodrich saying that people, generally, and school board members, specifically, may be rational creatures?
>
> *Richard:* Don't you agree? Let's suggest to our readers that they try an "action" experiment. They should select a current issue in their school/community. After gathering data on the community's feelings on the issue, our readers should present their findings to a school board member(s). The reader should encourage friends in other districts to do the same task; a comparison of findings will enable them to develop firmer conclusions about the effect of objective information on the decision-making process of board members.

Past experience with citizen participation in policy making (Van Meter 1975) also suggests that increasing participation by community members in implementing their opinions is an effective starting point. The conclusions of one researcher who studied participation by neighborhood organizations in Cincinnati, Ohio, included the point that "the Metro project has demonstrated beyond any doubt that citizen participation in the budget process is desirable and feasible."[12]

The third exploratory study of members of the educational community which offers a means of determining what the next step should be in building communication was based on an inventory of the teacher's social technologist role, which is discussed further in chapter 7. Initial field testing in urban, rural, and suburban areas showed that teachers, administrators, school board members, parents, and student teachers agree that involvement in public relations programs, lobbying, and challenging established systems in order to deliver professional services to the victims are appropriate activities for teachers (Wallat 1976).

Whether these studies will contribute to helping the victims depends on whether or not we can pierce the "vacuum" in school/community interaction and explore some fresh ideas of what the focus of building school/community communication could be.

---

[12]E. C. Van Meter, "Citizen Participation in Policy Management," *Public Administration Review* 35 (1975): 804–11.

The Vacuum

The vacuum in school/community relations is the implementation of what we know. We "know" that parent involvement adds to student achievement. However, we have tended to consider an idealized image, such as cooperation, in isolation from the social context of the school/community and then have expected the ideal to work out. On the whole, we have not recognized the fact that one scheduled PTA meeting a month or two classroom mothers per grade level cannot provide a system of community involvement that will help to sustain families and schools in their growth over time. The results of the National Assessment of Educational Progress, published by the Educational Commission of the States, suggest that Americans of all ages have contributed to the vacuum in home/school interrelationships.[13]

The myth that education can remain "above politics" has helped to create a vacuum in our awareness of how a child's adulthood participation in school/community affairs can be fostered. It has long been assumed that the transmission of political values rests in the "private" arena of parent-child interaction. Yet recent reevaluation of this assumption suggests that the parents' influence is not on their children's future implementation of participation in political activity. The family's primary effect is to support the status quo. This observation is in no way intended as a negative value judgment. The family's transmission of the status quo means that they are recognized as the primary influence for promoting attachment to this country and, as such, contributors to social order. "Our point is that the absence of impressive parent-child transmission of political values"[14] heightens the responsibility of the school in the realm of learning to implement political roles.

> A third model has not yet loomed large in civic instruction. Termed segmented-organizational by Litt, this seeks to develop skills of technical intellectual analysis, such as political management, and technical concepts and analytic tools. (The model) emphasizes the technical ability to understand the nature of the political world in order that one may manage it.[15]

A great deal needs to be accomplished before the possible extensions and ramifications of Litt's (1965) thesis is recognized in the preparation of teachers. Some writers caution against trying to develop a training pro-

---

[13]"National Assessment of Educational Progress," A Project of the Education Commission of the States, *National Assessment Report 9: Citizenship* (Washington, D.C.: U.S. Government Printing Office, 1972).

[14]M. Kent Jennings and R. C. Niemi, "The Transmission of Political Values from Parent to Child," *Socialization to Politics,* ed. Jack Dennis (New York: John Wiley, 1973), p. 348.

[15]Wirt and Kirst, *The Political Web of American Schools,* p. 28.

gram that is based on Wirt and Kirst's call for courses that focus on the "social foundations of political behavior and the cultural forces that shape political roles and decisions."[16] Friedenberg (1973) states that the functions of socialization and social analysis may be incompatible:

A program of practice teaching that encouraged its practice teachers to view the school as an anthropologist might, becoming consciously aware of its folkways, sanctions, and rituals, would impede their identification as teachers. They would be encouraged to remain marginal men, detached intellectuals, which would pose a severe threat to the existing power structure of the profession. Since teacher education programs are so largely the agent of existing school systems, no such program is likely to be encouraged.[17]

Katz (1964) also has warned that new ways of conceptualizing teacher preparation courses and use of new methods can become a threat to schools "because it is liable to emphasize a teacher's autonomy over a teacher's compliance with existing school constraints."[18] While recognizing the hazards, Friedenberg (1973) contends that the purpose of student teaching should be to study the school as a micro-social system. He suggests that the conflict between making the move from student role to teacher role might be worked through with this method.

Thelen's (1973) answer to the move from student role to citizen role is presented in his definition of a professional. Vocational concern for authenticity, legitimacy, and productivity are the main characteristics of the professional role. While far from taking a negative stand on all educational research, Thelen contends that a professional will not allow intuitive reservations to be overridden by the prestige of scientific findings. Since the concerns of education will continue to change, members must participate in legitimizing their own concerns for effective education. Concerns are legitimated according to

group purposes, disciplines of knowledge, career demands, test objectives, societal issues, laws, or by any other larger organized context that enables the activity to go beyond its own particulars to become a prototype or model for a broad class of enterprises throughout life.[19]

Although it has long been recognized that "teachers are political agents by the very fact that they serve in an institution which is structured to

---

[16]Ibid., p. 30.

[17]Edgar Friedenberg, "Critique of Current Practice," in *New Perspectives on Teacher Education,* ed. D. J. McCarty (San Francisco: Jossey-Bass, 1973), p. 36.

[18]Fred Katz, "The School as a Complex Social Organization," *Harvard Educational Review* 34 (1964): 428–55.

[19]Herbert Thelen, "Profession Anyone?" in *New Perspectives on Teacher Education,* ed. D. J. McCarty (San Francisco: Jossey-Bass, 1973), pp. 194–213.

politicize and acculturate,"[20] most training programs are concerned with development of technical knowledge in the form of collection of scientific data and records rather than development of social-political-ideological intelligence.[21] Although the "teaching and learning of attitudes are accepted as a teleological educational objective,"[22] there is need for recognizing that the consequences of more and more professionals working directly with values may affect the entire social system.

It is the possible significance of every act of the teacher that distinguishes him from the artisan or craftsman and that necessitates both more extended educational qualifications and more latitude in governing his own work.[23]

Christie (1969) contends that the issue of teacher development must be concerned with what strategies can be developed for professionals who face an ethical dilemma when they recognize the need for change in specific parts of a social system without changing the whole.[24] Haberman (1970) supports this viewpoint through his thesis that the issue is beyond whether conflict between the individual and the system "should be."

It is vital to recognize that the conflict "is" and to develop criteria and mechanisms for helping organizations change in response to selected individual pressures but to continue to resist others.[25]

Richard: We'd better take a break. As soon as you mentioned that change must be in some areas but not in others our readers probably thought "here we go again."
Cynthia: OK. I'll take a break, but I'll do it through sharing how Goodlad described the vacuum in his chapter on stability and change in American education.

A five-year research project sponsored by the Study of Educational Change and School Improvement (Goodlad 1975) suggests that the vac-

---

[20]Normand Bernier and Jack Williams, *Beyond Beliefs: Ideological Foundations of American Education* (New Jersey: Prentice-Hall, 1973), p. 10.

[21]Harold Wilensky, "Problems in Application of Social Sciences," in *Agents of Change: Professionals in Developing Countries,* ed. G. Benveniste and W. Illchman (New York: Praeger, 1969), pp. 62–77.

[22]David Barbee and A. Bouck, *Accountability in Education* (New York: Petrocelli Books, 1974), p. 78.

[23]Donald Contrell, *Teacher Education for a Free People* (Oneonta, N.Y.: American Association of Colleges for Teacher Education, 1956), p. 393.

[24]Nils Christie, "Relativity in Development," in *Agents of Change: Professionals in Developing Countries,* ed. G. Benveniste and W. Illchman (New York: Praeger, 1969).

[25]Martin Haberman, *The Art of Schoolmanship* (St. Louis, Mo.: Warren H. Green, 1970), p. 13.

uum is in part due to misconceptions of the change process. Goodlad would no doubt agree with the ideas of Christie and Haberman, but he manages to present his ideas with clearer illustrations. When a student begins to analyze the concept of change by looking at specific aspects, such as teachers, students, curriculum, financing, governance, facilities, or equipment, he might get caught in the trap of thinking that he now

"understood" the workings of the schools and was prepared to start changing them. . . . He might select one of these components as his point of attack for change. Improve teacher training, he might decide, and you improve all . . . or improve curriculum, that's the key to everything. (Or) . . . he would produce a more complex program for change, involving several components and frequently illustrated by charts filled out with bold lines, dotted lines, arrows going in several directions, and terms such as "input," "feedback network," and "evaluation-revision loop."[26]

Goodlad believes that the reason for the vacuum in home/school relationships is because we have looked at schools as if they were a mechanical system. We break them apart into small pieces and try to find a new part that will keep the "fragile, vulnerable organism" working. We have forgotten in our preoccupation with acquiring the newest technology, be it curriculum or facilities, that each school is a natural, not a mechanical, system.

The single school with its principal, teachers, pupils, parents and community links is the key to education change. . . . The reconstruction must occur school by school. This means that it will move forward on a broken front and not as part of a national grand strategy.[27]

As we have suggested earlier, the vacuum in school/community relations is in implementing what we know. However, lack of implementation and citizen involvement cannot be considered in isolation from the social context of American citizens' feeling of powerlessness[28] or through over-simplified change strategies employed in the past. Nor can we place the blame solely on the fact that democracy has been an object of study rather than experience in participation. We still have a long way to go in translating the goal of aiding individuals in analysis and examination of societal values and institutions. Illuzzi and Milstein (1975) have reported inconsistencies between teachers' recognition of responsibility for citizenship education and their implementation of this goal in their teaching

---

[26]John I. Goodlad, *The Dynamics of Educational Change: Towards Responsive Schools* (New York: McGraw-Hill, 1975), p. xiii.

[27]Ibid., pp. 20, 81.

[28]Donald W. Robinson, "Citizen Education and the Revolution at the Department of HEW," *Phi Delta Kappan* 58 (1976): 355–56.

15

strategies. Many institutions, such as those described in Appendix C, have been venturesome enough to provide support for their teachers to try to fill the vacuum. At the same time, many critics have been primarily concerned with advancing hypotheses and collecting data as to whose fault lack of communication, lack of trust, and lack of interest are. The next section addresses the various targets of criticism and is concerned with the "verdict."

Cynthia: Teachers have prided themselves (and perhaps been "programmed" by their training) to be apolitical, neutral individuals. It seems to me that the above section of the book states that not only should teachers be involved in the political process, but that they have an obligation as democrats (notice the small "d") to participate actively in the political process.

Richard: I have a suggestion for you and me. (Our readers can join us if they desire.) Let's interview our public school and university colleagues on their perceptions of the educational issues in the Carter-Ford election. Then we will ask them how they participated. Finally, we'll ask our colleagues how educators should be involved politically with issues related to education on local, state, and national levels.

Cynthia: Richard, I think I am going to nominate you for a new award to be called "Professor whose students have accomplished the greatest number of interviews." The reason you'll win (in addition to the fact that I will be in charge of making the selection) is because you take the time to give your students dozens of ideas about gaining access to people. The point we have to keep in mind, however, is that some of our readers have gone through what Litt (1966) described as the integrative-consensual model of civic instruction (p. 15). Before we move to Litt's third model, i.e., "segmented-organizational," we have to concentrate on developing the ability to understand the nature of the political world in order to begin to manage it (i.e., education as an apolitical process and/or society as a melting pot).

The point of all this rambling is that we should give an alternative to our readers for accomplishing the third step in your suggested interview.

One alternative is to read through the following description of the state of Oregon's graduation requirements. After reading the description, go back to each competency listed and discuss how you think educators filled the vac-

uum and fulfilled the state mandate for accomplishing these competencies.

Oregon Graduation Requirements

Models and Guidelines for Social Responsibility Education, Section III
Oregon State Department of Education

Available from: Eric File ED 085 066, 1973
                or
           Documents Clerk
           State Department of Education
           942 Lancaster Drive
           NE Salem, Oregon   97310 $1.50

Beginning in 1969 identification of "survival" competencies essential for functioning at citizen level were prepared by a graduation requirement task force. The requirements were passed on September 22, 1972, by the Oregon State Board of Education. It was left to school districts to evaluate credit by exam, by off campus study, or through issuing certificates that all students beginning with the class of 1978 will have fulfilled the requirements outlined below.

GOAL:

Students accept responsibility in social, economic, and political affairs.

COMPETENCIES:

1. Identify values exhibited in typical individual behavior and in legal codes (e.g. given case studies, identify values).
2. Given description of everyday situation, list values exhibited.
3. Given list of five basic values, identify and defend the values that would guide your resolution of conflict.
4. Given a list of student responsibilities and everyday conflict situations, identify sources of conflict and identify alternative solutions.
5. Given a list of agencies and organizations, identify those which are involved in protection of rights.
6. Given case studies of legal action, suggest methods of appeal, e.g., file lawsuit, letter to newspaper, etc.
7. Given descriptions of consumer activities, identify three causes of scarcity or abundance of consumer items.

8. Given a list of several American values, identify those which are generally learned in the family setting.
9. Given a list of American group values, identify those which influence your opinions and actions.

The Verdict

Herbert Kohl (1976) has suggested that the reason we don't know more about community and parent involvement in education is because it exists only on paper "or [has been] forced to lead a fugitive and defensive life."[29] His analysis of the struggle for community control of schools in New York City focused on the type of conflict that may result when school issues bring union members, central administration, and parents together. Before reaching the conclusion that "community control could not have failed in New York, because it was never allowed to happen,"[30] Kohl described the chaos. He observed that while the union was manipulating public sentiment with emotional charges that community control would heighten prejudice against certain ethnic groups and the central administration attempted to block the power struggle by tying up funds, parents spent their energy on battles with hostile media.

Similar themes of professional, administrative, and interest group obstruction have been described by Henry Resnik (1970) and Allan Ornstein (1974). While Resnick's description is primarily a personal interpretation of events, Ornstein is concerned with assessment of the status of decentralization and community control in sixty-seven school systems. His summary of five major reviews of literature on issues related to community control includes the following arguments:

Arguments For	Arguments Against
1. Community control is positively correlated with accountability.	It is difficult, if not impossible, to evaluate teachers and administrators with reliability and validity.
2. Community control will lead to greater public participation.	The majority of parents are indifferent or, inept and inexperienced. Those who are concerned are only concerned with their own group.
3. Community control will raise student achievement.	There is no proof that this will happen.
4. Community control will lead to educational reform.	It is a distraction from the greater need for money to educate children.

---

[29]Herbert Kohl, "Community Control—Failed or Undermined?" *Phi Delta Kappan* 57 (1976): 429.
[30]Ibid., p. 370.

5. Community control will motivate parents to seek self-government and high quality education for‍ their children.

It is a return to the myth of separate but equal.[31]

While researchers have been concerned with a multitude of ramifications in attempts at community control, others have delimited their studies to analyzing mechanisms such as advisory groups. For example, Clark (1975) presents a review of a school-community commission in a large West Coast city. The purpose of inviting 110 individuals, representing sixty community organizations, to form a commission was to study violence in the schools. Based on content analysis of the final report submitted to the commission and observations at all the meetings held, Clark concluded that "the entire report neither reflected the community nor suggested viable solutions to violence in public schools."[32] In addition to the suggestion that the meetings had a worse dropout problem than the schools, he contends that community involvement is a myth.

> *Richard:* Wow! Do you think the readers may feel that we support "community control" of the schools? If they do (especially those readers who are professional educators) I think they'll stop reading now and return the book for a refund.
>
> *Cynthia:* Where's your honesty? You recently told me that there are certain aspects of community control that you support. For example, ...
>
> *Richard:* Wait a minute! OK, I understand your point. I have a suggestion. Let's encourage our readers to (a) develop a list of pros and cons of community control, (b) develop a list of pros and cons of community participation, (c) present the lists to parents and educators for their comments.
>
> *Cynthia:* What are the goals for this task?
>
> *Richard:* It is not to convert our readers to one type of commuity involvement or another but to help them to understand the issues involved in an objective way.

Arguments concerning the success or failure of parental involvement ventures can, of course, continue indefinitely. The vacuum seems to be in the criteria we are using to judge the success or failure of parental involvement. We know that due to the political nature of education some

---

[31]Allan C. Ornstein, *Race and Politics in School/Community Organization* (Pacific Palisades, Calif.: Goodyear, 1974), pp. 11–13.

[32]W. W. Clark, *An Analytic Review of a School-Community Commission,* ERIC File ED 114 418, 1975, p. 26.

interest groups will be more "successful" than others in having their curriculum ideas recognized (e.g., banning of books in West Virginia). We also know that some groups have been successful in having their input on collective negotiations included in new contracts (e.g., Fairfax, Virginia, citizens are given six months to respond before ratifications of new contracts).

We wonder, therefore, whether it is not premature to render the verdict that parent involvement exists only on paper. Have we been asking the right questions concerning the success or failure of the means employed to involve the community? Do the questions contribute to recognition that children are affected by all strata of our social system? Do the questions contribute to developing public expectations that parents, the community, and other social institutions have taken steps toward working out effective strategies for dealing with "all the stresses, social as well as personal, for which the modern world provides no other regular outlets?"[33] Last, but not least, do the questions help to clarify how parents and educators have had to build mechanisms toward involvement step-by-step and inch-by-inch?

> Richard: Cynthia, we can't leave the readers "up in the air" with the questions that end the chapter. Let's give them some answers.
> Cynthia: OK, start answering.
> Richard: Well, I can't. The questions are so complex. But won't our lack of conclusion frustrate the readers? They are looking to us for the answers.
> Cynthia: I'm not sure that's our task. As a first step, we're trying to help the readers to clarify the verdict that community involvement in schools is a myth.
> Richard: So their task is . . . ?
> Cynthia: You guessed it—to decide whether the verdict may be premature. You set them on one track in the last activity by suggesting developing a list of pros and cons of community control and community participation. I'd like to set them on another track by suggesting they review the ten plans developed by Harvey Scribner (1975) in Make Your Schools Work.
> Richard: Didn't you write a letter to Dr. Scribner about his request in his book for people to share their plans with him?
> Cynthia: Yes, I asked him if he had received a lot of ideas from

[33]Rowland Berthoff, *An Unsettled People: Social Order and Disorder in American History* (New York: Harper & Row, 1971), p. 410.

people who agreed with him that we can make our schools
work.

Richard: What happened?

Cynthia: Well, I was hoping I'd hear that lots of people had answered so I could say the verdict that community involvement is a myth was wrong and call for a mistrial. But . . .
wait! Let's share the letter with our readers. The activity he
describes in the letter builds on the one you suggested.

Cynthia: For those readers who developed and used a program
based on Scribner's recommendations, I suggest that they
respond to Scribner's plea and write him a letter describing
what happened. Scribner suggested guidelines for the response to him:

a. Explore the pros and cons of the plan selected;
b. Spell out the implications the plan had on the built-in
   interest groups in the school establishment;
c. Identify the plan's direct and indirect effects on the
   children;
d. Prepare a policy for adoption of the plan by the local
   board of education.

Richard: You mentioned Scribner's plea. What about ours? We
promise to respond in writing to any program description
sent to us. Perhaps our recommendations may even be
helpful!

**The Commonwealth of Massachusetts
University of Massachusetts
Amherst   01002**
SCHOOL OF EDUCATION

July 26, 1976

Dear Dr. Wallat,

    Thanks for your letter of 7/23/76. Obviously, it
was pleasing to note your interest in "Make Your
Schools Work" and to learn of your desire to find
out if further plans had been submitted as a result
of our invitation. Very little positive motion has
been manifested by anyone at this date. Many letters
have come to me but they deal mostly with a few

21

gripes and a lot of persons who relate to the book via beefs about their children being in what they sense to be bad situations. The lack of positive effort to an honest call for further action appears to me to further indicate how bankrupt the educational establishment is. I hope you can stir some interest on the part of your teacher trainees.

As a result of the book I did approximately thirty-one radio and T. V. interviews from five minutes to four hours in length. The book is in the process of coming out in paper-back this fall. It has been used by a few, at least, as a text in teacher education courses but has been even more popular for adult study groups.

A Professor friend of mine at Rutgers used the book as a text last year and he approached it as follows: He had each of the members of the class volunteer for one of the ten plans and the groups were asked to: (1) Explore the pros and cons of the plan they had selected, (2) Spell out the various implications the plan had on the built in interest groups in the school establishment, (3) Identify the plan's direct and indirect effect on the children in the school system and (4) Prepare a policy for adoption of the plan by their local school Board complete with rationale. I had the pleasure of meeting with the group after their explorations for a good "no holds barred" two hour discussion. (Lest one wonders about the profits from such an experience, I had been paid in advance to publish the book and I went to Rutgers for the discussion at my own expense).

Again, thanks for your inquiry. If I can be of any further assistance, please write.

Best wishes for a good school year.

                  Sincerely,

Harvey Scribner

The authors wish to thank Dr. Scribner for permission to reprint his letter.

The Venue

To place the total blame on one sector of the school community is a narrow view of our social system.

> The problems of American public education are not separate and distinct from the conditions, problems, and changes of the larger society. . . . A great deal of criticism of education stems from the frustration of facing apparently unresolvable social problems plus over-expectations regarding what education might do about them. [34]

If the public expects too much from education, one would expect that educators would be anxious to have any help they could muster from members of the community and from other public agencies. Yet past studies of the extent of elementary school teachers' participation in the community (Carson, Goldhammer, and Pelligrin 1967) and studies of university faculty reports of community service (Kanun 1975) suggest that teachers have not availed themselves of opportunities for becoming involved in decision-making processes in community affairs. The reasons for lack of involvement in decision-making processes are decidedly involved, yet researchers suggest that teachers perceive parents as the "greatest threat" to their taking a stand on controversial actions (Zeigler 1966).

It is partly in recognition of the threat of public sanctions that one hears boasts such as the following which aim toward channeling all decisions through one interest group.

> The American Federation of Teachers is determined to control the public schools of the United States. And someday it will. Just as the American Medical Association controls American medicine and the American Bar Association controls the legal profession. [35]

It appears that the originator of this statement has failed to look into the most "priceless" characteristic of a profession: the manner in which a profession accepts and carries out its public responsibility. [36] A group concerned with professional development and recognition by the public must attend not only to the technical aspects of the work to be performed but also to the idea that professions are developed in the "marketplace" [37]

---

[34]C. T. Thomas and W. Harman, *Critical Issues in the Future of American Education* (Menlo Park, Calif.: Stanford Research Institute, Educational Policy Research Center, 1972), p. 1.

[35]Braun, *Teachers and Power*, p. 10.

[36]Seymour, "What is Professionalism?", p. 179.

[37]William Goode, "Professions and Non-Professions," in *Professionalism,* ed. H. M. Voelner and D. L. Mills (Englewood Cliffs, N. J.: 1966), pp. 34–45.

where competition for resources is keen. Since the very fact of striving for recognition is political, those who are naïve enough to think that power, such as that held by the AMA, will eventually accrue to teachers' associations and establish a new elite should rethink their tactics for gaining that power.

The first item of business might be how to deal with the U.S. Department of Labor grants to the National Civil Service League to study the extent of representation of the public interest in public sector collective bargaining. It appears that the question of whether the public should be represented has already jumped to the second point of how effectively they can be represented. The next item for attention would be that the days of independent profession have long passed. The growth of specialities within education has been described by Guthrie and Craig (1973). The authors also suggest another item which they think demands cooperation in educational policy implementation:

> The relative political success of teachers (in working conditions and economic benefits) . . . is awesome. Yet, the consequences of their actions may not have all accrued to the benefit of educators. It may be that the curtain has dropped on Act I. There are certain constraints upon the power of teachers to act effectively within the new political context.[38]

Various opinions have been offered for teachers' lack of participation in political decisions and their perception that the public would not consider community involvement as appropriate. While some authors have suggested that lack of involvement is due to personality characteristics, e.g., "timidity—or lack of competence—in the face of controversy,"[39] others have suggested that despite the availability of a score of "desirable" competency descriptions, codes of ethics, and state requirements for certification, the teaching profession has not

> established any generally understood standards of teacher performance or a definition of the duties that should be performed competently by one who assumes the title of teacher.[40]

Although the complexity of describing the teacher's instructional role has been extensively reviewed (Dunkin and Biddle 1974), the complexity of measuring expectations toward teachers' roles as citizens and social technologists has been a recent concern (Wallat 1976). One indicator of the problem involved in overcoming the myth of education as apolitical

---

[38] Guthrie and Craig, *Teachers and Politics*, p. 16.

[39] Wirt and Kirst, *The Political Web of American Schools*, p. 32.

[40] R. K. Sparks and H. Strauss, "The Naggingly Logical Question: How Soon Before Those 'Professional Teachers' of Yours Can Be Sued for Malpractice," *American School Board Journal* 159 (1972): 19–21.

can be seen in statements printed in *The Congressional Quarterly*. In general, education groups shy away from the label of "lobbyists."

> I virtually never go to the Hill except on request. I don't walk the halls. . . . we lobby by invitation.[41]

It appears, however, from the following reaction by a member of Congress that invitations aren't often forthcoming.

> Never in his 20 years in Congress, he said, had he seen "anything so brazen by any group coming here trying to influence legislation." His reaction to these citizens informing their representative that they would be in the House gallery during the vote was paramount to "Big Brother will be watching." On hearing that the citizens were also planning to tell the representative, if he promised to vote to override, that the constituent and his associates would do everything they could to assist him locally, Ayres commented, "in other words, in his next election. By inference, if you do not vote with them, you know what they are going to try to do. I think this is a disgrace to . . . education."[42]

Lack of effective lobbyists interested in building school/community relations does not appear to be a problem only on the federal level. Only fourteen states have passed legislation measures pertaining to parent involvement.[43] Analysis of the twenty-three laws passed in these states reveals that fourteen of them are concerned with parent involvement in planning, evaluating, or advising, seven are concerned with program implementation, and four are concerned with administration procedures involving discipline and classifying students. For the most part, as one can see in the names of the legislation presented in table 2–1, parent involvement is limited to a particular area, such as bilingual education, career education, migrant education, or expulsion of pupils.

> Cynthia: I'm going to read you section one of the Early Childhood Education Act (California 6445.01):
> Parent participation shall be included in a manner which: (a) involves parents in the formal education of their children directly in the classroom and through the decision making process of the California Public School System; (b) maximizes the opportunity for teachers and parents to cooperatively develop the learning process and its subject

[41]"Education for a Nation," *Congressional Quarterly* (Washington, D.C.: Superintendent of Documents, 1972), p. 29.
[42]Ibid.
[43]Safran, *State Education Agencies and Parent Involvement*, pp. 15–16.

TABLE 2–1.   State Laws According to Categories of Parent Involvement Legislation

Category	Name of Legislation (State)
Planning, evaluating, and advising	Early Childhood Education (California)
	Bilingual Education (California)
	Educationally Disadvantaged Youth Programs (California)
	Educational Accountability (Colorado)
	School Advisory Committee (Florida)
	Parent-Student Evaluation Committee (Hawaii)
	School Reorganization (Indiana)
	Career Education (Louisiana)
	State School Aid (Michigan)
	Regional Vocational Education (New Hampshire)
	Joint Resolution (Oklahoma)
	Education Act of 1973 (Rhode Island)
	Special Education (Wisconsin)
	Special Educational Needs (Wisconsin)
Program implementation	McAteer Act (California)
	Early Childhood Education (California)
	Bilingual Education (California)
	Educationally Disadvantaged Youth Programs (California)
	Migrant Education (California)
	Community School Act (Florida)
	Parent Educational Participation (Tennessee)
Administrative procedures	Student Due Process (Indiana)
	House Bill No. 5004 (Michigan)
	Public Education Basic Support (Nevada)
	Expulsion of Pupils (Wisconsin)
Unknown	Standard and Procedure for Family Life (Maryland)
	Citizen Advisory Committee (Maryland)

SOURCE: From Daniel Safran, *State Education Agencies and Parent Involvement* (Oakland, Calif.: Center for the Study of Parent Involvement, 1974) p. 16. Reprinted by permission.

> matter. This opportunity shall be a continuous permanent process.
>
> *Richard:* It's about time that a state legislature recognized the rights of parents and children.
>
> *Cynthia:* I agree. But I have a problem with the legislation. As I view the legislation in my role of "parent," I feel that parents are not given enough real decision-making power. On the other hand, in my role of "educator," I feel that many parents don't have the competencies needed to assume the responsibilities described.

> *Richard: Interesting point. Do we have the obligation as profes-*
> *sional educators to help parents acquire the skills neces-*
> *sary for full participation in their children's learning? A task*
> *for our readers—they will share the above description of*
> *the California legislation with parents and teachers. If a*
> *feeling exists that parents may need assistance to learn the*
> *skills necessary to participate fully in their children's edu-*
> *cation, our readers who are professionals will suggest*
> *specific procedures for working with parents.*
>
> *Cynthia: I agree with your suggestion and want to add another*
> *dimension—perhaps the "helpers" for the parents could*
> *include educators and parents who are skilled in "plan-*
> *ning, evaluation, and advising."*
>
> *Richard: My elitism is showing through again. Parents are a resource*
> *that educators and other parents must use.*

One cannot blame only teachers for failing to ensure implementation of public involvement in education. Perceptions of political activity as inappropriate are not limited to teachers. Although political analysts have long admonished all members of the American public to assume an active citizenship role, most fail to convince the public that politics is a human activity.

> This definition implies much. It is meant to make politics have something to do with morality. What is implied is that politics means taking a stand, being passionate about something, defining what you believe to be right or wrong . . . and then acting on that belief. It is not an easy kind of activity, especially when one is taught to reject just such propositions. But it seems to me that politics involve the inner tension of trying to figure out—and then doing —good in a world where we do not know what good is and where no choices seem clearcut.[44]

Howard James (1975) seems to doubt whether the American public will be able to overcome the perception that politics is "dirty." He also believes that rather than working together in solving problems, members of the education community will continue to blame each other or pass the buck.

> To put it another way, the social system hurts many children, but few Americans know this. Even if they found out how damaging the system is, and even if they cared, they would not know what to do about the problem. . . .

---

[44]David Schuman, *A Preface to Politics* (Lexington, Mass.: D. C. Heath, 1973), p. 25.

27

Citizen anger has not changed the system—partly because the American people do not know how to exercise power.[45]

Holleman (1975) has suggested that one of the reasons that many Americans do not know how to exercise power is because community activities often do not lend themselves to systematic analysis. The illusiveness of power has led to research models which attempt to describe the activities shared by groups with different interests. The purpose of the models is to help individuals interested in developing parent and community involvement to make judgments about what areas show the most possibility for agreement rather than to continue to voice often foundless sentiments, such as "school boards don't listen," "parents are apathetic," or "teachers don't care." An overview of useful models for contributing to resolution of issues is presented in Appendix A. Rather than concentrating on areas of disagreement, these inexpensive source books focus on planning, organizing, and publicizing the following specific activities:

1. Encourage your club, church, or friends to sponsor a conference on children.
2. Encourage your school board to sponsor seminars for teachers to discuss what you have collected.
3. Establish a family of the year recognition dinner and reward those who have done the most in the community to help children.
4. Form a committee to prepare a community checklist of things every community should have for children. Then call on civic groups, churches, wealthy families, clubs, school groups, and others to help.
5. Join an advocacy group—better yet start one by writing for literature on children with problems and distributing it to friends and neighbors.
6. Open schools during the evening and on weekends.
7. Monitor programs already available.
8. Start a fact finding group and gather information on children in need of help, resources available, community needs, and community problems. Then lecture at service clubs, churches and before other groups.
9. Persuade local newspapers and T.V. to look into services for children. Provide them with standards and guidelines that their reporter can use to measure local facilities against.
10. Use your imagination. Put your talents, interests, skills and experience to work.[46]

---

[45]James, *The Little Victims: How America Treats Its Children*, p. 42. Reprinted by permission of David McKay Co., Inc.

[46]Ibid., pp. 352–57. Reprinted by permission of David McKay Co., Inc.

> *Richard:* Is James suggesting in the above steps that these are ac-
> tivities for parents to organize? If so, I disagree with the
> process. Why not have parents and educators plan and
> carry out the above suggestions together?
>
> *Cynthia:* Good point. Both groups together will create a positive
> power block for children.
>
> *Richard:* Our readers should design and implement one of James's
> suggestions (or a related suggestion). One guideline—a
> reader who is a parent must work with a professional
> educator; the reader who is the professional educator must
> work with a parent.

In order to escape the vicious cycle of "blame the parents, blame the schools," we "know" that the problem of how to motivate the power structure cannot be tackled until one knows how to locate the power structure in meetings where many interest groups are involved.[47] Partly as a result of recognition that members of the public need help in exercising their power and partly as a result of the growing recognition that curriculum changes and more teacher training are not enough to ensure efficient education, various organizations and individuals in addition to James and Holleman have offered specific suggestions.

1969 Scheinfeld, David. "On Developing Developmental Families." In E. Grotberg, ed. *Critical Issues Related to Disadvantaged Children*. Princeton, N. J.: Educational Testing Service, 1969.

Outlines the need for a developmental community to sustain changes over time. The impact on one family may spread to other families if a system of community support is developed.

1970 Lurie, Ellen. *How to Change the Schools: A Parent's Action Handbook to Fight the System*. New York: Random House, 1970.

As in Resnick's book, this is a description of the educational system's restraints on change in a particular area. One will be heartened by Lurie's acknowledgment of people who helped her attempt to improve education in New York City. The acknowledgments are the best data on attacking the argument that people are not interested.

1970 Resnick, Henry. *Turning on the System: War in the Philadelphia Schools*. New York: Pantheon Books, 1970.

An inside view of the struggle in Philadelphia for educational reform. The author's impressions of political struggles ranges from the board of education to the classroom.

---

[47]. T. Holleman, *The Use of Power Structure in the Attainment of Educational Goals,* ERIC File ED 116 266, 1975.

1970 Totten, W. Fred. *The Power of Community Education.* Midland, Mich.: Pendell, 1970.

Totten offers proof that the school can be a meeting house for individuals, families, social agencies, communications media, and service clubs concerned with better understanding of social trends, reduction of poverty, improved cultural tone, and reduction of dropouts, delinquency, and crime. Best of all he cites proof that school bonds can be passed for individual and community improvement.

1973 Bromwich, Rose. "Working with Parents of Preschool Children." In Robert Friedman, ed. *Family Roots of School Learning and Behavior Disorders.* Springfield, Ill.: Charles C. Thomas, 1973, pp. 225–83.

Feelings of self-worth, a sense of adequacy, and a feeling of competence are necessary for both adults and the child. Bromwich offers notes on conferences and on working with groups to help them realize that they are resourceful and can be actively involved.

1974 Almy, Millie. *The Early Childhood Educator at Work.* New York: McGraw-Hill, 1974.

"From the point of view of research . . . the lesson is that 'socioeconomic status' measured by such indices as income and place of residence, masks a number of other factors, such as the adult's perception of his ability to control his environment, that . . . shape and limit their expectations for both themselves and their children." (p. 248)

1975 Buskin, Martin. *Parent Power.* New York: Walker and Co., 1975.

Reviews the growth of the parent advisory committees and warns that it involves a long-term commitment, may be ignored, lacks the excitement and drama of a group formed to solve a particular issue and can *do more* to bring about change than any other kind of group.

1975 Newman, Fred. *Education for Citizen Action.* Berkeley, Calif.: McCutchan Publishing, 1975.

Seventeen pages of addresses of organizations and schools supporting community involvement curriculum, projects, and action.

1975 Scribner, Harvey, and Stevens, Leonard. *Make Your Schools Work.* New York: Simon & Schuster, 1975.

Based on their administrative service to New York City schools, the authors suggest ten plans that they believe could work. Among the suggestions are for parents to select their children's teachers and each family to have one vote on the success of their school in meeting objectives.

1976 Gordon, Ira, and Breivogel, William. *Building Effective Home-School Relationships.* Boston: Allyn and Bacon, 1976.

In addition to defining the parent's role as audience, teacher at home, volunteer, and decision maker, a central aspect of Gordon's program is the Parent as Paid Employee. Parents would be paid to come to learn particular techniques for managing or teaching their child.

1976 Talbot, Nathan. *Raising Children in Modern America, Vol. II: What Parents and Society Should be Doing for Their Schools.* New York: Little, Brown, 1976.

Talbot presents the following suggestions of a Harvard University Seminar concerned with establishing child-rearing support systems: (a) subsidize public broadcasting programs concerned with child rearing; (b) support marriage and child-rearing courses.

The suggestions outlined by the authors listed above mirror Howard James's objectives:

Our goal must be . . . to change our culture. That change must take place first in our hearts and minds and in our own homes . . . it only takes a few people in each neighborhood to produce lasting change.[48]

In order to evaluate the feasibility of these suggestions in your particular community, we would like to share with you what we have learned in the sixties and seventies in early childhood program development. We now know that if we think of the schools as a mechanical system we can easily begin to think that if we have a good plan for updating curricula or teacher preparation or financial support from Washington, all our problems will be solved. Well, in 1965 all of the above began to take place on a wide scale with funds available for curriculum development and teacher development. Bettye Caldwell (1975) has summarized what we have learned since plans and federal funds became available in 1965.

1. We learned that people with different kinds of backgrounds could work together.
2. We learned that we talked too much. We promised too quickly that we could develop positive self-concepts and new levels of language competence after only six weeks of summer school.
3. We learned that we were too narrow by letting ourselves get locked into using IQ tests.
4. In legislative and funding defeat we learned about the necessity of being citizens as well as professionals.
5. We learned to take a stand on controversial issues.[49]

Whether Dr. Caldwell's analysis of what we have learned in the past will contribute to building school/community relations depends on whether or not educators and parents recognize the issues surrounding these five points.

---

[48]James, *The Little Victims*, p. 357.
[49]Bettye M. Caldwell, "A Decade of Early Intervention Programs: What We Have Learned," *American Journal of Orthopsychiatry* 44 (1974): 491–96.

Just as one can quickly read the words "we need each other," so we can quickly accept the assumption that people with different kinds of training and background could work together. It seems to the authors, however, that working together requires a common framework on which to build. Concern for children appears to give the home and school a head start in establishing communication, but we also have to go through some soul searching. Do we really believe that educators have done their best, or have they wasted funds? Do we involve parents in the school because we are convinced that parents are educators and capable decision makers or because they save us from all that paperwork and cleanup after parties? Do we realize the extent of our role as professionals? Do we continue to profess that we "should be" recognized as professionals and "would be" if we had a better income? Do we recognize that fulfilling citizenship and professional responsibilities as social technologists requires a commitment of whether or not we really want to expend that much time and effort on school/community relations?

In order to establish a basis for answering the question of whether or not we *really* want to expend time and effort on school/community relations, and to establish a context for viewing what's going on in school/community relations in part II, we have asked a professional who has recognized and accepted (a) that we *definitely* need each other, (b) that people with different kinds of training and background *must* work together, and (c) that a level of commitment to teaching and learning is necessary before a professional *takes a stand* on controversial issues, to share her voyage toward building school/community interaction.

The Voyage

"If only Johnny's parents would help him at home with his flash cards, I know he could learn his facts! But they say they're *too* busy, and besides, teaching is what *I* get paid for! If they don't care about their child, why should I?"

Schools sometimes seem to resemble a football field where teachers and parents play against one another while the ball (or child) is thrown back and forth with both sides fighting for control. And after a play has been called, each side argues with the referee (or principal) to step in and recall the play in their favor. It seems to me that the whole educating process would be much more effective if all concerned would work together as one team striving for a common goal. Research has shown that

---

*"The Voyage" was written by Michele LeLaidier Krisher (Kent, Ohio: Kent State University, Department of Early Childhood Education, 1978). Used with permission.

parents and teachers working together for the benefit of children can be accomplished in a variety of ways.

Thomas Gordon says, "Parents are blamed, not trained." It seems that this is the key factor that lies beneath the whole parent-teacher controversy. In order to turn this around, we first need to help parents realize that their skills are valuable and that they are effective educators of their children. Teachers need to accept this fact and help train and give encouragement to parents. It calls for a changing of roles whereby parents view themselves as educators and teachers view themselves as parent educators.

When making changes of this type, it is important that we (teachers or trainers) don't imply that what parents already do with their child is wrong or unimportant. Parents need to know how vitally important their role is and that they are their child's best teacher. Too much emphasis of this point cannot be made. We need to be viewed by parents as a support system to which they can defer when needed.

One way in which we can begin to help is to provide means by which parents are actively involved in their children's education. Parents can help plan curricula, take part as parent volunteers in the classroom, or share their "special talents" in the classroom (cooking, hobbies, etc.). Parent meetings can be held in which films can be shown, learning activities shared, and discussion groups held with the teachers acting as group leaders.

Of course, one other fact must be realized—not all teachers will be comfortable in the role of parent educator. These people should not be directly responsible for some of the above-mentioned activities. They, like the parents, need some training through workshops and the like to help them be more comfortable in their new role.

The restructuring and/or development of attitudes is the only viable means of fostering home/school/community interaction. To change or develop attitudes, one must begin as early as possible with building positive parent-teacher interaction. I would like to take this opportunity to share the development of how I learned to take a stand such as the above on home/school/community interaction.

It's difficult to pinpoint the exact moment when one decides to embark on a voyage—or choose a career. There is so much charting and plotting that must occur before the sails can be set. Certain provisions must be laid in, and the vessel must prove seaworthy. But even before that, one must examine where she's going and why.

I guess I've always wanted to be a teacher. I can vividly recall how much I loved staying after school to help Miss Sloan in her classroom. It began when I was in second grade. I would stop by her door and ask, "Is there anything you want me to do tonight?" She would let me rearrange

33

bulletin boards, clean the blackboards, and each Christmas we'd decorate the tree to surprise her first graders. I imagine that thinking up little chores I could do must have been bothersome for her at times! She introduced me to tea with lemon and honeydew melon. During summer vacations she always sent me postcards from her trips across the United States, and she never forgot my birthday. That's probably where it began—my voyage—my desire to be a teacher. In fact, I'm sure of it.

As a teenager, I discovered that I easily developed a very good rapport with little children. I was an excellent babysitter, always able to think up little games or to tell stories to appease my charges. Also, during this time, I began working in a primary EMR unit as a Future Teacher volunteer. Perhaps this is when I realized that if I did become a teacher, I would enjoy working with the younger children. It seemed like a very natural and comfortable role for me.

As the fourth of seven children in a working class family, I found no money available for a college education when the time arrived. However, my father was always a person who believed that if you really wanted something badly enough that you could get it—if you were willing to work. So, work I did. I began my job as a receptionist the day after my high school graduation. I discovered that I might be eligible for college sponsorship by the Ohio Bureau of Vocational Rehabilitation due to a childhood accident. It was like a dream come true when they informed me that they would pay my college tuition for two years. So I started school that fall. I worked forty-four hours per week and took thirteen quarter hours of classes at the Trumbull Campus of Kent State University. I was tired nights, but I always believed it was worth it. A year and a half later, I quit my job and was married. At the start of my junior year, my husband and I moved to Kent so I could finish school as quickly as possible. That's when I really began to feel as though I was training for my career.

It was exciting to be on campus and begin work in my major, early childhood education. I thought I wanted to be a kindergarten teacher, and now I was sure of it. The professors in the early childhood department were so full of enthusiasm and ideas that it spilled over and made you want to work harder than ever. It was required that we spend part of our time in classroom field experiences—and I was thrilled to do so. I was determined to spend every extra moment I had at the University Lab School kindergarten to prepare myself for my career. After all, I'd heard so many stories of people who discovered too late that they didn't really enjoy teaching. I'll never forget my first lesson at the University School. I read a story to the children; then they did a follow-up art lesson and an experience chart. The children responded so well, and the teacher invited me to work with her at any time. I became very involved with the afternoon social studies program in the kindergarten and was sure I'd "found my calling."

The time flew so quickly and before I knew it, another year had gone by and I was ready to do my kindergarten student teaching. My husband and I moved back to Warren, Ohio, and I was assigned to a kindergarten classroom of thirty-six children. Standing alone before them, I was really grateful for the experiences I had in Kent. It was a half-day assignment for ten weeks. For the first three weeks of school, I went home and slept each afternoon. What I wasn't prepared for was just how exhausting it can be to single-handedly deal with thirty-six five-year-olds. But I loved it!

During my kindergarten student teaching, I encountered my first experience in becoming involved with my students' parents. Open House was scheduled for the second week of October. The format was such that parents attended their children's classroom during regular school hours in order to observe the children in their daily school routine. My cooperating teacher asked me if I wanted to teach during Open House. I can't explain how nervous I was! I simply ignored the parents and focused only on the faces of the children. I was amazed at how well behaved the children were under such unnatural circumstances. Afterwards, I talked with parents and was flattered that many of them complimented me on my teaching skills. It seemed as though I had just begun feeling at home when it was time to move on to another student teaching assignment.

This time, I was in a delightful first grade classroom in another Warren city school. What a switch from kindergarten! I think I finally learned phonics while trying to teach reading to my first graders. This school was much different from the one I had just come from. The environment was less structured and more open (after being in many schools, I came to realize this was in great part due to the tone that is set by the building principal). And for a second time, I was fortunate to have a very good and personable cooperating teacher.

Miss Bahr was very organized and specific about lesson plans. (To this day, my plan book resembles hers!) She taught me a good deal about how one relates positively with parents, other staff members, the principal, the secretary, and, of course, the custodian. I've often been thankful that she made me aware of some of the "political realities" that teachers need to cope with and understand.

While working under Miss Bahr, I held my first parent conference. I remember preparing very carefully what points I needed to cover with each parent. I was very nervous and concerned about my appearance. Little did I know, at that time, that the parents were sharing some of my same feelings. All the time I had spent preparing for the conferences was certainly worthwhile. They went very smoothly, providing me with a positive first parent-conference experience. In March of that school year, I finished my student teaching and graduated from Kent.

Graduating in March proved to be very beneficial. I was able to make personal appearances when applying for jobs, and I was three months ahead of most new graduates. Perhaps more importantly, though, I was able to become a substitute teacher for nearly four months. Apparently, during the spring, it is very difficult to obtain substitute teachers for a variety of reasons. Therefore, I worked all but two days during the time I was available for substitute work. It enabled me to teach in approximately eighteen different schools, in six different grade levels, and become acquainted with principals who might later remember me when job opportunities became available.

The old adage, "Being at the right place at the right time," certainly applied to my securing the job interview that led to my present teaching position. I happened to be in the county board of education office talking over my credentials with the man in charge of personnel, when his phone rang. After a few moments, he covered the mouthpiece and asked, "You did say you wanted kindergarten, didn't you?" I then overheard him say he had an interviewee right here that he'd send over for an interview. I remember quite clearly that my interview was scheduled for April 8th.

When I met Mr. Bell, I was immediately comfortable. He looked over my credentials and letters of recommendation, asking questions in reference to them. We then discussed kindergarten philosophies and some of my ideas for implementing a kindergarten program. Near the end of the interview he asked me if I would be available to substitute for one of his teachers in May. As I drove home, I felt that the interview had gone well, but I was sure that I would not be hired since I had no experience. Meanwhile, I went about filling more applications and hoping I'd be called for more interviews.

Mr. Bell's kindergarten teacher became ill in May, and I substituted for her several times. During the time I was teaching, Mr. Bell would come into the room often—but he never mentioned the job! Then he finally informed me that I was being considered for three positions, either a kindergarten, first, or second grade classroom. He then asked if I could finish out the year for his kindergarten teacher. It was as though the roof had caved in on me! Here I was, being offered a chance to prove my teaching skills for the job I wanted and I knew I had to turn down the offer. Two weeks earlier, I had promised to finish out the year in the school where I had done my first grade student teaching. However, one month later, I was hired for the kindergarten position I wanted so much. I couldn't believe it, I had been so afraid I wouldn't get hired my first year out of school. I've always wondered what those letters from my Kent professors and cooperating teacher had in them—working hard really had paid off.

That summer, I spent every possible moment thinking about and planning for my first year as a teacher. I wanted to be the best—I wanted to prove to those who had expressed their confidence in my ability that they had not made a mistake. I must have spent two weeks in my new classroom—organizing, arranging, and rearranging furniture—trying to prepare the best learning environment for my new students.

The bulletin boards were ready, the room was finally arranged to my satisfaction, the name tags were neatly printed, all was prepared for the first day when I was to greet my children. But I couldn't sleep the night before! I had mailed a letter introducing myself to each parent, but I hadn't met them yet. Would they like me? After all, the teacher I was replacing had been well-liked by the community, and I was brand new and they were aware of it. I'd heard people had been asking about "the new kindergarten teacher." And the children—I'd been prepared for the way kindergarten children might react to the first day of school—but would they be comfortable with me? I knew how important this first day would be for them. Would I ever fall asleep! "I'll look terrible tomorrow if I don't!" That morning I wore the special dress I had bought, hoping I'd look "like a teacher." Then at 8:15 they begin to arrive. The children were so cute —new clothes, new shoes, and new haircuts. Some were frightened and hid behind their parents. Others, well, they couldn't wait to begin. I began to realize that this was new for all of us, the children and their parents, as well as for me.

I worked very hard those first weeks—again I rearranged the furniture, realizing things weren't exactly as I thought they'd be. Gradually, I began to receive some feedback that my principal and the parents were pleased with my teaching. It was a good beginning.

The teacher before me had utilized parent volunteers in the kindergarten. When I was approached by the principal concerning this, I told him that this would be new for me, but that I wanted to give it a try, with his help. Actually, I thought to myself, "How am I going to teach and deal with discipline when there is a parent constantly watching me? And what will I do with them?" It was a little awkward at first, but I came to depend on my parent volunteers and looked forward to their participation. During my first year, fourteen mothers originally volunteered. By the end of the year, twelve of them were still participating once a week in the program. I realized that I did have to be very organized so that I could get the maximum advantage of a classroom volunteer. But it was a worthwhile program then and now. I have found that parents are willing to help out in any and all capacities. They work at learning centers, cut paper for art activities, and help out with clerical work—among many other duties. Participating parents have related to me how much they enjoy being able to take part in their child's classroom and *thank me* for letting them participate! I have become so accustomed to having parents in my classroom that I can't imagine ever being hesitant about the volunteer program. Last year, I spoke to some fellow kindergarten teachers at a county kindergarten meeting on the pros and cons of a volunteer program and ways to go about establishing such a program.

As anyone who teaches kindergarten knows, there is a lot of room for teacher creativity and flexibility in establishing a curriculum. This has always been one of the most appealing aspects of kindergarten for me.

However, during my first year of teaching, I began to feel that I would appreciate some type of readiness program. I wanted something well-researched and field-tested that would offer more scope and sequence to our existing curriculum. My principal felt that I should examine a number of readiness programs, choose a few that I liked, and then get back to him. That spring I attended an Elementary/Kindergarten/Nursery Educators Conference in Columbus, Ohio. There was a large array of readiness programs on display for teachers to examine. I talked with salespeople, looked at materials, and collected brochures from many of the programs. One in particular seemed appealing to me. I talked with my principal about two programs and told him which one I preferred. We then contacted a sales representative and arranged to meet with her and a reading consultant to review the program with us. Then Mr. Bell talked with a principal in a nearby district which was currently using the program. My principal arranged for me to visit a classroom to see a teacher and the children using the program. I was already partial to this approach; now I wanted to see how the children responded to the lessons and the materials. Our reading teacher confirmed that the program was sound, and we purchased it. I began to use the new readiness program during my second year of teaching.

I felt that there were unique aspects of this approach which needed to be explained to the parents. I planned a parent meeting on a weekday evening to discuss the program as well as kindergarten philosophy and other aspects of the curriculum. Last year, about 50 percent of the parents attended the meeting. This year, 90 percent of the parents attended. As a result of this type of meeting, I felt that the parents better understood the rationale behind the kinds of activities their children do in kindergarten. It also serves to familiarize parents with some of the materials their children are using in school.

I was extremely pleased with the progress the children were making in prereading skills as a result of the new program. However, this fall when the children who had gone through this program entered first grade, some unexpected circumstances arose. The first grade teachers had not been properly familiarized with this kindergarten readiness approach and its goals. As a result, they were not fully aware of the kinds of skills the children had worked on in kindergarten. The children knew sound-letter associations, but they did not in all cases know the names of the letters of the alphabet. At first, I was upset and felt personally injured when the teachers were criticizing the program which I had advocated. However, I realized that it was a situation in which lack of communication could cause some real personal friction and arranged time to articulate and support the rationale behind the new program and explain it more fully to the first grade teachers. The key to being able to accomplish this was to emotionally detach myself and deal with the problem rationally.

I really do love teaching kindergarten. The children are so responsive and eager to try new things. And there *is* something to be said about being their first teacher. Just the other day, a little second grade girl, who had been my student, walked through my room. She paused and looked around, then turned to me and said, "You know, Mrs. Krisher, I love this room and I love you. You were the bestest teacher I ever had." It's nice to know that along the way we've not only taught the children some academic skills, but provided them with happy memories of their childhood.

In the spring of my first year of teaching I began to work toward my master's degree. I found that while I loved working with the children, I also missed the stimulation of a college environment. Now that I had my own classroom, some of the theory began to make even better sense and I wanted to learn more about the nature of the child I was trying to teach.

This is my third year teaching, and in the spring of this year I will graduate again. Funny, I always thought that the voyage would end when I became a teacher. But it didn't. I saw that I needed to keep moving and growing. It's difficult to pinpoint what's in the offing . . . perhaps I'll start a family . . . perhaps I'll continue my education. After all, I'm only 25, and there are many more seas to sail yet—the voyage has only begun!

P.S.
Honey–
The leftover roast is for your supper. Please don't eat the chicken, it's for tomorrow.
      Love,
      M.

What's Going On: PART II
The Venturesome

Community Development Studies 3

In taking the time to describe' the launching of a professional role, Michele LeLaidier Krisher shared the development of her commitment to teaching young children and her embarkation into the professional scene of action where she took a stand on an educational concern. The narrative was important because it highlighted the fact that the dimension of personal relationships with parents and with teachers at all levels of our education influences our attitudes toward teaching. However, in the introduction to her voyage, Michele also shared another dimension that is equally as important as personal relationships. That dimension was reflected in her knowledge and awareness of the complexities of change processes in home/school/community interaction.

Several statements in Michele's introduction emphasized the fact that the voyage toward becoming an effective professional educator requires more than positive experiences with adults and children. Those statements point to the intellectual dimension in becoming an educator and serve to highlight material to be covered in part II.

—It seems to me that the whole educating process would be much more effective if all concerned could work together as one team striving for a common goal. . . . We need to be viewed by parents as a support system. . . . (see chapter 3).

—One way in which we can begin to help is to provide means by which parents are actively involved in their children's education. Parents can help plan curricula. . . . (see chapter 4).

—. . . we first need to help parents realize that their skills are valuable

43

and that they are effective educators of their children (see chapter 5).

—The restructuring and/or development of attitudes is the only viable means of fostering home/school/community interaction. (It calls for a changing of roles [see chapter 6 and chapter 7]).

The fact that Michele began with her belief that the whole education process would be more effective if all concerned would work together as one team striving for a common goal is not a surprise. We have had the opportunity to work with Michele and to be heartened by her ability to draw on current knowledge of social foundations and community development. Michele's statements concerning the active involvement of parents in their children's education reflect her awareness of research by social scientists who recognized that clearness of goals is a critical factor that can either activate and/or limit change. It has been noted that change breeds change—that attention to provisions for adequate food, clothing, shelter, and social arrangements for employment and involvement of the people who are to change in the planning and education of projects may cause subsequent awareness of alternatives in attitude toward life and education.

Building Support Mechanisms at the Local Community Level

Past research in the relationship between civic and educational attitudes and levels of involvement in resolution of educational issues (Lynn and Flora 1973; Cibulka 1975; Holleman 1975; Mesa 1976) has shown that when parents and teachers perceive local institutions as helping rather than hindering, their participation increases. Howard James (1975) has said that reform must begin in the community; he has described local ventures concerned with building up the local community so that members of the public have organizations about which they can make decisions. The Lafayette, Indiana, plan, which James describes, rests on his position that reform must begin in the community. The premises in the plan include:

1. While federal and state programs may affect children, the crucial decisions are made in the community. Reform must begin there.

2. Services in the community are fragmented, selective, or nonexistent. Since services usually compete for funds, attention must be given to developing a plan to which all groups contribute.

3. Even when services exist, parents must be motivated to seek help. Attention must be given to recruitment.[1]

[1]Howard James, *The Little Victims: How America Treats Its Children* (New York: David McKay, 1975), p. 344. Reprinted by permission.

Freidman (1973) has addressed the issue of recruitment. The recruiter or the interviewer needs to be aware of the greater potential for projecting his own needs onto the family, and for coming across as a blaming rather than as a helping person. In this regard, the designation of parents as potentially positive change agents (in terms of specific ways the parents can improve the child's school situation) can allay guilt and alleviate upset.[2]

Scribner and Stevens (1975) also have described a mechanism which a group might adopt for giving the school-community a focus. The mechanism is public awareness of agreed-upon criteria for evaluating a school's success. The criteria, described by the authors as the Vermont Design, include the following measures of accountability:

1. The emphasis is on each child's own way of learning through discovery and exploration.

2. Each individual is working according to his own ability.

3. Each child is working toward evolving a set of personal values and developing responsibility.

4. The school environment is continually expanding from classroom to environment.

5. The environment provides for students and adults to learn from each other.[3]

Although one advocate of parent involvement contends that any intelligent parent can sit in on a class for thirty minutes and get a halfway decent idea of what is going on,[4] one should keep in mind that the concept of accountability is a touchy subject.* Advocates of the position that parents should be involved in selection of their children's teachers warn that it is "critical if parents are to make decisions they have not had the opportunity to make before, (that) they need some basic training and briefing."[5]

What can happen without a thorough briefing period for both parents and educators concerning the goal of parent involvement is apparent in the following interview of some parents. It reviews the global provisions of parent involvement established by Title I funding legislation and, at the same time, points out that we have to attend to parental role clarification in order to get at the subject of working together as one team striving for a

[2]Robert Friedman, ed., *Family Roots of School Learning and Behavior Disorders* (Springfield, Ill.: Charles C. Thomas, 1973), p. 91.

[3]Harvey B. Scribner and Leonard B. Stevens, *Make Your Schools Work* (New York: Simon and Schuster, 1975), pp. 82–83.

*See Henry C. Johnson, "Court, Craft, and Competence: A Re-Examination of Teacher Evaluation Procedures," *Phi Delta Kappan* 57 (1976): 606–10.

[4]Martin Buskin, *Parent Power* (New York: Walker and Co., 1975), p. 15.

[5]Scribner and Stevens, *Make Your Schools Work*, p. 40.

common goal. The interview was originally published in *Kaleidoscope* (Winter 1977). The purpose of the magazine, which is produced by the Massachusetts Board of Educational Information Services, is to provide a vehicle for coverage of new projects that are successfully fitting federal and state legislation to community needs throughout the state of Massachusetts. At the same time, the editor, Jennifer Skeele, is concerned with "coverage of particular projects that may stimulate more precise thinking about the sort of innovative projects that could be implemented elsewhere."[6]

Title I Parents Discuss Their Role in Effecting Educational Change

Title I of the Elementary and Secondary Education Act was passed in 1965 to supplement and improve the educational opportunities of educationally deprived children in low income areas. These are children who need assistance to perform at the grade level for their age. Although concentration of low income families identifies the area Title I will serve, educational need determines who is to participate in the program.

Parental involvement has always been an understood part of Title I, and it became part of the law in 1971. The United States Commissioner of Education Sidney P. Marland, Jr. indicated that such involvement is essential to the success of Title I. Therefore, each school district must have a system-wide council, half the members of which must be Title I parents whose task is to participate in the planning, operation, and evaluation of the district's Title I program. The United States Office of Education also recommends that parent councils be organized at each Title I school.

The local Parent Advisory Council (PAC) is a policy advisory body consisting, usually, of seven to fifteen members, but all parents at a target school are invited to participate. A city PAC may send one representative and one alternate to the state PAC for every $500,000 it receives. Cities and towns not qualifying, are represented by a county delegate. Elections to the state PAC are held every October by each county or district, which elects the people eligible to represent them for one year.

Kaleidoscope met with six members of the State Parent Advisory Council of Title I to discuss their role as parents and PAC members in serving Title I and Title I children. The following article is taken from a recorded interview; unfortunately, the discussion was too long to be included in its entirety. Kaleidoscope has, on occasion, provided a synopsis of background information for clarity and brevity. Present for the interview were Virginia Canty, Title I parent from Chicopee and president of the state PAC; Ann Bailey, Title I

---

[6]J. K. Skeele, *Kaleidoscope 18: Fruits of Cooperation* (Winter 1977): 5.

parent from Springfield, secretary to the state PAC and ex-president to the state PAC; Beverly Mitchell, Title I parent from Boston, president of the Boston PAC and chairman of the legislative committee; Cindy Tatelman, Title I parent from Revere and Head Start teacher; Judith Fisher, Title I parent from Mashpee and corresponding secretary of the program committee, and Alice Pagliorulo, Title I parent from Revere and member of the program committee.

Kaleidoscope: *Many believe parental involvement has a positive effect on students' academic achievement. There has been no conclusive study made, but we would be interested in hearing what you, as parents and parent advisory council members, think about this.*

Ann: If there is any effect on children, it has to be at the local school level. We at the state level are monitoring and evaluating programs, but we're not actually making a difference on children's achievements.

Cindy: I think one of the good effects of parental involvement is the positive attitudes that participating parents convey to the children.

Beverly: And because Title I is federally funded, Title I classrooms are accessible to parents, which has not always been true of in-school projects. With this contact, parents are exposed to teaching techniques and games they can take back into the home. Unfortunately, teachers and administrators see parents as a threat because they have not yet come to terms with the fact that parents can help teach their children.

Ann: I don't think there's any doubt that a parent's involvement helps his own children. But how much is a PAC helping all the Title I children in its district? What do we as a PAC, as a group, do for all the kids? That's the question.

Kaleidoscope was interested in hearing how parents who were not participating could be reached by either a local or state PAC.

Beverly Mitchell replied:
One of the biggest problems any city has is getting parents involved. This program is for educationally deprived children in low income areas who are that way because they have parents who don't care. To ferret out the parents who do care is quite a task. You'll find them, but you have to first dig them out and then educate them about Title I.

Cindy: I think rather than not caring, they're "innocently ignorant" of how they can help their children's education.

Virginia: I live in a housing project where parents don't care what their children are doing, in school or anywhere else. And they're not about to commit themselves to go to meetings and find out about their kids' education.

Beverly: I think another factor is the stigma that's attached. A parent may care, but he's terrified of being labelled a "poor parent."

Virginia: Or an "ignorant parent."

Ann: I have to disagree with all these things. Poor parents have been

47

systematically excluded from any part of school. They have been intimidated; they have been put down; they have been insulted. The only time they are ever asked to school is when their child's in trouble, and then they're told what rotten parents they are and what rotten children they have. You can't talk about these parents as you would upper middle class parents who sit on the school committee with the people who run the school, who are the teachers, who are the administrators, who are the business people, the lawyers, the doctors. We're talking about people who have been excluded from every part of society they could be excluded from. And school is just one more place. There they tell the parents, "We don't want anything to do with you unless we call you." You don't get parents involved because they know they're not wanted. And on a Title I PAC, you feel this even more for a long, long, time. It takes a lot of really hard fighting.

And poor parents don't have the time to volunteer to spend time at the schools, because they're out earning a buck so their kids can eat. That's what comes first. So that is why you don't get parent involvement.

Alice: And you get a lot of people who are afraid to attend a meeting because they've only gone to the eighth grade and are afraid of making fools of themselves.

Cindy: I don't think finances have anything to do with it. Schools have alienated parents regardless of financial status. They have never wanted parents to get involved because they pose a threat. But what I see today is very exciting. The Head Start program has made real progress in the past five years, and this, too, is a low income group. I have seen parents who were never interested who, each year these special services are in effect, become less alienated and less reluctant to come to schools, to come to meetings to learn. They are now genuinely interested in participating and in helping their children.

Virginia Canty reminded us that while the federal regulations dictate parent participation, they don't clearly specify who is to be responsible for soliciting this support. She voiced her concern that somehow the job had been relegated to the parents themselves, while the schools remained insensitive to their own role in inciting parent participation.

The school system's responsibility to the PAC consists of providing the council with all the information it needs to function, of establishing specific means for answering parents' questions, of indicating the council's views in the Title I applications, and, at least once a year, of evaluating the effectiveness of its funded programs in meeting stated goals.

The panel offered the following views:
Beverly and Ann agreed that since a school system is being paid to comply with federal regulations requiring a local PAC, it is the responsibility of the school system to ensure participation. PAC members can act effectively as advisors, but should not be expected to undertake the entire effort.

Beverly: In May of 1975, Boston's federal court ordered parent participation as a part of the desegregation program. There are now parent groups operating in every school in this city, with mandated educational plans. So, if the federal court can mandate such that the school system knows it means business, why hasn't the federal government, H.E.W., been in here mandating PAC participation, and standing behind the regulations it passed?

Ann: The Local Education Agencies can do it, but the federal government lets them off. It is felt that as long as they seem to be making an effort, it's okay. But unless the PAC has help, it may turn into nothing but a recruiting council.

Kaleidoscope: *A further problem of the relationship between the local Title I Director and the PAC was also mentioned; Judith Fisher explained that some directors who were new to the job never learned to use parents, while still others merely tried to placate them with "pats on the back" and first name friendliness. Ann Bailey ruefully acknowledged that the less formal education a parent had, the more likely he was to receive such treatment.*

On the subject of community involvement outside of the PAC, the panel had a number of interesting comments. Apparently, a collaboration of community groups had originally established the PAC guidelines, and in a Title I proposal, a checklist of other involved agencies is required. Some members felt that while other agencies could be of great help, such as neighborhood health centers, providing resources and helping to assess needs, it was generally agreed that, at times, Title I funds were awarded to agencies unable to fulfill their obligations. Greater care taken in the awarding of monies would produce improved cooperation and collaboration between Title I and other agencies.

Cindy added:
PACs learn where their friends are. PAC developed a relationship with the Boston Teachers Union, for example, and what we couldn't get from the school department, we got from the union. If you can't deal with the school system, you deal with the union, and if you can't deal with the union, then you find somebody else.

Vehement disagreement arose over the question of what actual power the state PAC had to effect changes. Voting power in the elections was a reality for some at the local level, but not for others, and a few felt that because they worked with the state Department of Education, they were more influential with their local school systems. Others lamented that even this did little or nothing to enhance their powers to effect change.

Cindy outlined her understanding of PAC's responsibilities and powers:
We're watchdogs. We oversee that the money allotted is used to the fullest, even though we can't make any demands of the school system. We try to advise, but the school system has the right to ignore it. It takes a great deal of time and work. You can't expect every Title I parent to participate, but that doesn't mean other children should be penalized. Our job is to see that the programs run correctly and smoothly. And the state PAC makes sure that the local PACs are functioning, which requires a great deal of dissemination about the rights of parents.

Beverly: I see our role as state PAC people as one of watching what the state Department of Education is doing with the Title I monies, and disseminating information to the local PAC: letting them know what the regulations mean, what Washington is saying, what we find out about programs, and supplying them the information necessary to function as an autonomous body at the local level. The state PAC needs to be constantly aware of what the state education agency is doing.

Ann: And we have to watch the school systems because they don't always know what's going on.

Virginia: That's right. We ran into a problem with the school committee in my community. One member who knew nothing about Title I, asked, "If it's going to cause this kind of a hassle, can't we do without the money?" It was obviously time to do some educating about Title I. And now we have a very good working relationship with them. They have the final say on how any Title I money is spent, but we can make suggestions, and never once has an educational suggestion been rejected. There have been other things over which we've had heated discussions, but never over an educational suggestion from the local PAC.

Ann: As a state PAC we had a voice in hiring the state Title I Director Joaquim Baptista and that's something more than if we hadn't had a PAC at the state level. State PAC members also go on program reviews which offers us an excellent chance to see what happens with Title I and then get back to the parents.

Cindy: We also have observation committees, an idea we have been able to share with other locals through the state PAC. Different approaches will be appropriate with different local districts. The observation committees make suggestions and recommendations to the school system. Revere, for example, has a screening committee, something which came about through parent pressure. No staff members, including the director, can be hired or fired without the screening committee's involvement. Now, not just anybody will staff our Title I program. This is not mandatory, so other cities may not have it, but we share ideas and achievements like this, and other places use them as dictated by their particular needs.

Ann: A number of us are on committees to draw up new Title I policy. And our training sessions are important.

Kaleidoscope: *What kind of training?*

Virginia: Procedure, What Title I is. What's expected of parents. What they, as parents on local or city or local PACs, can do, and so forth.

Ann: We also set an example. We run workshops, and people who see us can say, "There's a parent who hasn't been to college, who's not rich, and she's doing something. She's been able to learn, so I can too." When only administrators talk to parents, the parents say, "I'm not going to be able to do this." So the state PAC serves as an example and an incentive.

Cindy: I think we also serve to demonstrate certain responsibility a parent has toward his children. The dissemination of information of rights and responsibilities is extremely important at any level.

Kaleidoscope: *Finally, what advice would you give other advisory councils?*

Beverly: Stand up behind what you believe in.

Ann: And stay together—don't let them separate you. Divide and conquer, they do it time after time. Stick together when you've decided on something. Stay by it and stay by each other.

Cindy: Demand communication. Demand it.

Ann: Demand respect.

Cindy: Right. And you must understand how to approach certain situations, and then follow through.

Ann: I guess it takes information and courage.

Virginia: Say that louder, Ann, it takes information and courage.[7]

Dangers in Using Predetermined Goals

The statement ". . . you must understand how to approach certain community situations and then follow through," has been the subject of study in the social sciences for many years. Much of our knowledge about how to approach community situations has come from anthropologists who have enacted the role of participant-observer in thousands of communities. Margaret Mead shared her conclusions concerning community development several years ago. In 1953 Mead suggested that those who hope to be successful in creating team work in a community must present objectives in a way that allows the community to see the overall goal as compatible with the rest of their personal goals.[8] More recently, Wilensky's (1969) review of community development studies concluded with the observation that "substantial change will not occur unless the target people themselves are involved in the action.[9]

What Wilensky's conclusion means should be read as a sound of warning. Just talking about a predetermined list of goals at parent meetings

---

[7]Reprinted from *Kaleidoscope* (Winter 1977), pp. 14–16 with permission of Jennifer Skeele, Editor, *Kaleidoscope* magazine, Nancy Hewitt, Editorial Assistant, Bureau of Curriculum Services, Massachusetts Department of Education.

[8]Margaret Mead, ed., *Cultural Patterns and Technical Change* (Paris: UNESCO, 1953), p. 312.

[9]Harold Wilensky, "Problems in Application of Social Science," in *Agents of Change*, ed. G. Benveniste and W. F. Illchman (New York: Praeger, 1969), p. 77.

or sending a list of a school's goals home in September or even measuring the amount of congruence or compatibility in goals in a community through preset questions on questionnaires still leaves us at the level of what we know and why we don't know more. We know that substantial change will not occur until the school community is involved in planning and enactment of goals. One need only examine the topics of parent-teacher organization meetings to get some idea of why most communities don't view the school as a support system. Let's look at some substantive and nonsubstantive questions. Do parents and teachers discuss how they can help children by working together, or do they simply give our "particularly useful" (Miller 1971) lists of parent responsibilities such as the following (which was prepared without any consideration of parental resources or, for that matter, parental anxieties about whether they are effective forces in their children's lives)?

> Talk to your child.
> Listen to your child.
> Read to your child.
> Take him on trips.
> Tune in on thoughtful programs on T.V.
> Join the public library—make his first trip a joy.
> Buy books for your child.
> Keep your child well.
> Guide your child towards better movie going.
> Accept your child as he is.[10]

Do parents and teachers discuss how to help each other and their children develop the capacity to contribute to social cohesion, or do they give out reference lists such as the following, which help to entrench the attitude that "school children have always been cheated."[11]

> 1957 Goldenson   *Helping Your Child to Read Better*
> 1962 Strang   *Helping Your Child Improve His Reading*
> 1971 Smith   *Parents and Reading*
> 1975 Smethurst   *Teaching Young Children to Read*

Finally, what do parent-teacher organizations do about the reams of data collected on student achievement? Do they accept labels such as "a poor self-image," "lack of language development," or "negative attitude toward school and authority," or do the parent-teacher organizations seek out resources to solve the problems?

---

[10]Burley Miller, "What Parents Can Do for the School," in *Parents and Reading,* ed. Carl B. Smith (Newark, Del.: International Reading Association, 1971), pp. 107–11.

[11]Stella Chess and Jane Whitbread, *How to Help Your Child Get the Most Out of School* (New York: Doubleday, 1974), p. 283.

> Cynthia: Richard, HELP!! I'm trying to explain that Michelle's statements about striving for a common goal and the need to view schools as a support system opens a Pandora's box labelled "change."
>
> Richard: That's OK, open it. Several people associate change with overnight remedies or changes in curriculum material and don't get to the business of change as the difficult business of attitude change.
>
> Cynthia: That's the problem. As soon as I open the box, I'm tempted to fall into the trap of lecturing about the change process. As a fail-safe I remind myself of two things. First is a wise old professor's advice: "If you want to understand something: try to change it," and second is a list of 400 hypotheses called What Accounts for Sociocultural Change that I had an exam on as an undergraduate.[12]
>
> Richard: I like the first. What do you remember most about the second?
>
> Cynthia: That change causes tension.
>
> Richard: What else?
>
> Cynthia: That there is no operational definition that will help you predict which of the 400-plus variables associated with change are the most important to deal with in every local home/school/community situation.
>
> Richard: OK. Then we restate the fact that we don't know more because we can't predict what will occur in every community, and we'll leave the discussion of striving for a common goal in the background for this chapter. Then we can continue the chapter with a discussion of community development studies in roles and support systems.

A Selected Review of Community Studies

Discussion of the roles of community members and parents in building a support system for home/school/community interaction has, until recently, been presented at a theoretical rather than an applied level. In 1972, the Center for the Advanced Study of Education invited twenty leaders in early childhood education to present their views and share information on what they believed to be the role of parents and educators

---

[12]Gilbert Kushner et al., What Accounts for Sociocultural Change? A Propositional Inventory (Chapel Hill, N.C.: Institute for Research in Social Science, University of North Carolina, 1962).

in fostering home/school interaction. The major forms of teamwork identified by these educational leaders can be summarized into three areas:

1. Familiarizing parents with the content and techniques of the program.
2. Involving parents in programs designed to provide both general information about child development and specific information about their own children.
3. Including parents in decision making processes regarding goals and operation of the program.[13]

The task of judging the extent of implementation of these areas of parental involvement in early childhood programs is somewhat lightened by the publication *40 Innovative Programs in Early Childhood Education* (Fallon 1973). This book provides detailed descriptions of current practices in programs in twenty-seven states. Each description was compiled by program personnel and was, according to Fallon, submitted with a willingness to subject program efforts "to scrutiny by a wide reading audience."[14] Our scrutiny was concerned with finding answers to the following questions:

Questions	Answers	*Total* Programs = 40
Do you include parent participation in your program?	Yes	27
Do you think parents are solely responsible for preparing children for schools?	Yes	1
Do you set aside 2 or 3 conferences, meetings, or home visits every year?	Yes	7
Do you supply parents with activities and materials to use with their children at home?	Yes	3
Does your staff offer parents workshops in human relations and construction of teaching aids?	Yes	1
You have stated that you did not know right from the beginning what role your parents were going to play. Did this		

---

[13]Ronald K. Parker and Mary C. Day, "Comparisons of Preschool Curricula," in *The Preschool in Action,* ed. Ronald K. Parker (Boston: Allyn and Bacon, 1972), p. 498.
[14]Berlie J. Fallon, ed., *40 Innovative Programs in Early Childhood Education* (Belmont, Calif.: Fearan, 1973), p. xii.

then involve being flexible and gradually making parents feel comfortable?	Yes	2
Do you believe that parent involvement is essential?	Yes	5
Do you ask parents to submit an end of the year evaluation?	Yes	3
Do parents' votes count on policy issues such as staff selection?	Yes	5
Can you specify what is essential?	No	40

Our conclusion that a gap exists between theory and practice in the forty programs outlined in Fallon's review was based on the following steps. First, we read through program descriptions in order to find any references to parent participation and/or parent involvement. As shown, twenty-seven of the forty programs mentioned that parent participation was included in their program. The second step was to identify how these twenty-seven programs defined and/or enacted parent participation. Once again we went through the program descriptions and found that one program associated participation with their belief that parents are solely responsible for preparing children for school. Seven programs associated participation with conferences, meetings, or home visits. Three programs described participation as telling parents what to do with their children at home, while one program offered workshops to help parents learn what they can do in order to be involved in their children's education. Refreshingly, the staff of two programs admitted that they did not know right from the beginning what role parents were going to play and therefore concentrated on making them feel comfortable. Although in reading through the review of these forty innovative programs we found that five programs described parent involvement as essential, we could not find a clearly stated reason as to how the program organizers arrived at this conclusion. Without having the opportunity to consider a clear rationale for mechanisms, such as end of the year evaluations and voting on staff selection or curriculum material selection, the reader is left with the impression that a gap exists between theoretical "ought to be" statements of home/school/community interaction and the reality of "what is" going on.

One further example of the gap between theory and practice in teamwork in community development will be used as an introduction to what associations and organizations are available to help parents and educators build a support system for home/school/community interaction at the local level. In 1974 Litwak and Meyer offered a theoretical description of linking mechanisms that can be created to foster home/school/community interaction. The linking mechanisms they described were outlined in specific roles that they believe can close

55

the social distance between the home, school, and community and, therefore, create change in communities where the schools have a closed-door policy.

Building on past research findings that the clearness of goals is a critical factor that can either activate or limit cooperation, Litwak and Meyer (1974) attempted to share with those concerned with the practice of school/community relations that different roles, or linking mechanisms, have different effects on either activating or limiting the attainment of specific goals. If, for example, your goal is to close the social distance between the home, school, and community and open communication channels, then the role of a "detached worker" is more important than getting an "opinion leader" in the community on your side or even having someone in a position of "formal authority" on your side. Litwak and Meyer (1974) delimited their description of mechanisms of cooperation, or links, between the community and the schools into eight areas.

1. Detached worker: Send a professional to the home for the purpose of bringing values and norms into harmony, i.e., attempt to influence the family.
2. Opinion leader: Find the spokesperson in the community, i.e., work through him or her.
3. Physical facilities: Work through community agencies already established, i.e., attempt to influence through educational or therapeutic programs.
4. Voluntary associations or groups: Present your school program to already established groups in the community.
5. Common messenger: Cultivate cooperation through persons who work in schools and are also members of community organizations.
6. Mass media: Arrange for coverage of programs and events.
7. Formal authority: Use administrators of public agencies and institutions as spokespeople for relating how their facilities support community involvement.
8. Delegated function: Set up middle-people, i.e., those connected to the schools only in the sense of having been charged with the responsibility of linking themselves to the community groups the school seeks to affect.[15]

As you can see in table 3–1, Litwak and Meyer offer evaluations of each mechanism. The basis of their evaluation is whether or not the mechanism hinders or helps to meet the following objective:

A school may be said to have a "program" of school-community relations, by

[15]Eugene Litwak and H. J. Meyer, *School, Family and Neighborhood: The Theory and Practice of School/Community Relations* (New York: Columbia University Press, 1974), pp. 16–19.

our definition, when some deliberate effort is made on the part of the school families to affect the relationship to one another. . . .[16]

Table 3–1 includes six of the linking mechanisms defined above as well as the authors' suggestions for what linking mechanisms to use in different situations.

Whether Litwak and Meyer are right or wrong about the high and low effect of the roles they specify is not the question at this time. The theory they present serves as a useful framework because it highlights the fact that

TABLE 3–1. Comparative Usefulness of Linking Mechanisms for School/Community Relations

School Position	"Open door"	"Closed door"
Interaction Goal	Close social distance	Create social distance
Linking Mechanism		
Detached worker	very high	very low
Opinion leader	potentially moderate, e.g., when community is friendly, or when coupled with another mechanism (e.g., detached worker or mass media) and when used for recruitment.	very low
Voluntary association	moderate; potentially very high when community is friendly.	moderate
Common messenger	low	high
Mass media	low; potentially high only when community is friendly	high
Formal authority	very low	very high

SOURCE: Adapted from E. Litwak and H. Meyer, *School, Family and Neighborhood: The Theory and Practice of School/Community Relations* (New York: Columbia University Press, 1974), pp. 27–28. Copyright 1974 by Columbia University Press. Reprinted by permission.

[16]Ibid., pp. 3, 27.

a school district cannot insure they will have an effect on the community just because they have lots of public relations committees or high attendance at public meetings. Different roles have different effects on communication and community development. Litwak and Meyer's work is valuable insofar as it helps us to specify roles, tasks, and possible effects of various roles on the community viewing the school as a support system. Their work can also serve as a discussion point to help parents and teachers decide whether or not to seek outside help from voluntary associations concerned with educational issues and parent involvement.

Sources of Help for Home/School/Community Development

Just what form the outside help might take depends, of course, on the level of community development you believe your neighborhood is ready for. If you are concerned primarily with increasing the awareness of individuals so that they may choose among alternatives and later implement those choices, we suggest you write to the following associations for information about current activities and publications in home/school/community interaction.

Center for the Study of Parent Involvement
5240 Boyd Street
Oakland, California   94618

Institute for Responsive Education
704 Commonwealth Avenue
Boston, Massachusetts   02215

National Committee for Citizens in Education
Wilde Lake Village Green
Columbia, Maryland   21044

A recent copy of *Network,* published by the National Committee for Citizens in Education (NCCE), included checklists on Organizing for Action, A Readers Exchange of Ideas, and How to Rate Yourself as a Parent (e.g., you lose thirty points every time you fall asleep at a parent-teacher meeting). Columns entitled "Learn What Teachers Know" and "Home Learning Materials" were also included. Arguments in favor of release time from work for parents who contributed their time to schools and a call for an ERIC Clearinghouse* for parents were set on either side of a review of organizations' positions on current federal legislation. In addi-

*See Appendix B.

tion, the spread of literature attacking the Child and Family Services Act of 1975 was traced down to its original source.

The letter reproduced below gives a clear idea of the purpose and strategies of NCCE.

NATIONAL COMMITTEE FOR CITIZENS IN EDUCATION
Suite 410, Wilde Lake Village Green
Columbia, Maryland   21044
301-997-9300

October 6, 1976

Dr. Cynthia Wallat
Dep't. of Early Childhood Education
Kent State University
Kent, Ohio 44242

Dear Dr. Wallat:

Thanks for writing to us. I would like to tell you how NCCE works with local parent groups and ask that you relay this information directly to the Parent Advisory Board.

Last year NCCE started a nation-wide program to mobilize citizens for action to improve the quality of public education. This campaign is called the Parents' Network.

We are convinced that the key to continued public support of public education is the active participation and a real share in decision-making by parents and other citizens. Many groups have been working toward this goal, but until now there has been no way of communication and sharing information, experience and skills. This is the purpose of the Parents' Network.

In the last year more than one hundred and fifty organizations in thirty-two states have joined. (see enclosed list in the back page of our newspaper, NETWORK) By participating in the network, groups receive names of people who call us on our toll-free telephone line (800-NET-WORK).

In addition, all groups are invited:

—to participate in a Citizens' Training
Institute to share skills and improve organizational
effectiveness;

—to subscribe to NETWORK, a new school year
newspaper for parents;

—to participate in NCCE research studies like
the privacy of student records and violence in the
schools.

Parents' Network is not another bureaucracy. It
has no by-laws, no constitution, no executive board.
Individual groups are not considered chapters of
NCCE. Organizations with dues paying members may
join the Parents' Network with a minimum fee of $15
and a maximum fee of $50 on the basis of 10¢ a
member. Other groups with no formal dues structure
may join at the minimum fee of $15.

Any parent or citizen group can join in the
Parents' Network. Membership requests are accepted
as long as the organization seeking to join is
concerned about the improvement of public education
for all children.

Sincerely,

Stanley Salett
Senior Associate

SS/rb

The Institute for Responsive Education also systematically publishes information pertaining to community development studies. The quarterly journal of the institute, *Citizen Action in Education,* reports on new models and ideas for citizen involvement in school decision making. In *Schools Where Parents Make a Difference* (Davies 1976), eleven success stories have been published together in one volume, available from the address printed above.

One can find descriptions of the Center for the Study of Parent Involvement (CSPI) in its monthly bulletin *Apple Pie.* The growth of organizations concerned with school/community interaction is exemplified by the center's sponsorship of annual national conferences on parent involve-

---

The authors wish to thank Mr. Salett for permission to reprint his letter.

ment. For current information concerning conference reports you may write directly to Dr. Daniel Safran at 5240 Boyd Street, Oakland, California 94618. The first annual conference report (November 7–10, 1976) was entitled *Parent Involvement: An Inalienable Right*. The second annual conference (November 3–6, 1977) explored the theme of Parent Involvement and Children's Rights. Parent leaders, parent/community workers, and educators from all over the country discussed issues relating to parents' roles as advocates for children's rights. The leaflet reproduced below overviews the objectives and services of CSPI.

The Center for the Study of Parent Involvement has been established to:

- Identify and examine parent involvement activities and accomplishments which enhance the value of formal education
- Provide consultation and training to national, state and local education agencies in
    - —preparation of teachers for meaningful interaction with and utilization of parents in various roles as volunteers, decision makers and partners in the education and development of children
    - —preparation of administrators for effective management and implementation of parent and community involvement programs
    - —organization, development and orientation of parent and community advisory committees
    - —planning, implementing and evaluating staff development in the "community domain" for teachers and administrators
    - —policy development for effective parent and community participation in school site, district and state education planning, programming and evaluation
    - —identification of parent and community resources to complement and enrich local educational activities
- Collect information on parent involvement research, action methodology, legislation, administrative innovation and parent and teacher education
- Investigate unique problems of parent involvement in special education and in the educational programs of developing nations rural areas and oppressed peoples
- Prepare and disseminate materials and monographs which con-

tribute to the work of practitioners, researchers, community developers, administrators and students in educational and community affairs

- Bring together the considerable experience of professionals, laypeople and academicians in encouraging the participation of parents in every aspect of their children's education

* * *

CSPI has been working with the Parent Development Project of Pacific Oaks College to provide workshop and conference opportunities for parent/community workers, teachers, administrators, and involved parents. Write to us for information about workshops, inservice training and other educational activities (many of which provide extension credit).

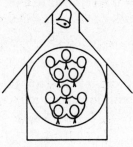

CSPI
5240 Boyd Street
Oakland, CA   94618

Daniel Safran, Director

Richard: That was a lot of information about community development in one chapter—how about summing it up?

Cynthia: Perhaps our readers would rather see how a school that cares about community development can win a writeup in part II.

Richard: OK, after they read it they can go back through this chapter and point out all the mechanisms that might have been à la Litwak and Meyer; organizations mentioned in this chapter that might have been contacted; answers to the extent of parental involvement à la Fallon; and finally how the Weston Plan compares to the steps of the Lafayette Plan and the Vermont Design.

Community 4 Development in Practice

In chapter 3 we discussed various aspects of affecting change that have been pointed out in community development studies. This chapter will be concerned with presenting examples of mechanisms created in a school district that recognizes and acts upon a major point presented in the previous chapter:

—substantial change will not occur in the educational community unless the target people (i.e., parents, students, educators) are involved in the action.

To give direction to the description of community development in practice, we will focus on the three forms of parent involvement described in chapter 3:

—Involving parents in programs designed to provide information about child development.
—Familiarizing parents with the content and techniques of the program.
—Including parents in decision-making processes regarding goals and operation of the program.

From Theory to Practice

You have had a chance to judge some of the complexities of the voyage from theory to practice earlier; Michele LeLaidier Krisher began a voyage in home/school communication when she acted on the theory that learning isolated letters and sounds is not the most important prerequisite for learning to read. We would now like to share with you one further example of professional commitment to community development in practice.

Weston Public Schools

In her keynote speech at a research meeting sponsored by the Department of Learning, Development, and Social Foundations at the University of Cincinnati, Cazden (1977) referred to a school district that has realized that program improvement is not a magical solution such as buying a new curriculum series. The school district further realizes that the complexity of the two simple questions—Who does what? At what time?—depends upon the problem identified in each school by professionals including parents. Realizing that what can be done at this point in time depends upon the availability of information for our readers, the Weston Public Schools have given their permission for reproducing the mechanisms they have created for enactment of community involvement. The enactment of the three forms of involvement described on the first page of this chapter are, as you will see, the product of many sources of cooperation. It would be impossible to thank all the administrators, teachers, parents, students, professors, and community members who helped to build these mechanisms. Succinctly stated, they serve as an inspiration.

Any reader who wishes to communicate with the school system will find that the program director of Weston Public Schools will help put you in touch with the right person.

> Dr. Donald G. Kennedy, Program Director
> Weston Public Schools
> Weston, Massachusetts   02193

INVOLVING THE TARGET PEOPLE TO EFFECT CHANGE

Since the school year 1974–1975, the Weston Public Schools have undertaken extensive program evaluation reviews in the areas of Physical Education K-12, Math K-6, Foreign Language 7-12, Special Education, and Reading, Language Arts, and English K-12. The collection and analysis of data concerning these areas of the curriculum has involved members of the community, the administration, and the faculty of all schools in the district.

In order to establish a shared context with the reader concerning the mechanisms that are used to provide information about community involvement in the change process we have reprinted, with permission, the full text of the public announcement of the 1977–1978 program evaluation on Reading, Language Arts, and English K-12. As you read through the report which appeared in the *School Issues* newsletter that is sent to every resident in the town, you will see that the authors of the report have not fallen into the trap of word inflation. The details concerning the types of data collection and the stages of analysis in the review are clear enough to be replicated in other locations that recognize, as Weston does, that educational objectives must change continuously in order to remain viable. Besides providing the number of individuals on the committee, the report lists the types of data collection mechanisms that have been used in addition to interviews with graduates and parents. These mechanisms for monitoring what needs to be updated and eventually changed included:

> 140 classroom visitations,
> 212 interviews with teachers and administrators,
> 15 interviews with whole classes, and
> 158 individual interviews with students.

The data collection figures presented above are impressive. Yet the compilers of the report are fully aware of the fact that continuing support for school/community interaction depends upon more than the collection of figures. Several statements in the *School Issues* report speak directly to issues that were raised in chapter 2 regarding the victims and the verdict. These statements show awareness of phenomena such as:

1. Teachers being judged as technicians rather than professionals,
2. Teachers being perceived as being at odds with parents,
3. Teachers being judged as not facing the fact that conflict in perceptions of education exist.

Table 4–1 lists a number of examples from the Weston *School Issues* which speak to these three phenomena. As you read the text of the *School Issues* newsletter, you will be able to spot additional examples of Weston's concern for breaking the vicious cycle of blame as well as their concern for involving the target populations of educational change in the change process.

65

TABLE 4–1. Descriptors Used in the Weston Report Regarding Teachers

Descriptor	Examples
Diligent	Committed to instructional improvement
Hardworking	Time and energy expended
Conscientious	Willing to respond to the community
Clearly/Care	Absence of indifference
Candor/Openness	Desire to obtain reactions to improve their program

> **Richard:** I've looked ahead and I'm impressed with Weston! Have you put together a task for the reader as they go through the School Issues? If not, I've got one.
>
> **Cynthia:** No, it's my turn. The School Issues report is for general information on types of data collection mechanisms that can be built as well as an example of the format for reports to the community. In addition to general information, the reader will find this report is useful for several specific purposes:
>
> 1. Read through the report for information that helps you make decisions concerning time requirements, number of individuals you will have to recruit for the review committee, possible reward mechanisms for participants, and the means built in for sharing the report results with the community.
> 2. List the specific phrases that you believe capture the problem identified. For example, "attention to discrete skills and conventions of language is often misdirected and counter-productive."
> 3. Describe why you think that after all the time and effort spent on program evaluations in the district, the recommendations included the phrase "a program for improving school/community relations" must be instituted.

School Issues: May 1977

REPORT OF ENGLISH REVIEW

Background

Beginning with the Physical Education Task Force of 1974-1975, the Weston School Committee has undertaken a series of program evaluations/reviews as part of its commitment to program planning and budgeting in the light of established needs and objectives. So far, there have been program reviews of Physical Education K-12, Math K-6, Foreign Language 7-12 and—most recently—Reading, Language Arts and English 1-12.

Dr. James Squire served as chairman of the English Review Committee, a group of collegiate and secondary school educators and writers, two of them Weston residents, who were assigned the task of evaluating program at both the elementary and secondary levels.

The Review Committee were provided with a 250 page handbook of materials to read prior to their observation of classes in Weston. These background materials included: curriculum guides, test data, staff profiles, statements of Goals and Objectives, Attitudinal Survey responses and Private School Survey results, course outlines and enrollment statistics.

The English Review Committee held its first session on January 9 and visited the elementary, junior high and high schools on the three succeeding days. In the course of their visit, they:

  made 140 separate classroom visitations
  held 145 interviews with teachers of English and Language Arts
  held 60 interviews with counselors, librarians and teachers in other
     subject areas
  held 15 interviews with complete classes
  held 158 individual student interviews
  examined 521 sets of student writing
  interviewed parents, graduates and the School Committee
  visited all support facilities, including the town library
  read the parent responses to the Attitudinal Survey
  interviewed the 5 principals and 2 program directors

On March 14, 1977, the Report of the English Review Committee was presented to the School Committee by Dr. Squire. We are impressed with the professionalism of the review and the quality of the Report, as we were with the qualifications of the Review Committee itself.

Because of your interest in our English program, we would like to invite you to become more informed as to the program's current strengths and weaknesses and to participate in discussions leading to the implementation of the many thoughtful recommendations found in the Report.

We believe that the Report deals with a complex subject extremely well, going beyond such simple solutions as "more basics" or "more creativity".

The Report should serve us well as we plan program development in the Language Arts.

In cooperation with the PTO, we have arranged for Dr. Squire to discuss the Report and respond to questions in a public meeting on May 25 in the Country School auditorium at 8 p.m. We hope you can join us at that meeting.

Recognizing that extracting parts of the Report could lead to misinterpretation, we nevertheless believe that an overview would be useful in providing the community with an understanding of the conclusions. In the remainder of this **School Issues,** we provide a list of the English Review Committee members, their comments on the general strengths of the present program and a summary of their recommendations. Copies of the complete report are available in the Town Library.

ENGLISH REVIEW COMMITTEE

Dr. James R. Squire, Chairman, Ginn-Xerox, Senior Vice President and Publisher; Executive Secretary, National Council of Teachers of English, 1960-1967; Professor of English, University of Illinois, 1959-1968.

Dr. Arthur Daigon, University of Connecticut, Professor of Education.

David Dickinson, Harvard Graduate School, Doctoral Student in Language Development; former teacher.

Dr. Larry Dougherty, Heath Elementary School, Brookline, Principal; Weston Resident.

Dr. Walker Gibson, University of Massachusetts, Amherst, Professor of English Rhetoric, Director of Freshman Composition.

Dr. Donald Graves, University of New Hampshire, Associate Professor of Education.

Mrs. Ardena Manahan, Highland School, Needham, Elementary Teacher; Consultant for Elementary Language Arts.

Ms. Betty Murray, Franklin School, Lexington, Principal.

Richard Niebling, Exeter, New Hampshire, Former Department Chairman, Phillips Exeter Academy, Former School Committee Member.

Mrs. Adrienne Richard, Weston, Professional Writer; Weston Resident.

Dr. Betty Ricker, Cambridge Public Schools, Coordinator of Cultural Arts, Former State English Coordinator, Commonwealth of Massachusetts.

Ms. Frances Russell, Winchester Public Schools, Director of English, K-12; Former State English Coordinator, State of Maine.

General Comments
"The Review Committee identified both strengths and weaknesses in the K-12 program in Weston and discusses these in the report that follows. In spite

of criticisms in specific areas, the Committee believes the Weston community and the administrative and teaching faculty should be well aware of general strengths that virtually all members of the Review Committee agreed were characteristic of the present program.

1. **Teachers in Weston are exceptionally diligent, hardworking, and eager to respond to the wishes of the community.** At every educational level and in almost every classroom, observers found conscientious teachers committing unusual time and resources to instructional improvement. Even as we questioned some of the practices, we were aware of the time and energy being expended to make the educational program work. Experienced school observers were particularly impressed with the absence of indifference or laxity in these schools. Clearly the Weston teachers care.

2. **Teachers in Weston are exceptionally well prepared academically.** Many elementary school teachers have completed college courses in composition and literature beyond the minimal introductory courses required for a baccalaureate degree. Many high school teachers have taken degrees beyond the B.A. level and many have completed college courses in language and composition (and sometimes film, speech, and drama) in addition to undergraduate majors in literature. In sum, the Weston faculty is impressively prepared to teach the English Language Arts.

3. **A major strength is the desire of the School Committee, the administrative staff and the teaching faculty to evaluate and appraise their own programs.** Again and again, Committee members commented favorably on the candor and openness of staff members and their desire to obtain reactions to improve the teaching program. Advance preparation for the review was superb, especially preparation by the Program Directors, who write with a lucidity and directness too seldom found in American education. The principals, too, seemed supportive and helpful. A desire for excellence was apparent everywhere.

4. **The stated curriculum goals and written curriculum are commendable in their commitment to engaging pupils actively in the production of language rather than stressing the independent analysis and study of language.** While the Committee found the concepts imperfectly executed in many classrooms and over the complete K-12 program, it seemed clear that a number of teachers, as well as the Program Directors themselves, see writing as a significant outcome in education.

5. **Teachers and administrators in Weston have a major commitment to teaching the skills of language.** Whether in a first grade classroom or in the twelfth, observers found a strong commitment to teaching the skills and conventions of language. Moreover, "basic skills" seemed to be the primary focus of most classrooms observed and whatever the quality and kind of young people's writing, it seems clear that mechanical and sentence errors on papers are noted, corrected, and revised. As this report makes clear, observers felt that such overt attention to the discrete skills

and conventions of language is often misdirected and frequently counter productive. But the Committee recognizes that teachers presently are responding to what they believe the community wishes. There is no question that the Weston Public Schools are giving more than ample attention to what they see as "basic skills" in reading, spelling, usage, handwriting, and taking dictation. There is good reason to believe that test scores of Weston children are due to something more than innate intelligence and favored background. (A neighboring community with students of roughly comparable backgrounds was ranked in the lowest 10% of all school systems in the State on tests given to all fourth graders.) Clearly the emphasis on skills in Weston has resulted in a substantial level of achievement as measured by standardized tests. Thus, many members of the Committee would commend Weston teachers for their well intended response to community wishes to teach the basic skills. However, the entire Committee believes that the present stress needs to be redirected. The community must realize that teachers are doing a very good job but must further understand that classrooms today cannot and should not be replicas of our own student experiences of some decades ago.

No review of English Language Arts and Reading instruction in the Weston Public Schools conducted over three days can identify with certainty all the opportunities and problems that confront teachers and administrators in the system. Even when supplemented by intensive study of documents, reports, questionnaires, testing results and background materials laboriously gathered and generously submitted by the school staff, such a review at best is likely to be fragmentary, to focus on much information already known to the community and to emphasize certain concerns at the expense of others. Nevertheless, the completeness of the documentation, the openness of teachers at every level, and the interest of staff members in answering fully the many inquiries of the Committee ensured that the report would be reasonably balanced and comprehensive.

This report has been read by all members of the Review Committee and their individual suggestions, modifications, and reservations have been included. The Chairman of the Review Committee emphasizes that members of the Committee are virtually in unanimous agreement on the recommendations. Those differences which did emerge resulted largely from variations in what was seen and observed, not over the interpretation of what was seen. Despite considerable differences in background, members of the Review Committee achieved a surprising degree of consensus.

The charges to the Committee with respect to the various areas of inquiry have been reproduced and underlined at the beginning of each section. The Committee's findings and recommendations then follow.

Given the quality of the student population, the competence of the staff, and the commitment of the community to excellence in education, language and literature education in the Weston Schools should be a continuously stimulating experience for virtually all students. Unfortunately, such stimulation occurs only occasionally in selected classrooms, rather than continuously throughout the program. This was a major concern of the Review Committee and inevitably raises questions to be addressed by those responsible for the education in these schools. . . ."

Summary of Recommendations

1. **"Administration and Supervision**
   - That fragmented scheduling of reading and language arts in grades 1-6 be eliminated and substantial time blocks be provided for integrated learning of the English language arts directed by a single teacher.
   - That instructional supervision be identified as a priority for the Program Directors and for the elementary school principals and that a language arts specialist be employed to assist in inservice education in grades 1-6.
   - That an internal program for monitoring instruction, consistent with Weston's goals, be developed to provide continuing "feedback" information to teachers and instructional supervisors on pupils' progress in reading and language arts.
   - That coordination and communication between grades 6 and 7 and grades 8 and 9 be improved and that intervisitation of classes be encouraged among teachers at different levels.
   - That inservice programs be developed in several areas of critical needs: attending to individual difference within classrooms, the art of questioning, developmental reading in the secondary school, the teaching and writing of poetry.
   - That paraprofessionals, parent volunteers, and aides be employed or secured to provide more time for teachers to attend to individual needs.
   - That a program for monitoring student writing folders be developed for grades 1-6.
   - That heterogeneous grouping be used as the basis of reading and language arts instruction in grades 3-6, unless, through careful inservice education and instructional supervision, an "open-ended" homogeneity can be established within which teachers are able to attend to individual needs.
   - That at all levels ways be found for teachers to spend more time conferring with individual pupils about their writing problems.
   - That a program for improving school-community relations be instituted at the earliest possible opportunity.

2. **Curriculum**
   - That at all levels practice and drill in the basic conventions and skills of language be directly related to actual uses of language.
   - That the focus of the kindergarten program be redefined to emphasize instruction basic to reading and language development.

71

- That far more extensive and far more varied writing experience be provided in grades 2-6 and that a program in writing be initiated for grade 1.
- That the emphasis on the single mode of expository writing in grades 9-12 be expanded to include narrative, poetic, personal and other forms of writing.
- That guidelines be developed to provide for adequate attention to oral language development in grades 1-6.
- That more emphasis be placed in grades 3-8 on skills involved in reading in content areas.
- That a continuous six-year program in composition be developed for grades 7-12 with outcomes clearly specified.
- That a program of developmental reading be developed in grades 7-12 for the 25 percent of all students who seem to require such instruction.
- That a few more selected works of literature be read in common at the junior high school.
- That the goals of ninth grade English be more clearly articulated and that instruction be more clearly related to the capabilities and interests of the entering high school students.
- That the program in literature in grades 9-12 be expanded to include much reading of non-fiction prose, including magazines and newspapers.
- That the teaching of extremely mature works of literature be deem-phasized in grades 10-12 and greater stress be placed on the teaching of worthwhile books that speak to students at this age level, including works of poetry and non-fiction prose.
- That at all levels attention be directed to the reading, writing and oral interpretation of poetry and that a poetry collection be developed in the high school library.
- That rigorous and disciplined study of ideas in the visual media be included in English at all levels of instruction.
- That the AP course be made more rigorous and selective or that it be abandoned."

The Weston School Committee

Becoming Aware of and Identifying Information About Child Development

Confirmation of Squire's report of a high level of professionalism among Weston teachers was soon available within the community. The report recommendations for meeting individual needs, providing more varied writing experiences, and developing a program for monitoring instruction were acted upon immediately after the report was made public. Meetings were scheduled so that all faculty could be involved in discussing organizational issues and planning summer workshops. The workshops were designed to give teachers the opportunity to identify recent information from child development research in order to have the opportunity to verify among themselves what could be fostered in the schools and what could be taught. Plans also were made during the meetings for scheduling workshops for parents who would be "writing consultants" in grades six, seven, and eight. The involvement of parents as "writing consultants" spoke directly to the recommendation for a program for improving school/community relations.

The primary target for the first summer workshop for teachers also spoke to ongoing improvement in school/community relations. The targets set by the staff included:

1. The need for a philosophical framework,
2. The need for a clear statement of expectations according to the children's developmental level,
3. The need for elaboration of techniques to diagnose and teach specific skills,
4. The need for development of strategies that could be used by parents and teachers to assess the activities of step 3 and therefore prevent potential learning problems.

The *Weston Elementary Language Arts Handbook* that was created by over two dozen teachers and administrative staff in the summer of 1977 laid the groundwork for all four of the areas outlined above. The handbook included sections entitled:

1. Philosophical Foundations of Weston Language Arts
2. The Language Arts Experience Chart
3. Explanations and Activities for Oral Language Components
4. Sequences of Writing Development K-6
5. Student Skills Checklist
6. Expectations Concerning Conventions such as Punctuation and Grammatical Terms for Each Grade Level K-6
7. Strategies to Prevent Potential Learning Disabilities

Samples from several of the above areas will be presented later. Before going further, we wish to reiterate at this point that "we know" that substantial change will not occur in communities unless the target populations are involved. The teachers in Weston could have saved themselves a great deal of time and energy if they had not acted on "what we know" about community development. They could have easily voted in a curriculum committee who would have been responsible for searching out textbooks or curriculum guides from other school districts. After looking at the materials they could have simply voted on which series or guide seemed to take care of the weaknesses outlined by the Squire report. But they didn't! The Weston teachers acted on the basis of their knowledge of change processes and theories from community studies. They played the major role in designing and determining the nature of goals and objectives after taking the time for community input into decisions about current practices and needs.

As you will see in the following excerpts from the "Philosophical Framework of Weston Language Arts," "The Language Arts Experience Chart," and "Chart Explanation," the teachers spent time identifying and verifying recent developmental research concerning what can be fostered and what can be taught in language arts.

We have retraced the steps of their development of philosophical statements and have identified those words and statements that can be included in a category entitled **teach** and those words and statements that can be included in a category entitled *foster*. In the following reprint from the philosophical framework, we have italicized items that can be included in the "foster" area and set in boldface type the items in the "teach" area. The items that the Weston teachers have accepted teaching responsibility for are set in bold type. The items that the teachers believe can be fostered in the home and school and community are italicized.

In Appendix D you will find excerpts from the curriculum section "Oral Language." The distinctions between *what can be taught* and *what can be fostered* are not made for you in these sections. As you read through the excerpts from the oral language section you should continue making distinctions for phrases that you think describe something to be fostered (by underscoring once) or for activities that you think can be taught directly (by underscoring twice). We do not expect 100 percent agreement on these judgments of *foster* and **teach** among members of the classes using this book or among parents and teachers who are reading the book together. The fact is that conflict in perceptions of education exists. The problem to begin to work with is to reach consensus on how these varying perceptions can be dealt with, i.e., should conflict in perceptions be camouflaged or communicated?

The Weston *School Issues* newsletter spoke directly to the issue of conflict in perceptions existing in the following statements from the report:

This report has been read by all members of the Review Committee and their individual suggestions, modifications and reservations have been included. The Chairman of the Review Committee emphasizes that members of the Committee are virtually in unanimous agreement on the recommendations. Those differences which did emerge resulted largely from variations in what was seen and observed, not over the interpretation of what was seen. . . . We believe that the report deals with a complex subject extremely well, going beyond simple solutions such as "more basics" or "more creativity."

Richard: *I have an idea that might cut down any anxiety on the part of our readers who might be worried about identifying what can be fostered and what can be taught in the Weston excerpts from "Oral Language."*

Cynthia: *I knew you'd come through. Our readers might be unclear about why certain phrases and words in the philosophical framework section are judged "can be fostered and not taught" if they haven't had much opportunity to work with children. This task needs the same structure as you gave the readers in chapter 3 as they attempted to work through the complexity of the change process.*

Richard: *As you go through the section on oral language, you can make a list of all the activities either a parent or a teacher can do. The list should be shared first with a parent and then with a teacher. (Hopefully you will ask a teacher that you know and s/he can help you get in touch with one of the parents.) This exercise will give you a clear idea of areas of agreement between the teacher and parent. Hopefully you will follow through by sharing the areas of agreement with both the teacher and the parent. The use of this concrete example can serve as a focus of discussion between parents and educators on what they have found they can teach directly, what they found they can both foster, and what they found they have no control over. The latter point could be a spark for more community involvement in specific problems identified.*

Cynthia: *Lists such as the one you outlined could also be set up at the beginning of each school year. Parents and teachers could meet early in September to go over the first three months' curriculum and identify these three areas (i.e., teach, foster, no control). Then they could use the teach and foster list as a checklist and compare what types of activities can be scheduled at home and school and in the community to reinforce the goals identified by the teachers and parents together.*

Philosophical Foundation of the Weston
Language Arts & Write On Program

The goal of education in the elementary schools is to teach children *to think*. Long after a child forgets **the name, structure,** and **function of a biological organ, a historical date, the plot of a story,** or the development of a specific **mathematical algorithm,** the child's success in the world will be dependent upon his or her ability to *intake information, process it, assimilate it,* examine it in light of past experiences, and react to it—*to think*.

Because a teacher cannot enter into a child's head to determine the quantity of his thought, the teacher must evaluate that thought on the basis of what the child does. The child reveals his or her thinking by engaging in language. *Reading, writing, speaking,* and *listening* are the child's language repertoire by which teachers may evaluate the depth of thought.

Oral language is the foundation of all language activities. *Reading* is dependent upon something to read. The "something to read" is the printed page—oral language written down. *Listening* can be accomplished only if oral language is transmitted. *Writing* is the encoding of inner, oral language.

Because each child comes to the educational setting with different life and language experiences—because the child is an individual in a particular stage of development—educators must be cognizant of stages of development in the language modes. Educators must begin with the knowledge that the child's life and language experience is unique and with the knowledge that at any given time, the child is in his or her particular stage of language development.

> In planning a *language arts* curriculum, it is crucial to distinguish between those things which are innate and those which are imposed, between the analytic and the synthetic, between what can be taught and what can only be motivated.

> Failure to make and act on these distinctions confuses us and parents. It muddles our pedagogy. It turns off our students.

> Simply because some things cannot be taught, but are dependent on what nature and experience have done to children, the teacher cannot give up responsibility for teaching those other things which are **arbitrary conventions,** quite unrelated to cognitive development.

> On the other hand, the teacher who sets out to directly "teach" something which is dependent on preconscious, nonrational capacities frustrates herself as well as the child and inhibits learning both in and beyond the language arts class in which the crime is committed.

> Here, as elsewhere in education, we should always ask:
>   Is this something I can teach directly?
>   Is this something I can only encourage?
>   Is this something over which I have no control at all?

Some suppose that empty-handed children arrive in first grade and the teacher passes out the language arts—the same set to each child—and then proceeds to follow the curriculum preestablished in the editorial offices of Scott Foresman and Company.

In fact, the children arrive at first grade, bringing their language arts with them, and present them to the teacher. Her curriculum is what she does with this motley assortment of gifts.

Explanation of the Language Chart

The language chart [see fig. 4–1] provides a framework into which we logically fit theoretical model and practical application. According to the theoretical model, all language acquisition is based on a child's experiences from his earliest years on. In a hierarchical progression, the child goes through the following stages: inner language (sound-concept formation); auditory receptive (listening); auditory expressive (speaking); visual receptive (reading); and visual expressive (writing). The highest level of sophisticated language use is verbal symbolic behavior. The child can integrate past and present experiences, make inferences, draw conclusions, and handle abstractions and metaphorical language.

Each stage of development is necessarily dependent on successful manipulation of the preceding stage: to express himself orally, a child must have developed inner language (sound-concept formation) and auditory receptive language (comprehension of the spoken word). If at some point there has been a breakdown in the successful manipulation of experiences, the subsequent stages of development will be adversely affected. In order to ensure success, the teacher introduces and progresses with the child from tasks which are general, simple, undifferentiated or concrete toward those which are increasingly specific, complex, differentiated or abstract.

In the chart, various modes of expression are suggested. The classroom teacher can help provide modes of expression for auditory-verbal (oral) experiences and visual-verbal (written) experiences in all curriculum areas. Whatever the mode of expression, integral to the child's feeling of success is an audience with which to share his ideas.

Communication skills will benefit from careful teaching but not overskill. Input experiences (listening and reading) and output experiences (speaking and writing) are made a part of the child's verbal symbolic behavior as they are consistently practiced and refined.

Positive reinforcement must permeate whatever teaching method is used. A child may meet success as long as he is challenged at his own level of performance. Necessary to a child's success in language is a model to emulate, interaction with peers and adults to sound out ideas, an audience with which to share his work, publication of the finished product (often involving revision beforehand), integration of auditory/visual input and out-

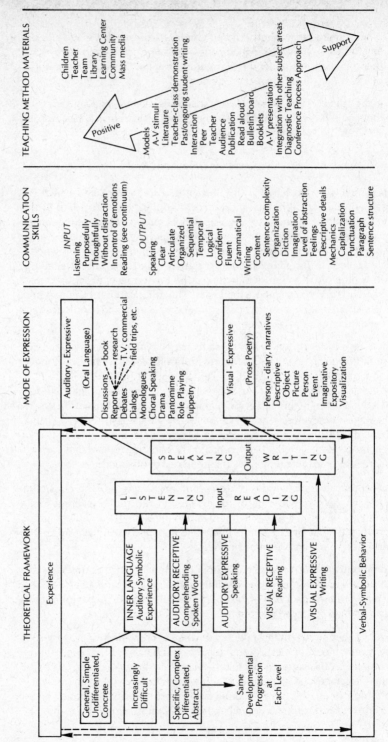

FIGURE 4–1. Language arts experience chart

put skills into all areas of the curriculum and diagnostic teaching to the individual child's needs and the process which is effective for him.

Materials for all language experiences are available wherever there are people and things happening. They are formal (printed and packaged) or informal (catch the moment). It is not so much the mastery of materials that are used, but the mastery of the *processes* of thinking and doing that are tantamount to success with one's language.

The hypothesis of the chart is that language is all-encompassing—it pervades all experiences and interactions of an individual. The teaching of language is, therefore, an integral part of all social and academic areas and cannot be considered as a fragmented section of the curriculum.

All levels of communication are interrelated and interdependent. Therefore, crucial to a child's progress in oral and written language is the feeling of success at whatever level of development he or she is presently functioning. Children will draw from their experience, environment, and imagination and apply their language skills in order to receive and express their ideas in a meaningful way.

Richard: As I read through the Weston handbook sections on oral language (see Appendix D) I found dozens of ideas about activities that parents and teachers can use to reinforce the areas outlined. I decided to look at the possibilities for parent and teacher joint assessment of the activities described.

Teacher/Parent Goal Identification	Teacher/Parent Joint Assessment
a) Describing	*Establish criteria for describing, e.g., animals and birds in the area.* *1. Describe physical structure and shape.* *2. Share child's conclusions about the way the animal or bird eats, lives, and moves based on the description of the animal or bird.*
b) Explaining and/or directions	*A project on technology could provide a record of children's explanations of tools found at home and school. The descriptions would include the uses of the tool and the directions for its use.*
c) Questioning and discussion	*These two areas of oral language can be merged into one area of assessment.*

79

> *Parents and teachers can keep records of the types of questions the children create to gain the attention of their playmates and classmates for discussions as well as the types of questions the children use over a period of time during participation and interaction.*

Cynthia: Looks good. You've captured areas directly related to implementing the criteria of successful programs. The parent/teacher areas outlined touch on criteria including modeling, rehearsal, pre- and post-behavior record keeping, goal setting, and feedback mechanisms for program personnel and parents.

ARTICULATING AND IMPLEMENTING CURRICULUM DECISIONS

As we went through the *Weston Language Arts Handbook,* we realized that the Weston schools had managed to cut through the complexity of building home/school/community interaction by attending to four steps. The content of the Language Arts program is set up in such a way that teachers have a ready source of information that can be shared with all members of the target population of interaction (i.e., child/teacher, teacher/teacher, teacher/staff, and home/school). Each component of the curriculum can be identified across grade levels. Having accomplished the task of identifying curriculum components, each teacher can attend to the remaining steps of communication including informing, verifying, and resolving.

In order to describe how the Weston curriculum, or, for that matter, any curriculum can be articulated and implemented in a school community, we have put together a visual model for dealing with what we know about home/school/community interaction. The model includes a total of only four steps that are repeated continuously with the four target audiences of child, colleagues, staff, and parents.

The first step of figure 4–2 is concerned with *awareness.* The function of this step is to *identify* what can be taught and what can be fostered. This first step (as well as the remaining three steps of implementing curriculum decisions) must be repeated for every target population in the educational community. The distinction between what can be fostered and what can be taught must be communicated at the micro-level of child/teacher interaction and teacher/teacher interaction and at the macro-level of teacher/staff interaction and home/school interaction. What might appear to be a complex undertaking is reduced by the fact that every teacher can go through the same four steps of articulating and implementing the curriculum for every target population. A simple paper-and-pencil poll such as "What is reading?" or "What is Social Studies?" in the classroom can serve as a catalyst for building communication.* The answers can be written on 3" × 5" index cards and arranged in piles for individual classrooms.

The second step would be to *inform* the class members of the discrepancies and *verify* whether a consensus on the goals of reading could be a target for the year.

The *resolvement* step can be accomplished through the teacher's assessment and diagnostic measures. As these steps are being accomplished in individual classrooms the same steps can be going on between teacher/staff and home/school. The same device, i.e., a paper-and-pencil test such as "What Is Reading?" can be the focus of a note sent home to parents. As mentioned earlier, the steps for building home/school/community interaction are the same for each target population. The process of resolving whether a child has indeed learned a new skill can be the focus of parent/teacher meetings. The meeting can end with returning to the first step, i.e., identifying the next curriculum goal and the parents' position on what can be fostered and what can be taught in terms of that goal.

INCLUDING PARENTS IN DECISION-MAKING PROCESSES REGARDING
GOALS AND OPERATIONS OF THE PROGRAM

Figure 4–3 summarizes the steps presented above and also summarizes information we have covered so far in the book above what we know. The information outlined takes into account the victims, the vacuum, and the venue. The four steps outlined are based on our analysis of Weston's success in community development in practice and our analysis of community development studies.

Following figure 4–3 we have included select samples from the *Weston Language Arts Handbook*. Our purpose in sharing these sections called "Sequences of Writing Development K-6," "Student Writing Skills Checklist," and the lists of expectations concerning language mechanics, grammar, and composition correction is to provide examples of mechanisms that provide for Steps 2, 3, and 4 of implementing school/community interaction. The availability of well-thought-out sequences insures a firm basis for interaction and communication between child/teacher, teacher/teacher, teacher/staff, and home/school. For example, following the articulation of writing guidelines, the Weston

---

*An example of this approach is described in J. Green and C. Wallat, "From Theory to Practice: What Is Social Studies?" *Contemporary Education* 49 (1978): 85–90.

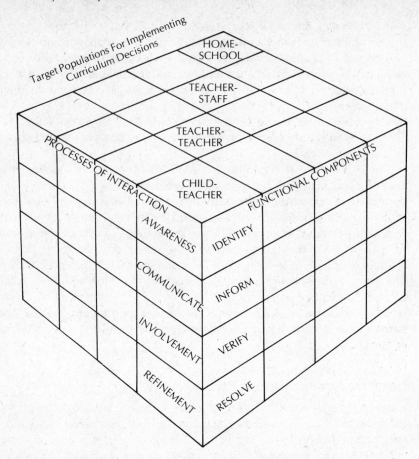

FIGURE 4-2. A tridimensional model for dealing with discrepancies

teachers trained a group of parents to be "writing consultants" in grades six, seven, and eight. Without creation of sections such as the following there would have been little basis for the functional components of *identify, inform, verify,* and *resolve.*

As you go through the samples from the Weston handbook which follow you can identify answers to the questions and substeps in figure 4-3. We have used the material with our students as a basis for reviewing the strengths of current programs. We also have shared the material with parents as a basis for building structures that pull together the strengths of their children's schools. Some readers may want to read through specific examples of how the material has been used by our students before they use the guide as a basis for analyzing the excerpts from the Weston curriculum. The samples of how our students used this material are included in Appendix B.

An Introduction to Developmental Writing
(Weston Public Schools)

The Sequences of Writing Development K-6 Chart depicts conceptual and structural (writing activity) stages in a continuum from basic levels to the more complex. Categories in the conceptual and writing activity columns are intended to correlate so that if a student has reached, for example, the sequencing stage of development, #3 in the left column, his writing can be expected to show the characteristics listed in the corresponding level of the right column. Conversely, if a student's writing shows certain features listed in the structural column, the teacher may presume that the equivalent level of conceptual development has been reached.

Caution: These remarks concerning the interpretation and use of the S.W.D. Chart apply in general terms only! That is, the teacher must not expect that, for instance, writing activities 3, 4, and 5 will always follow each other for every child in an exactly defined and easily identified sequence. Many, in fact most, of the conceptual and structural levels overlap and may occur to a certain extent simultaneously. Moreover, children are individuals and will show vital differences in development as well as temporary regressions in development which will seem to nullify the usefulness of the chart. The teacher must bear in mind that the S.W.D. model is intended as a guideline only and should utilize it as such.

We have described the developmental stages according to students' capacities rather than by age or grade. Given the tremendous range of variation within any single classroom, we feel that breakdowns by grades would be impractical. These levels apply to writing across all curriculum areas.

The following guidelines will clarify the use of this chart:

1. Writing is not delayed until a child is ready to write complete sentences independently. There are many steps which children go through before they are ready to write a simple story. These steps are the essence of written language in the primary years.

2. When the student is able to write at some length, he must know something of what he is writing about. This information base must be great enough to allow him to select relevant materials which support his general statement.

    In order to write meaningfully and with a purpose, the student should write with an audience in mind, sharing his writing skills and/or information with other students in the same or different classrooms or grade levels. The publication in books, pamphlets, etc. of student writing is encouraged. Rarely, if ever, should the teacher be the sole audience for student writing.

    Rehearsal is necessary before actual writing begins. This can take the form of drawing, painting, A-V presentations, group discussions, role

NEED FOR A FRAMEWORK

Failure to do so muddles our pedagogy; confuses us and parents; and turns off students.

STAGES OF IMPLEMENTATION

STEP 1
Awareness/Identify

Distinguish between what can be taught and what can be fostered:

Is this something I can teach directly?
Is this something I can only encourage?
Is this something over which I have no control?

STEP 2
Communicate/Inform

A clear statement of expectations according to the child's level:

What model will be available to emulate?
What new roles will he learn?
When and where will interaction with peers and adults take place?
Who will be the audience for sharing and sounding out ideas?

FIGURE 4-3.

STEP 3
Involvement/Verify

Elaboration of techniques to diagnose and teach specific skills

Sample Problem: Processing of Information

Observe and Diagnose:

Teaching Techniques:

Attention fluctuates?
Needs time to process info?
Afraid of new tasks?

Break input into small steps.
Provide an activity at each step.
Mediate task verbally to provide reinforcement.

STEP 4
Refinement/Resolve

Parent and teacher's joint assessment of activities from Step 3. Diagnose and develop prescription of next stage of implementation, i.e., return to Step 1.

FIGURE 4–3—Continued

85

playing, pantomime, simply thinking it over and/or outlining. Writing is the culmination of the rehearsal process.

3. Our focus has been on the conceptual developmental aspects of writing, not on the transcribing skills of handwriting, spelling, and punctuation. We have, however, given attention to the Continuum of Language Mechanics and Grammar (Summer Workshop '75)* because we wish to shift emphasis to the student's own awareness of his writing and to avoid teaching skills in isolation. It would be worthwhile to use the Continuum of Language Mechanics and Grammar along with a checklist so that the student can monitor his own progress in mastering mechanical and grammatical skills. (See suggested prototypes for the students' skills checklists.)

4. We hope to stress the teaching of writing, including syntax, mechanics, usage, organization and content, by using the student's own writing. This does not mean that we are rejecting the use of excellent literary models such as those from the Nebraska/Weston Program. It does mean that we believe writing is taught through writing.

Using the conference process approach prepared by Weston teachers, the teacher and student are able to concentrate on attaining writing skills appropriate to the individual child. For instance, the run-on sentence may very well indicate that a child is just reaching a new plateau of writing awareness and should be encouraged to refine this new writing technique rather than obliterate it from his writing. A run-on can be the bridge between simple sentences and sentences utilizing subordination or parallel elements. Or, it can show the student's lack of readiness to move from the simple, single clause construction to the more complex. Whether the first or second of these cases is true will be determined by the teacher and the student in the writing conference. Either way, the chart will provide a reference point for the teacher from which to set further writing goals. In this regard, it is important that the teacher concentrate on one or two problems evident in the student's writing rather than attempt to note every weakness in a composition. The Writing Development Chart will indicate which developmental level it is appropriate to be concerned with. It is a tool for analyzing students' writing, presenting an overview for the teacher. It is not intended as a correction device, but it will enable the teacher to make finer discriminations in her judgments of children's writing.

Sequences of Writing Development, K-6

Principles that apply at all levels: 1. Students should write from an informational base, 2. students should have a sense of audience, 3. students need adequate rehearsal[1] for writing.

---

*Included at the end of this section.

Conceptual	Structural (Writing Activity)
1. Relationship between spoken and written word	1. Uses 1 or 2 words for captions, titles, labels, lists. Uses longer fragments and experiments with word ordering: a. teacher written b. child written
2. Combines ideas in a meaningful way	2. Uses "semantic" sentences. Uses mechanics[2] Uses word endings
3. Sequencing	3. Lists serial order of events.
4. Differentiation or elaboration of sentences	4. Uses conjunctions and clauses. Uses fewer "run-ons." Uses proofreading (Steps 1 and 2)[3]
5. Expansion of territory[4]	5. Choice of writing topics is sex-related and changes as boys and girls grow.
6. Increasingly complex organization	6. Disorganized→chapter effect[5]→paragraphing
7. Temporal sense Perceptual→Conceptual Sense	7. Uses "before, during, while, after," etc. Uses language that shows a development from a sense of body and action space to a sense of geographical and representational space.
8. Tentative judgment	8. Uses "if, maybe, might, could," etc. Selects and rejects information.
9. Begins to infer	9. Synthesizes information. Uses advanced proofreading/editing/revising.

10. Sense of abstraction

10. Moves with ease from the concrete to the abstract. Uses metaphorical language.

---

[1]"rehearsal" - Refer to Introduction
[2]"mechanics" - Refer to Introduction
[3]"Proofreading - Steps 1 and 2"—simple proofreading word-by-word for mechanical correction, progressing to proofreading phrase-by-phrase for mechanics and completeness of thought.
[4]"Expansion of territory" - Refer to next page
[5]"Chapter effect" - stage in a child's writing when one idea at a time is clearly presented by brief, nonelaborated segments. ("I like trains. I like planes. I like tanks.") Progresses to a point where many ideas are dealt with and expanded.

Expansion of Territory

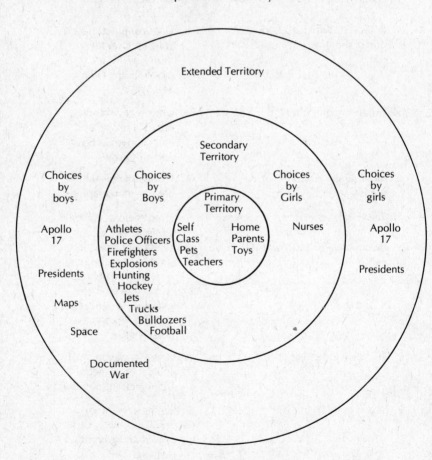

This model, based on recent studies, should aid the teacher in understanding the move from one "territory" to another in children's writing. Primary territory covers the areas of the greatest child experience, namely the home and school. It occupies the smallest concentric circle in the diagram. Secondary territory expands to the metropolitan area around the child and includes transportation, adult vocations, professional athletics, and community events. It occupies the second circle. Extended territory refers to national and world events and persons identified with them, and is found between the second and outer circles.

Choices of children's unassigned writing show that seven year old boys write more in secondary and extended territory, whereas seven year old girls write more in primary territory.

Boys ignore the use of the first person, I, and project themselves into a vicarious use of the third person. Their characters are always *doing* something, seldom show feeling, and are poorly described.

Girls, though territorially limited, express personal feelings, describe characters and use the first person in ways which are much more developed than boys.

The study concludes that there are developmental reasons for the writing choices of boys and girls which the teacher should be aware of in evaluating the unique needs and strengths of both sexes. With these factors in mind, the teacher should understand when it is a reasonable expectation for children to attempt to begin using new topics in their writing.

Suggestions for Writing Experiences

The teacher can stimulate much writing by building on the background of experiences that children bring with them to the classroom. The teacher should discover and foster each child's unique area of interest, and should encourage the child to "become an expert" in his area of interest. As a result, motivation for writing will be present. The teacher can take advantage of this "natural" motivation to build additional expertise, and as a child develops ever greater confidence and interest in writing, the teacher can direct him to new (but perhaps related) areas of interest, motivating further writing.

To develop a secure base of information from which to write, students should be encouraged to collect data through interviewing and through the use of surveys and questionnaires which they have constructed. Resulting writing assignments can range from "formal" reports to newspaper-style articles or "letters to the editor."

Students can also collect data through a note taking process of recording what they have seen, heard, felt, tasted, or smelled during a particular period of time (i.e. a field trip). Using their notes, students make experience charts. In the charts, teachers can encourage language ranging from the simply descriptive to the metaphorical, depending on the student's developmental level.

Writing Skills—Level A

Name _____

Performance Level

1. I cannot do this.
2. I know how to do this but don't always do it.
3. I usually do this.
4. I could teach this skill to others.

Skills

_____

1. use capital letters at the beginning of sentences.

2. use capital letters at the beginning of names, places, dates, titles.

3. use periods, exclamation points, and question marks at the ends of sentences.

4. form contractions.

5. use commas in a series.

6. keep my writing and paper neat.

Name _____

Performance Level

1. I cannot do this.
2. I know how to do it but don't always do it.
3. I usually do this.
4. I could teach this skill to others.

Skills

I

1. use capital letters at the beginning of sentences.

2. use capital letters at the beginning of names, places, dates, titles.

3. use periods, exclamation points, and question marks at the ends of sentences.

4. form contractions.

5. use commas in a series.

6. use commas where the sentence breaks.

In Addition, I _____

1. _____

2. _____

3. _____

4. _____

5. _____

6. _____

7. _____

Writing Skills—Level C

Name _____

1. I cannot do this.   3. I usually do this.
2. I know how to do it but don't always do it.   4. I could teach this skill to others.

Skills

I _____

1. use capital letters at the beginning of sentences.

2. use capital letters at the beginning of names, places, dates, titles.

3. use periods, exclamation points, and question marks at the ends of sentences.

4. form contractions.

5. use commas in a series.

6. use commas when needed.

7. use apostrophes to show possession.

In addition, I _____

1. _____

2. _____

3. _____

4. _____

5. _____

6. _____

7. _____

(Very small card note-taking helps some children focus on main ideas and recognize the value of brevity and organization.)

With secure backgrounds of experience and information, students' writing can take many forms, including memos, telegrams, classified ads and official cables and letters, perhaps forwarded through a school or grade level postal service set up in relation to a social studies or science unit.

Information can be entertainingly presented through the use of cartoon strip dialogs. Later transcription to direct quotation dialog form can provide firm reinforcement of mechanical skills.

Students' willingness to write can sometimes be enhanced by assigning many short writings, such as the ones just suggested, and perhaps including a series of a mini-reports on areas of interest. One line poems, couplets, and haikus are examples of excellent short poetic forms, while sentence combining and breaking down exercises build skill in prose writing without involving excessive length.

The ideas mentioned here scarcely skim the surface of writing possibilities. Two highly recommended texts for further investigation are:

Moffett, Student-Centered Language Arts and Reading, K-13, 2nd Edition, Houghton Mifflin, 1976

Petty, Petty, and Becking, Experiences In Language, Allyn and Bacon, 1976

Use of the Student's Skills Checklists

The Student's Skills Checklists may be used as an adjunct to the Sequences of Writing Development Chart and *should* be a part of student writing folders for use during writing conferences. The checklists indicate three levels in the development of mechanical and grammatical skills and are designed for utilization at grades 3 through 6.

It is intended that students, with teacher guidance, be responsible for the checklist. They should know at what level of performance they are currently functioning, and they will put the appropriate numeral for that level in the box next to the skill. Boxes have been left undated so that teachers can keep track of student progress in intervals suitable to individuals.

Continuum of Language Mechanics*

The chart which follows identifies the grade level at which punctuation symbols, grammatical terms, and letter writing should be familiar to and mastered by Weston elementary students.

Children are introduced (I) to punctuation through reading. At some point

---

*From *Write On! A Curriculum Guide to Writing in the Elementary Language Arts Program.* Summer Workshop 1971 (Revised 1975). Weston Public Schools. Bruce Mac-Donald, Program Director, August 1975. Reproduced by permission.

Continuum of Language Mechanics and Grammar

GRADE	INITIAL CAPITALIZATION IN SENTENCES	CAPITALIZATION OF PROPER NOUNS	TERMINAL PUNCTUATION	CONTRACTIONS	POSSESSIVE APOSTROPHE	COMMAS IN A SERIES	COMMAS IN SENTENCE BREAKS	SUBJECT AND PREDICATE SPLIT	SIMPLE VS. COMPLETE SUBJ, PRED.	PARTS OF SPEECH	FRIENDLY LETTERS	BUSINESS LETTERS USING COMPLETE SENTENCES AND PARAGRAPHS	QUOTATION MARKS (DIRECT ADDRESS)	CONSISTENT TENSE
1	I		I				I				As needed. Pre-Christmas brush-up advised.		I	
2	T	←—— as needed ——→	T	I			I						I	
3	R		R	T	I	I	I						I	
4	M		M	R	I	T	T						T	I
5	M	M	M	M	T	R	T		I	I		✓	T	T
6	M	M	M	M	R	M	T	T	T	T		✓	R	T

94

the teacher will set aside class time to teach (T) a particular symbol and its use to an entire class. Some review (R) of most mechanics issues will be required as students pass through the grades. Mastery (M) follows from use and reinforcement. When mastery is considered appropriate to an entire grade level, the teacher will do direct teaching with only those students who have not achieved mastery.

To move from introduction to mastery requires the conscious effort of the teacher in (1) pointing out the significance of punctuation in the reading class: "Which sentences are questions? How do we know Dick was excited when he said 'Wow!' What letter is left out of 'don't?'" and in (2) asking a child to write questions about the story or make up dialog. Reinforcement holds students responsible for punctuation appropriate to their grade.

Bi-weekly dictations will reinforce children's mastery of skills as well as provide diagnostic insight for teachers.

Key to Continuum of Language Mechanics

I—Introduction. Teachers should point out the use of these signals in reading classes.

Some students may use the signals in their own writing.

T—By the end of the year, most students should have mastered the use of these signals. Teachers will spend class time in deliberate teaching of the forms and their use.

AT NO POINT should this instruction become so concentrated as to consume more than three consecutive days in teaching mechanics.

Bi-weekly dictations will act as diagnostic tests for the teacher and reinforcement for the students.

R—Periodic brush-up and review of the use of the mechanics assigned to that level. Some work with individual students may be required.

M—Mastery. It is assumed that students have mastered the use of these symbols or skills. Errors should be noted in the correction of papers. Some work with individual students may still be required.

Continual use in composition and the bi-weekly dictation will reinforce this mastery.

√   A limited number of letters should be written at this level. Letter writing prior to Christmas is a useful way of teaching the form to some purpose.

When students are weak in mastery, individual work may be required to bring a particular student up to level. Infrequently, an entire class may need to review. When group review is required, it may be necessary to work with exercises gleaned from the various available texts.

95

AT NO TIME, however, should periods of four or five days be spent on punctuation exercises. The punctuation which clarifies a student's own writing (see CORRECTION) is meaningful. Punctuation in the abstract is not.

While teachers through grades four should not hesitate to use grammatical terms like "subject" or "adjective," only teachers in grades five and six will set out to teach the terms and concepts listed on the graph. Any decision to teach these is an arbitrary one—unlike the punctuation, which is required in writing—and no necessary "good" is served by knowing the terms except as they are made useful by some equally arbitrary design.

Teachers of students below the fifth grade have better things to do than teach terminology.

Correction of Composition

1. Have students leave an inch margin on the left of their papers for correction marks and comments.

2. Hold students to ONLY those punctuation requirements appropriate to their level. (See Continuum of Language Mechanics.) But insist on those requirements.

3. In general, ask spelling correction for only those words which are familiar enough to a child's *writing* vocabulary that accuracy in form can reasonably be demanded.

4. Don't inhibit a child's impulse to use a longer, more precise word whose spelling is uncertain. When students are writing, be cautious about saying, "Look it up." Often a child will settle for a second-best word he can spell. Spell words for students who ask help. If they care that much about "getting it right," why discourage them?

5. Prepare students for the use of punctuation in writing by pointing out its use and meaning in reading classes. Preliminary notions of paragraphing and use of quotations can be suggested by giving these issues attention as they show up in a text. For students who are already using them in their writing, such attention provides reinforcement.

6. Encourage the students to see that the conventions of spelling, punctuation and indentation make their own work more readily accessible to a wider audience. Failures in these areas are not moral problems, of course. Still, things do go better when the conventions are observed.

7. Some papers should be revised according to the comments in the margins, and a corrected copy should be submitted to the teacher.

8. Use a slash to indicate which line contains an error to be corrected. Use the appropriate correction symbol with the slash to indicate what sort of correction is needed. Let the child find the error. For example:

   ,/ means "Somewhere in that line you need a comma."

9. The purpose of correction is to get a child involved with his errors. If he can hunt down a line and find the mistake you indicated in the margin,

fine. If you have to circle the spot where things go wrong, do that. But in some cases, you may have to do most of the work and say, "That third word is spelled wrong."

As much as possible, put the burden of finding the error on the child. Our purpose, after all, is to promote self-editing on the child's part.

10. When there is to be no second draft, have students correct their papers, referring to the margin signs you used on the first reading. Glance over the corrected originals and let the students keep them.

11. Write comments about content anywhere on the paper.

12. Circle word choices which are particularly apt and write "good" next to them.

13. Use longer margin slashes next to sentences or sections which are effective and write some comment in the margin.

14. Write approving comments on papers as you are able. But nobody is convinced for very long by a routine sprinkling of "Good idea," "Interesting paper," and associated bromides.

15. Try using less academic comments where appropriate, like "Wow!" or "Great!"

16. Reward the effective word, the clever comment, the special effects.

17. If students ask for help in using semicolons or some punctuation mark beyond their level, help them.

18. Use these correction symbols:

capitalization needed	— C/
quotation marks	— " "/
terminal punctuation	— ./ ?/ !/
add apostrophe	— '/
comma*	— ,/
spelling error	— Sp/ or, failing that, circle the word
word left out	— ^
paragraph break	— ¶
unacceptable fragment	— inc/
use different word	— dw/
run-on sentence	— run-on/
incorrect capitalization	— ¢/

*Use only one comma in a series of three items.

Sample Correction—Third Grade

sp/   I think that the pictiture says

liberty is for everybody. The (medevel) *good!*

castle is a place that kings lived.

./c   Old fashioned people lived there the

sp/   big rocket shows that science experamits

∧   help our freedom. When I the Washington

sp/   Monument I knew the pictiture was

about America. Can't anyone figure

out that Washington is the center

?/   of freedom. You really don't have

to be (Einstine) *good* to know that! Every-

inc./   thing in the picture that you

showed us during class. It is

a good enough picture of liberty

good sentence/ but the one I carry around in

my own head is even better!

Why not try writing that picture
you carry around in your head?

This is better than Monday's paragraph;
you're improving.

Sample Correction—Sixth Grade

sp/   I think that the pictiture says
sp/ liberty is for everybody. The (medevel) *good!*
dev castle is a place that kings lived.
./c Old fashioned people lived there the
sp/ big rocket shows that science experamits
∧ help our freedom. When I ∧ the Washington
,/sp Monument I knew the pictiture was
c/ about America. Can't anyone figure
    out that Washington is the center
?/ of freedom. You really don't have
sp/ to be (Einstine) *good* to know that! Every-
inc/ thing in the picture that you
    showed us during class. It is
    a good enough picture of liberty
good sentence but the one I carry around in
    my own head is even better!

    This is better toward the end, especially that
last sentence. But you don't really prove
what you say in your first sentence. What
is the point of the castle? You just
describe it.

Parents as Educators 5

The English Review Committee recommendation that a program for improving school-community relations be instituted at the earliest possible opportunity did not specify a blueprint for involving parents in the recommended changes. In their case it was refreshing that the committee *did not* specify, for it would have belied the recognition given to the Weston teachers as professionals. The fact that a memo circulated by Bruce MacDonald and Donald Kennedy merely contained the phrase "Elementary and Secondary: Will implement/in process" next to the review recommendation for more parent involvement also serves as powerful testimony to the regard and high expectations Weston has for its teachers. The venturesome at Weston are ahead of their time. They have been convinced that parents are educators and have acted on implementing that conviction despite the fact that no blueprint exists for involving parents in the school. By the end of the next three chapters we hope to lead you to enough information to replicate that process. In order to accomplish that goal you will need to review what we know about parents as educators and where to locate additional sources on the hundreds of parent education programs that are available.

Historical Recognition

The recognition of parents as educators has appeared in historical reviews, reviews of early childhood education intervention program research, and reviews of child-rearing practices. Educational historians such as Gutek (1972) and Braun (1972) have been concerned primarily with tracing formal systems of American education back to early civilizations, yet they begin their review with the recognition that parents are the primary source of a child's integration into the social system to which he or she was born.

> While.... formal systems of education can be recognized, informal education goes on and must go on continuously, wherever a human society bridges the gap from one generation to the next. Without it no enduring society has ever existed. So education has been present wherever ... words and ideas were absorbed unselfconsciously day by day. For millenia every human passed on to its young its increment of knowledge with no need to designate a special place where this ought to happen.[1]

Historians, in addition to the authors cited above, also have been concerned with broad areas of parental teaching in the home (e.g., socialization, politicalization, and religious training). More specifically, Smethurst (1975) has traced the acquisition of reading skills through the 5,000 or so years that people have been reading. In addition to quoting passages from Roman literature which describe the responsibility of mothers for lessons, Smethurst quotes sixteenth century English editions which include reading instruction advice for parents. Among the author's conclusions in *Teaching Young Children to Read at Home* is the point that parental teaching of reading is by no means new. Agreeing with other authors cited in the text (Gedike 1791; Dewey 1898; Huey 1908; Hillman 1963; Bettleheim 1966; Hyme 1970), Smethurst summarized his position: "A child should be brought gradually into reading at home. This process is a natural one and starts very young with parents reading aloud to the child."[2]

Recognition in the Twentieth Century

Researchers concerned with parents as educators have not limited their concern to just one area. Increasing awareness of the parents' roles in a wide range of cognitive, physical, and social competencies has been supported by analysis of major characteristics of parental interaction with children. Schaeffer (1972) has outlined the following characteristics of parents as educators.

---

[1]Samuel J. Braun and E. P. Edwards, *History and Theory of Early Childhood Education* (Worthington, Ohio: Charles A. Jones, 1972), p. 2.

[2]W. Smethurst, *Teaching Young Children to Read at Home* (New York: McGraw-Hill, 1975), p. 40.

Priority	Parents influence the early development of relationships, language, interests, task-oriented behaviors, etc.
Duration	The parent's interactions with the child usually extend from birth to maturity.
Continuity	The parent-child interaction is usually not interrupted, particularly in early childhood, apart from brief separations. Concern about such interruptions has led to research on maternal separation and deprivation.
Amount	The total amount of time spent in parent-child interaction, particularly one-to-one interaction, is usually greater than with other adults.
Extensity	The parent shares more different situations and experiences with the child than do other adults.
Intensity	The degree of involvement between parent and child, whether that involvement is hostile or loving, is usually greater than between the child and other adults.
Pervasiveness	Parents potentially influence the child's use of the mass media, his social relationships, his exposure to social institutions and professions, and much of the child's total experience, both inside and outside the home.
Consistency	Parents develop consistent patterns of behavior with their children.
Responsibility	Both society and parents recognize the parent's primary reponsibility for the child.
Variability	Great variability exists in parental care of children, varying from extremes of parental neglect and abuse to extremes of parental acceptance, involvement, and stimulation.[3]

Each of the characteristics outlined by Schaeffer has received attention by researchers. Studies of the relationship between parental behavior and their child's moral values (Kay 1969), achievement (Jarvik, Eisdorfer, and Blum 1973), creativity (Groth 1975), learning styles (Walberg and Marjoribanks 1976), social development (Ainsworth, Bell, and Stayton 1974) aggression (Mussen, Conger, and Kogan 1969), political attitudes (Jennings and Niemi 1973), and occupational achievement (Leibowitz 1974) have increased recognition of parents as educators.

---

[3]Earl S. Schaeffer, *Parents as Educators: Evidence from Cross-Sectional, Longitudinal, Intervention Research,* Reprinted by permission from *Young Children,* Vol. XXVII, No. 4 (April 1972), pp. 227–239. Copyright © 1972, National Association for the Education of Young Children, 1834 Connecticut Avenue, N.W., Washington, D.C. 20009.

Although the above listing of parental influences on their children's behavior and attitudes is incomplete and has been criticized (Thomas and Chess 1973), it does support the view that parents are educators. However, as we have mentioned before, the availability of data does not insure action. This is apparent in the varying amounts of attention devoted to implementing what we know to support the family's role as educator. A consensus does not exist in public opinion "that strengthening and supporting family care and education of the child *should be* a major focus in child development programs."[4]

The phrase *strengthening and supporting* the family has had different interpretations in the history of early childhood education in the United States. Until the 1920s justification for those day nurseries that were organized was expressed primarily in terms of keeping families together.[5] Since poverty was viewed as an external condition in which people found themselves, those who could find places in day nurseries which were provided as a community service could be judged by their peers as attempting to improve their life. In the 1920s public opinion shifted to defining poverty as pathological. Those day nurseries that managed to stay open were viewed as a refuge for families who were intellectually, morally, and physically impoverished.

One can trace the frequent reinterpretations of "strengthening and supporting" to many influences. As economic conditions change, public opinion will change. In the 1930s there was an increase in the number of nurseries because of federal support under the Works Project Administration. In the 1940s the need for an increased labor force to handle war needs justified federal funds for support of day care. With postwar prosperity in the 1950s public opinion *not* to support and strengthen the family could be justified by Freudian emphasis on the importance of mother/child relationships as well as by studies on the effects of maternal deprivation. Studies that reported that children with nursery school experience progressed better than those without nursery school experience and studies which reported that foster children and orphans improved in achievement when placed in good homes and orphanages failed to loosen the assumptions of fixed general intelligence. Gardner (1970) has suggested that "had we listened, we might be further along today in understanding the issues on intellectual development raised . . . by Jensen."[6]

---

[4]Ibid., p. 187.

[5]Margaret O'Brien Steinfels, *Who's Minding the Children? The History and Politics of Day Care in America* (New York: Simon and Schuster, 1973), pp. 61–62.

[6]D. Bruce Gardner, *The Influence of Theoretical Conceptions of Human Development on the Practice of Theoretical Conceptions of Human Development on the Practice of Early Childhood Education.* ERIC File ED 033 766, 1970, p. 20.

Tucker's (1940) review of parent education between 1920 and 1940 examines the programs that were concerned with early education despite public indifference to day care and the opinion that a "mother's place was in the home." Although program developers recognized a range of concerns, from physical care and household management to problems of relationships between members of the family, programs were more concerned with sharing this recognition with parents than with helping parents acquire techniques to meet them. Tucker supports Gardner's evaluation:

> An examination of the problems included in parent education during this period revealed that the reasons why they (were) considered by the experts as pertinent to parent education are not clear.[7]

Steinfels's (1973) examination of the early childhood programs in operation today suggests that some programs involved in parent education could be charged with the same criticism. She has outlined the present state of day care into three areas:

1. Patchwork: Narrowly defined goals and/or "first aid" patches to the family's economic and/or emotional and educational problems.
2. Utopia: Change the family by instilling new values.
3. Realization: Attempt to bridge the gap between ideals of our society and the realities of today. Emphasis on affective objectives.[8]

Starting with the premise that "something must be done" in education, Follow Through and Head Start programs in the United States have been surrounded by controversy and have had to justify their existence on many levels. The objectives of federally funded programs in the United States were translated originally into compensatory education, i.e., change the child to fit the school or bring him or her up to par in language, reading, writing, and computation skills. The concept of compensatory education fitted neatly into a public opinion that had been shaped in the first half of this century by maternal deprivation studies. Rather than searching for the etiology of *deprived* or *disadvantaged* by pointing out specific instances of lack of societal support for families, researchers concentrated their efforts on the relationship of social class to child

---

[7]Clara Tucker, *A Study of Mother's Practices and Children's Activities in a Cooperative Nursery School* (New York: Columbia University Teachers College, 1940), p. 1.
[8]Steinfels, *Who's Minding the Children?*, pp. 14–15.

development. Although the bulk of class-linked literature which focused "on specific practices and routines, without any reference to context have been inconsistent and contradictory in their findings,"[9] the impressions gained from the studies have influenced the context of parent education.

Characteristics of Parent Education Literature Today

The existence of many theories of child rearing testifies to our concern with the effectiveness of the individual. Those theorists who have written books dealing with parents as educators have responded to social pressures and expressions of need in our society. The theories they describe are a way of combining a set of assumptions and communicating that knowledge to another person. The particular theory an author adopts is, of course, a free choice. As such, the reader can accept or reject what is reported on the basis of its utility to his/her particular interest. If an individual accepts a theory what s/he is saying is that s/he had made the decision to look at what the theory suggests is important. Since we can't possibly handle all events we can flag our intent, i.e., this is what I want to look at.

One of the reasons we do not have more answers from child-rearing studies is because researchers are still in the process of identifying variables that contribute to positive child development. One can see the scope of the research work involved in identifying factors that contribute to child development in table 5–1.

The scope of child development as outlined in this table points out one major fact. To accomplish development in these areas cannot be realized by a mother and father alone.

> The subtle complexities in parent-child processes are well-nigh overwhelming. Any simple set of rules to be followed would become irrelevant. We don't yet know how to program a computer to master the rules for generating language, so how could we possibly hope to give parents a set of rules for generating human beings? The books which purport to give detailed directions are not only leaving out essentials but are always operating with a multitude of unproven assumptions about human beings. As we shall see, "how to books" inevitably build a program upon some theory of human behavior which generally remains inexplicit and hidden.[10]

---

[9]J. A. Clausen and J. R. Williams, "Sociological Correlates of Child Behavior," in *Child Psychology*, ed. Harold W. Stevenson, 62nd Yearbook of the National Society for the Study of Education, Part I (Chicago: NSSE, 1963), p. 68.

[10]Sidney Cornelia Callahan, *Parenting: Principles and Politics of Parenthood* (Baltimore: Penguin Books, 1974), p. 33.

TABLE 5–1. Areas of Concern to Parents as Educators

The whole child from age 0 onward needs	to develop in these broad areas	to accomplish changes in these fields
An intact organism (this requires pre-natal and preparental care and information)	Physical Intellectual Personality Social	Cognitive Affective Physiological Psychological Spiritual Emotional
Health and physical safety (enough to develop normally includes nutrition)		Aspirational Attitudinal Interpersonal Conceptual Communicative Motivational
A warm and suppor-tive relationship		Aesthetical
Realistic experiences: a. with other people to arrive at self-other discrimination		
b. with materials and objects in the environment		
c. that increase in number and complexity with age		

SOURCE: *A Content Analysis of Early Childhood Development.* Final Report. Austin, Tex.: Educational Development Corporation, 1973. ERIC Document Reproduction Service No. ED 097 114.

As you review the books, you can pull out what you think are the assumptions concerning human nature. Once you pull out the authors' assumptions, you can make some decisions concerning how the methods suggested can meet your needs. Although we will be offering a critical analysis of the various child-rearing approaches we want to make it clear that we are in no way against the publication of these materials.

In light of the complexity of child development theories, the child-rearing books serve a useful purpose. Most parents can only find out about what's going on in child development research through a popular book. The books also serve as testimony to our optimistic American outlook that the future can be better and that it is possible to have successful children.

You can see these aspects in certain common features of the books. They all include reassurances that parents are capable; that they can increase their skills rather than sitting back because of the myth that parenthood is something natural which you have or don't have; that parents will make mistakes and it is OK to do so; and, finally, that parenting is a hard job for which they have the author's sympathy. The fact that they are written at all serves as testimony to belated recognition that "common sense and *instinct are not to be* trusted over knowledge and skills."[11]

In addition to attempting to build up parents' confidence in their view of themselves as someone who can be an effective influence in their children's lives, the books are all written on two levels: the first directed at parents trying to understand children better, and the second, at parents trying to understand themselves better.

A major criticism against the majority of the books is that the authors are lax in clearly stating their assumptions about human development. Since most of the authors have not offered any reasons why they have decided to concentrate on the family in isolation from the concept of human ecology, most of the books seem authoritarian in nature.

In her chapter "How to Read How-to Parent Books," Callahan (1974) offers the following major criticism against limited conceptualizations of the parent as educator.

> There is a persistent overconcentration upon early stages of child development (and early parenthood), so not enough is said about broader cultural education. Any idea of the political and social context in which parents raise children is (almost) totally absent. . . . How to get children involved in the community, and instill a sense of larger social and cultural purposes, is ignored.

> Parenting is always seen as a private concern focused within the four walls of the private utopian home. Within these walls, separated from the rest of the world, live the individuals who must relate to each other in the family. . . . The community may impinge on the family but mostly this is seen as a problem of TV in the home, not parents and children enmeshed in the community's struggles or purposes. . . .

> Even when schools, nursery or otherwise, enter into how-to-books, the emphasis is upon the school and the individual child, never a discussion of parents cooperating with fellow parents or children working with children. . . . The idea that parents might have to (work with) the school to affect the child's welfare is (almost) completely absent. . . . While the parent is encouraged to be the advocate of the child, giving emotional support, he is not often encouraged to band together with other parents or actually investi-

---

[11]Ibid., p. 72.

gate the objective situation with an eye to changing it. In other words horizontal relationships within the larger community are mostly non-existent; political social dimensions are ignored in favor of private solutions and adjustments.[12]

As you can see, neither our criticisms nor Callahan's revolve around the techniques or methods offered. As mentioned earlier, each person has the right to choose which theory s/he will use. The criticisms revolve around what the authors have omitted. As you go through the summaries of various approaches to parents as educators, you can begin to make some decisions about what has been left out. To help make those decisions we'll review what's going on in parent education programs.

Views of Coping and Communicating in Parenting Programs

Concern with the development of children is as old as humanity. What is new is the intensity in anxiety about how to raise children to become competent adults when we cannot predict what competencies they will need for the twenty-first century. One way of evaluating just how extensive the concern is for child rearing is to look at what researchers have been trying to find answers to. A review of a decade of research in parent-child relationships (Walters and Stinnett 1971) points to four major areas of concern:

1. To develop the ability of family members to tolerate conflict and to accept the hostility of others within the family with understanding and compassion.
2. To help children learn to respond to failure situations in a more positive manner.
3. To help parents and children learn more effective and satisfying ways of communicating.
4. To develop and communicate a true commitment and genuine sense of care, high regard, and respect between child and adult.[13]

These four areas of concern in child rearing can be summarized into two concepts: coping and communication. Various methods for those who are looking for help in building communication skills and coping with day-to-day problems are available.

---

[12]Ibid., pp. 92–93, 94, 95.
[13]J. Walters and N. Stinnett, "Parent-Child Relationships: A Decade Review of Research," *Journal of Marriage and the Family* 33 (1971): 70–111.

In recent years communication theory has emerged as a basic approach in working with parents. In this system many of the problems facing parents are considered to be the result of inadequate or distorted communication between parents and their children, or between the parents themselves.[14]

Some of the most popular child-rearing approaches concerned with parent/child communication and coping are Gordon's (1970) P.E.T. (Parent Effectiveness Training), Glasser's (1969) P.I.P. (Parent Involvement Program), Dreikurs' (1964) Parent Training Programs, and behavior modification programs such as the *Responsive Parent Training Program* (Clark et al. 1976). The continuing growth and popularity of these approaches is testimony to the fact that public opinion rates them as successful. Just what aspect of the programs is successful may come as a surprise. A parent education program concerned with "improvement of communication does not necessarily solve parent problems."[15] What this means is that the original problem which existed in the family may not have changed in any way that could be documented by the program organizers; what has changed is the parents' attitude toward the problem. It appears that even though a program may not be able to document specific differences in behavior after a course, the approach to child rearing will still be rated as successful by participants because they begin to feel closer to their children. The fact that participants feel closer to their children means that they have clarified the problem and/or had a change in attitude toward child rearing.

Possible areas of change in parent attitude have been documented in descriptions of parent/child programs (Walters and Stinnett 1971; Gildea 1973; Berlin and Berlin 1974; Grodner 1975; Morris 1975; Bromwich 1976). Among the frequently mentioned targets of attitude change that are discussed in evaluations of parent education programs are:

a) The parent's belief that there are multiple influences on a child's behavior and development.
b) The parent's belief that enhancing the quality of interaction depends not just on teaching the child specific skills but on assessing one's own as well as one's child's behavior.

The conclusion that the programs can be considered successful because they brought about a change in attitude might not appear at first to be very substantial. However, if one considers some of the myths, clichés,

---

[14]E. E. LeMasters, *Parents in Modern America*. (Homewood, Ill.: Dorsey Press, 1974), p. 203.
[15]Ibid., p. 224.

blame theories, and grand theories that have influenced our perceptions of the family, we will see that the phrase *change in attitude* is quite substantial. Reports of success in terms of change in attitude also take on additional significance when added to research findings that parental attitude is related to children's school achievement (Berlin and Berlin 1974). If the programs do in fact foster positive attitudes, parents might be more receptive to involvement in their children's schooling. Since parental involvement has been shown to contribute to the success of preschool programs, early childhood programs, and elementary and secondary programs (Butler 1970; Gray 1970; Adkins 1971; Gordon 1971; Roby 1973; Wittes 1971; King 1972; Pomfret 1972; Lille 1975; Gordon and Breivogel 1976), it again appears that programs which report evaluation statements included under the umbrella term *change in attitude* are worth our attention.

Characteristics of Successful Programs

Since the majority of parent education programs have not been able to document what specific characteristics or techniques of their programs are related to successful outcome, we have to turn to evaluations reported on other wide-scale programs to determine potential criteria for evaluating child-rearing approaches. A review of research findings in the area of group counseling with parents points to the first criterion.

"The parent's ability to transfer program skills to direct interaction with their children is unlikely" unless time is provided for modeling, rehearsals and comparing pre-program behavior with newly learned behavior.[16]

It also appears that adoption of the advice offered in the various approaches to child rearing is unlikely unless both the parent and child learn to engage in communication around a common activity (Bronfenbrenner 1974). Programs addressed only to the parent cannot insure sustaining effects on a long-term basis (Bronfenbrenner 1974). Shotgun approaches, such as once a year workshops, also cannot insure long-term effects unless provisions are made for insuring that the family

"is directly involved in problem delineation, goal setting and making changes they consider desirable."[17]

---

[16]W. Duehm and N. S. Mayadas, "Behavioral Rehearsals in Group Counseling with Parents," *American Journal of Orthopsychiatry* 45 (1975): 261–62.

[17]T. Leventhal and G. Weinbriger, "Evaluation of a Large Scale Brief Therapy Program for Children, *American Journal of Orthopsychiatry* 45, (1975): 121.

This second criterion is touched on in some of the programs we will review. We should keep in mind that we are still in an early stage of development in parent-child education programs and hopefully will not repeat past mistakes by building over-expectations about what can be accomplished. Doing just some kind of parent education may not benefit either the child or the parent. "Haphazard programs may operate to shake the confidence a parent has acquired."[18] We cannot assume that more is better. Nor can we assume, as we have in the past, that once the program is completed, any improvement in behavior will continue. We have had to learn the third criterion of successful programs the hard way.

"The essential prerequisite for the child's development requires continued communication and feedback between the program personnel and parents."[19]

We have learned that not all changes in social behavior or initial gains in cognitive performance will hold up without continued support for the child and his/her family. Evidence from therapy programs aimed at training parents as change agents points out that parents can learn to modify their children's behavior. But just as children who participated in Head Start programs need continued support, the parents who participated in child-rearing courses, such as behavior modification courses, still need support to continue treatment (Johnson and Katz 1973).

In addition to evaluations of Head Start (Bronfenbrenner 1974) and therapy programs (Johnson and Katz 1973) a review of research on programs designed to train parents as home teachers (Stevens 1976) points out that without systematic follow-up of programs we will not know whether parents have "acquired skills that transfer to their interaction with that same child when he is older."[20]

The essential criteria of (1) providing time for modeling, rehearsal, comparing pre- and post-program behavior, (2) providing for direct involvement in problem identification and goal setting, and (3) providing for continued communication and feedback between the program personnel and parents should be kept in mind by those people who are thinking about building a program or enrolling in a parent education course. The criteria may be used in the form of a checklist when you review program brochures or when you get in touch with the organization that is sponsoring the course.

---

[18]J. H. Stevens, *Training Parents as Home Teachers: A Review of Research.* Paper read at NAEYC (Anaheim, Calif.: November 1976).

[19]U. Bronfenbrenner, "Is Early Intervention Effective?" *The Family as Educator,* ed. H. J. Leichter (New York: Teachers College Press, 1974), p. 125.

[20]Stevens, *Training Parents as Home Teachers.*

Does the program provide time for modeling, rehearsal, and comparing pre- and post-program behavior?	Yes	No
Does the program provide for direct involvement in problem identification and goal setting?	Yes	No
Does the program provide for continued communication and feedback between the program personnel and parents?	Yes	No

Salient Features of Popular Parent Education Programs

In addition to the usefulness of the criteria as a means of assessing how various approaches can best meet parents' needs, we can also look at how these programs deal with the concepts of coping and communication. Table 5-2 is offered as a *simplistic* summary of the approaches. A pessimist might look at it and think, "Typical, all four programs continue to blame the parents." The optimist, on the other hand, might see the possibilities for building an ongoing support system in the community by combining the checklist presented with a year-round plan for offering, e.g., P.E.T. every fall; P.I.P. every winter; Dreikurs every spring, etc.

Advice from Experts Who Recognize Parents as Educators

Despite the various directions child development studies have pointed toward for parent education programs, the nucleus of the programs has been that "early learning is important, that the main burden falls on parents and that a bad start can ruin a child for life."[21] Advice on how to turn a "bad start" into a "good start" is available in paperbacks, such as those mentioned above, as well as in newspaper columns, talk shows, and periodicals. Interviews with leading psychologists and educators frequently find their way into national news magazines. The following pointers were solicited by *Newsweek* correspondents.

J. McVicker Hunt, professor of education at the University of Illinois: The best cue I know is the interest and excitement of the child. If a child is struggling to reach an object, and he is really working at it, the outstanding mother doesn't necessarily just kick the thing over to him. She kicks it closer,

---

[21]"What Parents Can Do to Help," *Newsweek*, 22 May 1972, p. 30. Used with permission.

so that he has a pretty good chance of getting it, but she doesn't put it in his hands. We should follow the child's lead, but you don't have to force him. When parents begin to feel that someone else's child is getting ahead of their's and they try to force him, then they have trouble.

Professor Earl S. Schaeffer of the University of North Carolina, former director of early child care research for the National Institute of Mental Health: If a mother said, "I'm a parent-educator," rather than a housewife, she would feel much better about her role. As educators, parents must try to promote shared activities, shared experiences—accentuated by language. You go to the grocery store and you talk about things that are happening. You cook and talk. You look at a book and talk. You talk at meals. Education works into life.

Ronald Lally, director of the Children's Center, Syracuse University: About 90 percent of the social interaction with a child from birth to eighteen months occurs during caretaking, such as taking off his clothes and feeding. For example, parents should not change diapers as quickly as possible, but should grasp this opportunity to communicate with the child. Smile and talk to him a lot while you do these things. They are the most important parts of a child's life.

Burton White, education professor at Harvard: The mother (of the superior child) is interested in what the child is interested in at the moment and spends a great deal of time talking to the child about it. These are not sustained sessions, but average about 20 seconds in length and are generally initiated by the child. The mother provides an interesting home, giving the child freedom to roam and follow his natural curiosity. There is an absence of restraining devices. That doesn't mean the mothers never use a playpen or crib, but never for long periods. The mothers average a little over an hour a day giving undivided attention to the child. (The minimum requirements for good child care are not too expensive for any human being. You don't need to be terribly bright to do a good job, you don't need to be wealthy, you don't need a happy marriage, and you don't need to spend the whole day doing it.)

Benjamin S. Bloom, professor of education at the University of Chicago: If I really wanted one thing, it would be that parents get together in voluntary groups to exchange information, the way they did for Great Books discussions. I would like early education to develop around the family rather than around institutions. Perhaps one of the parents would know a little bit more about the discussion subject than the others, but it would not have to be an "expert," and it would not have to be something from "big brother." The parents could exchange information, read books, see films, experiment with games and vent anxieties. You would have a way of checking by observing the feedback from the children.[22]

---

[22]Ibid. Copyright 1972 by Newsweek, Inc. All rights reserved. Reprinted by permission.

TABLE 5–2. Comparison of Various Approaches to Child Rearing

Approach	Coping	Communication	Methods
P.E.T. Thomas Gordon T. Gordon, *Parent Effectiveness Training* (New York: Prentice-Hall, 1970). T. Gordon, *P.E.T. in Action* (New York: Prentice-Hall, 1976).	Problems exist. Failure to solve problems exists (Not everyone who has a problem wants a solution—some would rather discover their own solutions.) Negative feelings exist. (Feelings of hate, anger, frustration are OK.) Uncertainty exists. (You can never be sure how the other is experiencing you.) Harsh realities exist. (Don't argue them away. You're hurt. You've had a bad day.) Inconsistency exists. (Our acceptance of children will vary depending upon the environment in which the behavior occurs (e.g., in public/in private); the characteristics of different children (e.g., mobile, aggressive, curious); and upon our own moods.	Identify your feelings. (Most parents have difficulty identifying what they feel. They're not accustomed to doing it. Our culture teaches that expressing feeling is impolite or immature or ego centered. So some people learn to deny and repress true feelings— (p. 122). Identify your mood. e.g., I'm mad. . . . Identify who owns the problem. ("It's your problem." "It's my problem." Associated with building self-responsibility. I'll help you find alternatives, but you must choose and implement them.)	Active listening—restatement. (a) Don't use unless you're free enough of your own problems. (b) Is not used for changing behavior you don't like; it's for showing acceptance. (c) Biggest problem is parental attitude toward trusting kids to solve their own problems. Passive listening. Acknowledge responses—uh huh—non verbal. Door openers.

114

Approach	Coping	Communication	Methods
P.I.P. (Parent Involvement Program)—based on Glasser's Methods of Reality Therapy	New priority in human motivation exists. The traditional struggle to reach a goal—a job, a home—still exists; however, the struggle for a role (an identity) takes precedence.	Involvement—anything is open to discussion. Don't dwell on just problems. "Nonessentials" are more important than discussing problems. Emphasize warm, involving conversations.	Involvement with at least one successful person is a prerequisite for growing up successfully, for maintaining success, or for changing from failure to success.
William Glasser, *Schools Without Failure* (New York: Harper and Row, 1969); *The Identity Society* (New York: Harper and Row, 1975), see especially Chapter 4, "Reality Therapy," pp. 69–98.	Children's behavior is not goal behavior and it is not acceptable to most parents. No parent can change a child's behavior without altering his own. Each must change his own behavior.	Current behavior. I believe you— You have convinced me you are upset. But what are you doing? What did you do to start the fight? What did you do to keep the fight going?	In attending to current behavior accept the feeling but emphasize behavior more than feeling. Develop plan. Ask for commitment (verbal or written). No punishment.
Contact source for program description & materials: Tom McGuinen, Ass't Director Educator Training Center 2140 W. Olympic Blvd. Los Angeles, CA 90006	Parents must take the lead for staying involved. Involvement alone does not lead to success. Parents must accept the primary responsibility to keep the involvement going at any one time.	Plan and commitment. If plan is not fulfilled don't punish—don't concentrate on failure. Not "it's your fault"—BUT are you still going to try to fulfill the commitment? Work for goals that will reinforce child's role—"Stop loafing and start working"—is a waste of breath.	

115

TABLE 5–2.—Continued

Approach	Coping	Communication	Methods
Dreikurs Rudolph Dreikurs, *Children—The Challenge* (New York: Hawthorne Books, 1964). *Logical Consequences* (New York: Hawthorne Books, 1968). *Maintaining Sanity in the Classroom* (New York: Hawthorne Books, 1971). *Discipline Without Tears* (New York: Hawthorne Books, 1972).	Our culture does not furnish sufficient means by which children can attain recognition through constructive activities. Parents need help in learning to cope with today's children on the basis of equality and mutual respect. Children cannot learn to take on responsibility unless it is given to them. We cannot train the child to take on responsibility: must give it to him. Today's children are free to do as they please while the adults have taken on the responsibility of their acts. Life is a continuous process of decision making. Unfortunately when faced with decisions we are almost never in possession of all the facts needed for an objective choice. Punishment is retaliatory not corrective—it usually has no connection with the misbehavior.	The essential theme must be cooperation not permissiveness. Cooperation is not possible without acceptance of responsibility. Success may be discouraging: the child may come to the conclusion that she is worthwhile only when successful. Encouragement is needed when the child fails. Neither parents nor teachers are prepared to deal with the child as an equal. They must be taught specific techniques. 34 principles in *Children—The Challenge*.	Capturing the ability to influence children depends upon parental enactment of the role of guide not boss. 1. Observation of the reactions the child evokes—not just the child! —to get attention? —to demonstrate power? —to hurt? —to be left alone? 2. Check the conclusion of your observation by trying to stop him or her—what happens? You have to check your own reactions a. "If annoyed, you give child attention b. If angry you fall into the trap of child's showing you that s/he can demonstrate power c. If you are hurt then child accomplished the goal of "I can hurt" d. If tempted to give up, you've given into the child's goal of being left alone. Decide who's responsible for: late for school not eating misplaced clothes, toys late night rules

116

Approach	Coping	Communication	Methods
Behavior Modification	Behavior not personality is the target of change.	Procedures outlined in the methods can be used to alter patterns of behavior.	Buy graph paper.
Marilyn L. Clark et al., *The Responsive Parent Training Manual* (Lawrence, Kan.: H & H Enterprise, 1976).	Children must be taught those behaviors they need for coping with behavioral requirements of the home or school.	Verbal, nonverbal, and concrete reinforcement. Respond to desirable behavior by issuing a token (reinforcement).	Determine baseline of incidents of current behavior.
Program description and materials are available from: H & H Enterprises Box 3342 Lawrence, Kansas 66044	The behavior modifier is not concerned with internal causes of behavior. Does not assume that the behavior is a symptom of a deeper problem.	Ignore undesirable behavior (extinction).	Determine schedule of reinforcement for new behavior.
Specific questions about the program may be addressed to: Marilyn Clark-Hall Special Services 5005 W. 95th Shawnee Mission, Kansas 66216	Who has the problem? Usually both the parent and the child. One party has the undesirable behavior; the other, the responsibility to do something about changing it.	Words spoken include *Yes, Good, Great, Wonderful*, etc.	Behavioral contracting (i.e. goal oriented as compared to Glasser's role identity).
		Sentences spoken include *You make me happy.* *Yes, I think you should continue.* *You make being your mother really fun.* *I like that.* *You're a good person.*	Behavioral rehearsal—role playing, modeling.
			Punishment includes: a. Separate the child from others until he is ready (time out from reinforcement). b. If you decide to use physical punishment it must be strong enough to stop the behavior immediately.
			Parents must be consistent. Plan out contingencies and rewards on a schedule!

> *Richard:* As I read the comments of Hunt, Schaeffer, White, and Bloom, I get the feeling that they are saying that professional educators should assume another role—helping parents to acquire skills needed to become excellent parents. I have a few questions:
>
> 1. Are we trying to have all parents act like middle-class parents?
> 2. How will professional educators find time to add this responsibility of parent educator to their already over-defined roles?
>
> *Cynthia:* Good questions. There has been some interesting work lately on the whole issue of "social class" (see Wandersman 1973). It also seems from the studies which pointed out the contribution of parent involvement to student achievement that the "time" might be well spent. However, our readers can select various parent programs from our Appendix B. From their reading, they can develop their own conclusions about the issues you raised. In addition, they can explore parent programs in their own community/regions.

The Challenge to Parenting Research: How Do We Study Developmental Change?

The advice from Hunt, Schaeffer, Lally, White, and Bloom touches only a small sampling of advice from prominent educators which is available to those concerned with the study of parents as educators. Many disagreements arise around what methods are appropriate for accomplishing cognitive and/or affective objectives, as well as on what theory of human development the program should be based. Those who argue against maturation and readiness theories can use evidence that formulation of the child's mental structure is determined by creating the correct environment. In *Intelligence and Experience,* J. McVicker Hunt (1961) offers his definition of the environment's influence in the term *genotype-environment.* Neither development nor intelligence is fixed at birth through inherited genes. What is transmitted through nature is potential, i.e., capability for processing information. Although the genes set limits, the environment develops or retards an individual's potential. On one hand are the individual's thought processes; on the other, external circumstances. Out of this situation arises the "problem of the match." If the external environment is too active, the child can be turned off or experience anxiety. In *Birth to Maturity* Jerome Kagan (1962) has attempted to analyze and define optimum levels of stimulation as "distinctive stimulation."

Within the context of these concerns numerous studies have taken place that attempt to measure the influences of the environment on the infant's life. The role of the mother in terms of feeding habits, amount of verbalization, and amount of time spent attending to her child as well as psychological testing of her attitudes during the prenatal period through the first two years has been investigated (Goodrich 1961). The role of the child in his own development has led to studies that measure such variables as activity level, rhythm of sleeping-waking, adaptability to new responses, quality of mood, distractability, and persistence (White 1968). The focus of some of these studies has been to determine whether the child's patterns of behavior influence his parents' attitude towards him or whether the parental attitudes and environment are the primary determiners of personality development (Thomas 1971).

> While all of this research is useful, the more basic question remains unanswered: What do parents do with their children on a day-to-day basis that effects the fairly consistent differences reported in (child rearing) studies? . . . Which specific features of parental behavior are really crucial? . . . Researchers attempting to observe and study the actual behaviors of a mother and child interacting together can obviously not record and analyze all the interactions over a lifetime. . . . It seems to us that a finer-grained analysis (is) needed of how a mother talks to her child when she really tries to teach him something, and how she structures a teaching situation . . . thereby making the interaction the focus of the research rather than the behavior of one person or the other.[23]

One might also add that while all of this research is useful, the basic question is: Who is responsible for sifting through all this advice and helping parents become effective in their role as educators? With a few years of training one can learn the curriculum techniques which are the outgrowth of child development studies. But it remains up to each teacher who is convinced that parents are the key to reform to sift through the research and ask questions. Williams (1974) has brought out the point that

> studies of child rearing practices and attitudes have been almost exclusively addressed to middle-class mothers between the ages of about 23 and 35 years who lived in nuclear family settings. Little, if any, information is available

---

[23]A. P. Streissguth and N. L. Bee, "Mother-Child Interactions and Cognitive Development," in *The Young Child, Review of Research*, Vol. 2, ed. W. W. Hartup (Washington, D.C.: NAEYC, 1972), pp. 167, 171, 181.

concerning the child rearing practices and attitudes of fathers, the upper class, older parents, very young parents, or single parents.[24]

One of the reasons for this broadening of view concerning parent education has been the slow recognition of global influences on childrearing in the wider society (Bronfenbrenner 1974). We are beginning to hear

guarded optimism about the long-range effects of two or three years work with the mothers, stating that the disadvantaged mother may be unable to provide a home situation that would maintain the development of the child and that the schools are, in general, unable to provide (alone) for the education of the child.[25]

One can trace the development of "guarded optimism" in both basic and applied research areas. Studies concerned with mother-child interaction and cognitive development and studies focused on the role of mother's language recognize that we still have a long way to go. Streissguth and Bee's (1972) review of past research on the relationship between intellectual outcomes of mother-child interactions concluded that

it is an unfortunate state of affairs that research has revealed more about the effects of mother-absence on children's intellectual development than about the effects of mother-presence.[26]

The latter summary of research on mother-child interactions is in no way intended as criticism. The amount of time and energy devoted to studying the role of mother's language has made significant contributions to parent education programs. Reviews of past studies have pointed out that both the mother's teaching style and the child's learning style is influenced by what can and cannot take place due to the structure of our social system.[27] This point of view offers hope in breaking the vicious cycle of blame the parents–blame the schools. The application of basic research to parent education programs has also offered a variety of techniques to foster cognitive, affective, and physical competencies of infants and young children as well as the fringe benefit of enriching the lives of parents. Succinctly, they offer new interpretations to the phrase *strengthening and supporting* family care and education.

---

[24]T. M. Williams, "Child-rearing Practices of Young Mothers: What We Know, How It Matters, Why It's so Little," *American Journal of Orthopsychiatry* 44 (1974): 70–75.

[25]Schaeffer, *Parents as Educators*, p. 196.

[26]Streissguth and Bee, "Mother-Child Interactions and Cognitive Development," p. 158.

[27]E. G. Olim, R. D. Hess, and V. C. Shipman, "Role of Mothers' Language Styles in Mediating Their Preschool Children's Cognitive Development," *The School Review* 75 (1967): 414–24.

The Challenge to Parenting Programs:
How Do We Deliver Services?

Rather than past emphasis on deprivation and compensatory education, parent education programs have accepted the possibility of unlimited potential in many areas of development rather than fixed innate potential. J. McVicker Hunt's (1971) review of thirty-six parent and child centers established by the federal government in 1967 for children under the age of three reported optimistic results in a variety of "demonstration studies that combine models for imitation and explanations of child rearing practices."[28] In 1972 Work visited parent-child centers in thirteen of the states described by Hunt. Although Work had some reservations about the expectations for behavior of fifteen-month-old children and the fact that some centers tolerated mothers not arriving with their children, his overall conclusion concerning the methods of application of cognitive techniques by parents and staff members was also positive.[29]

Work's main concern was the fact that the centers did not attend to the following aspects of the professional role of social technologists (see also chapter 7).

1. *Developing Public Expectations of Educational Services*
   In many of the ghetto centers there is a growing suspicion of research and the meaning of new findings to the political scene. This is most vividly demonstrated in the Boston area in the formation of a Black Research Review Council. . . . To date there has been some informal activity to cut down on research. Many of the parents have a long standing fear of research in their own neighborhoods. . . . In the Baltimore Center . . . the individuals served by the PCC (Parent Child Center) regard the latter as a potentially frightening place.

2. *Establishing the Nature of Professional Service and Criteria for Performance*
   There is a seemingly lack of intensive research activity focused on the processes and organization of the centers. This becomes crucial to the political scene since these are pilot centers and they will need to be duplicated if they are effective. A greater understanding of how they are organized . . . and how the process of staff relations, staff-parent relations, staff community relations, etc. may be carved out, is essential. Many of the people involved in these centers are concerned primarily with their day-to-day activities; they are loathe to look back. . . . There is (also) a general

[28]J. McVicker Hunt, "Parent and Child Centers: Their Basis in the Behavioral and Educational Sciences," *American Journal of Orthopsychiatry* 41 (1971): 13–38.

[29]H. H. Work, "Parent-Child Centers: A Working Reappraisal," *American Journal of Orthopsychiatry* 42 (1972): 582–95. Reprinted, with permission, from the *American Journal of Orthopsychiatry*: copyright 1972 by the American Orthopsychiatric Association, Inc.

lack of a relationship between various centers. . . . The Louisville and
Leithfield (Kentucky) Centers, located 60 miles apart, had no contact, no
communication, and no general means of working together to improve
their manner of function.[30]

Levenstein, Kochman, and Roth's (1973) examination of the processes
involved in replicating the laboratory model of the Mother-Child Home
Program (MCHP) in four organizations stands in contrast to how the
programs analyzed by Work enacted their professional roles in the community. Their implementation of school/community relations offers testimony to the fact that developing expectations of educational services
and establishing the nature of professional services can be implemented.
The MCHP Program in each organization included ninety-two home visits
over a two-year period to families with preschool aged children. The
Model Program was an outgrowth of research that suggested that intellectual development is closely tied to the child's verbal development
between twenty months and four years.[31] The program staff set about
convincing mothers that the service that both the mothers and the staff
could perform was beneficial. The salient features of the program, as
described by the authors, can be analyzed by the same method as the
programs reviewed by Work.

1. *Developing Public Expectations of Educational Services*
   The curriculum was demonstrated rather than taught to the mother, i.e.,
   didactic aspects were de-emphasized. The program was offered on a take
   it or leave it basis, i.e., the programmers acknowledged the fact that
   parents are the decision makers.

2. *Establishing the Nature of Professional Services and Criteria for
   Performance*
   The model program continues for research, demonstration, and evaluation purposes, i.e., methodology can be evaluated in longitudinal terms
   as the children progress through their formal school years. Communication and dissemination of new information between new and already
   established mother-child centers is facilitated through MCHP Coordinators; i.e., the coordinators can also work with local service organization personnel such as child psychologists who have not had experience
   with infant testing.

---

[30]Ibid., p. 590.
[31]Phyllis Levenstein, Arlene Kochman, and Helen Roth, "From Laboratory to Real World:
Service Delivery of the Mother-Child Home Program," *American Journal of Orthopsychiatry*
43 (1973): 73.

In examining the results of home delivery of service the authors extended Caldwell's observations of what we have learned after a decade of early childhood intervention.

> The overall lesson learned in the experience . . . was that there were few short-cuts in assisting an organization . . . every step, no matter how adapted to local needs, seemed necessary to ensure the achievement of either the scientific or practical goals of delivering this laboratory generated program to the "real world."[32]

One should keep in mind the two categories outlined above when reading any of the parent education programs listed in Appendix B. As you read through the programs, list all those items that describe services under the heading "Developing Public Expectations of Educational Services." Items describing how the program got started, how parents were recruited, and how parents were involved in decisions concerning the program can be listed under the heading "Establishing the Nature of Professional Services and Criteria for Performance."

Although many questions concerning samples, methods, and focus remain unanswered (Wandersman 1973), the venturesome know that the subject of parents as educators is far removed from a debate on whether or not parents do educate their children. The extent of recognition of parents as educators can be assessed in part by the beginning statement in a recent research report, "The Verbal Environment Provided by Mothers for Their Children" (Holzman 1973):

> Mothers take the explicit role of teacher. This has not been discussed in the introduction because it is such a well known aspect of the curriculum of the mother-child interaction.[33]

Another indicator of the growth in recognition of parents as educators is the organization of the Parenting Materials Information Center (PMIC), Southwest Education Development Laboratory, Austin, Texas.

In *Parenting in 1975* (ERIC File ED 110 153) materials, programs, kits, books, periodicals, audio-visual resources, and price and ordering information relevant to needs of parents and those working with parents were compiled. In addition, the Southwest Educational Development Laboratory will continue to collect, analyze, and disseminate information pertaining to parent education. Among the areas covered are

---

[32]Ibid., p. 77.
[33]M. Holzman, "The Verbal Environment Provided by Mothers for Their Children," *Merrill-Palmer Quarterly* 20 (1974): 13–42.

1. Academic content and skills
2. Child abuse
3. Discipline
4. Early childhood activities
5. Exceptional children
6. Family
7. Group relations and training
8. Health and safety
9. Language and intellectual development
10. Multiethnic, multicultural heritage
11. Parents, school and community involvement
12. Parenting
13. Physical and sensory development
14. Social and emotional development

Parents as Educators: Unanswered Questions

Many authors have suggested that parental involvement in preschool education practices, either at a center or at home, is associated with program success. Badger (1969) found that all the parent involvement programs she studied had succeeded. No one program was "clearly superior" to another. Although she worked with three groups of mothers in different types of structured and unstructured workshops, all the children involved gained in cognitive and verbal development areas. Wittes and Radin (1971) also found that despite differences in techniques used with parent groups (i.e., lecture versus activity oriented) all the children gained in academic achievement. Pomfret (1972) also has concluded that student achievement at elementary and secondary levels is associated with parents' *direct* involvement in education. Before jumping to the conclusion that parents and the school (may) "work at cross purposes no matter how valiantly the staff might try to make it otherwise,"[34] we should evaluate just how well we have interpreted to the public what is going on in schools and the fact that they are welcome.

Many possible reasons could be offered for the position that cross-purposes do exist. It appears that rather than searching for areas of agreement between the two systems of the home and school, studies have considered the adaptation of the entire family network to school entry. This type of study assumes that adaptation is a one-way street, i.e., children and their families must fit the school, and ignores exploration of how and why two systems are related. The opposite type of research has been described by Emlen.

---

[34]Bettye M. Caldwell, "Infant Day Care—The Outcast Gains Responsibility," in *Child Care—Who Cares,* ed. P. Roby (New York: Basic Books, 1973), p. 26.

We must discover across many settings how to favor the optimum development of the child as a whole person. (This means) making it easier for families to do the job of child care or of arranging for child care. (It means)
being concerned with . . . what kinds of support systems we should create in
order either to prevent or to strengthen the existing patterns of care that
families use.[35]

The educator who has accomplished the most toward developing our
awareness that we must consider human development across settings
within the social context is Urie Bronfenbrenner. Bronfenbrenner has
contributed to national commissions on child development, has testified
before senate committees concerned with American children, and has
headed delegations to countries in Europe, Asia, and the Soviet Union.
His model of the Ecology of Human Development offers a means for
understanding development as increasing awareness of alternatives, increasing ability to make choices, and increasing ability to implement
those choices.

The social context refers to the settings in which children actually live
and develop as well as people's conceptions of the appropriate means and
ends to foster development (i.e., ideology). The settings in which children
live and develop determine with whom and how he/she spends his/her
time. A child's development is influenced by the immediate setting (e.g.,
home, peer group, school) and the institutional systems and social dimensions in which the immediate setting is embedded (e.g., shopping centers,
public transportation facilities, political policies, economic policies and
conditions which affect the child's parents' work, legal decisions and their
implementation, and educational operations).[36]

Finally, underguiding both the encompassing social structure and its embedded immediate settings is an ideological system which, both explicitly and
implicitly, endorses motivational meaning to social networks, institutions,
roles, activities, and their interrelations. Whether or not children or youth
have a place and priority in such an ideology is of special importance in
determining how a particular system, including the entire society treats its
young and those responsible for their care.[37]

Research based on Bronfenbrenner's model has been considered prom-

[35]A. C. Emlen, "Slogans, Slots and Slander: The Myth of Day Care Need," *American Journal of Orthopsychiatry* 43 (1973): 35.
[36]Bronfenbrenner, "Developmental Research, Public Policy, and the Ecology of Child-hood, *Child Development* 45 (1974): 1–5.
[37]U. Bronfenbrenner, *Experimental Human Ecology: A Reorientation to Theory and Research on Socialization.* Paper presented at the 82nd Annual Convention of the American Psychological Association, New Orleans, 1974.

ising since it aids the researcher and those developing programs for school/community interactions in focusing on (1) the interrelatedness of just how "we need each other," (2) determining how the immediate setting nurtures parent-child-teacher interaction, and (3) determining which factors of economic and educational resources undermine or support the functioning of parents.[38] Future studies in school/community relations within the model of human ecology (see figures 5–1, 5–2, and 5–3) could help to illustrate that policy efforts need to concentrate on programs which provide adequate support systems for parents as educators.

Goodlad (1975) has described the advantages of an ecological view of educational improvement in the following way:

> One of the many advantages of an ecological theory is that it draws attention to what exists or is happening for purposes of information. What to do is not determined in advance but emerges out of diagnosis and consideration of alternatives. It may not be necessary to rip up the water system and replace it with another. Perhaps just a few leaks need to be repaired. Or, to use an analogy from schooling, it may not be necessary to install an entire new reading program; perhaps the teachers simply need more help with the present one.[39]

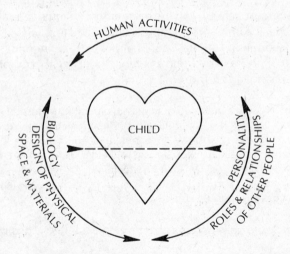

FIGURE 5–1. Analysis of human ecology: Dimensions of the immediate setting

---

[38]J. Garbarino, "A Preliminary Study of Some Ecological Correlates of Child Abuse: The Impact of Socioeconomic Stress on Mothers," *Child Development* 47 (1976): 178–85.

[39]J. I. Goodlad, *The Dynamics of Educational Change: Towards Responsive Schools* (New York: McGraw-Hill, 1975), p. 207.

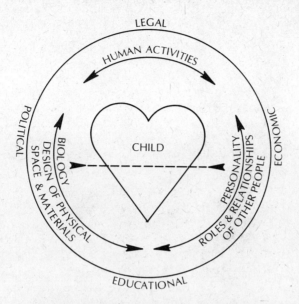

FIGURE 5–2. **Immediate setting embedded in the institution systems (limits and shapes what can and does occur in the immediate setting)**

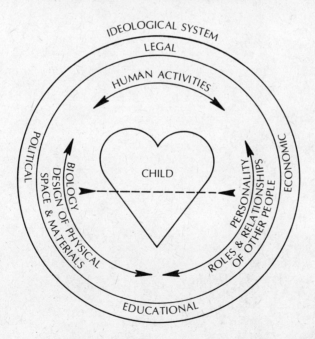

FIGURE 5–3. **Ideological system endows meaning and defines interrelationship of the child, the immediate setting, and the institutions**

127

Richard: I have always associated "ecology" with conversation and environmental issues. I like Bronfenbrenner's use of the term. Now I look at numerous situations—for example, the teacher who does not interact with parents may not be "anti-parent." If I look at the "ecology" of the situation, many factors may influence the decision: teacher is nervous when talking to adults; teacher is not aware that involvement with parents is part of his role; teacher is uncomfortable with people from class backgrounds different from his . . .

Cynthia: Well stated. I recommend that our readers select a specific situation in their schools and analyze the situation from an ecological approach and . . .

Richard: And try to develop numerous strategies (not just one) to deal with the situation.

Cynthia: You took the words out of my mouth.

Parents as Contributors to Decision Making 6

One of the fringe benefits for parents who have become involved in educating their children and educators who have helped them on their way has been an increase in knowledge for all involved. We know from operational definitions of democracy that an increase in knowledge is often associated with an increase in power over one's own life and the lives of one's family. Acquiring knowledge through parent education programs can be viewed in the following way:

1. Increasing awareness of alternatives,
2. Increasing ability to choose among alternatives,
3. Increasing ability to implement those choices.

Awareness of Alternatives

One would have a hard time defending the position that developers of parent education had as a primary objective increasing the ability to implement political choices. Those concerned with early childhood have had *to learn* to take a stand on controversial issues. Evidence of the fact that we have learned to take a stand is apparent in the organization of federal commissions concerned with the "victims." Two national commissions were organized in 1967 (The Gorham Committee and The Presidential Task Force), and others were held in 1969 (Joint Commission

129

on the Mental Health of Children), 1970 (White House Conference on Children), and 1972 (National Research Council Advisory Committee on Child Development). However, little if any information is available on all the details that had to be attended to in order to gain this recognition. If we had more information on how decisions were reached in these commissions, we might be further along in destroying the myth that politics is dirty.

Goodson and Hess (1975) have suggested that one of the reasons we are not further along in recognizing parents as contributors to decision making is that

> the extent of the home-involvement movement is not documented and probably cannot be, since many local programs operate without public recognition and with little printed material or records to make an inventory possible.[1]

Goodson and Hess also believe that the twenty-nine programs they reviewed were "usually not a response to the political issues of community control."[2] Although one could argue that the programs reviewed by the authors *were* a response to political issues since they were all "concerned with changing the parents—their knowledge, behavior, attitudes, or some combination of the three,"[3] Goodson and Hess do not consider these activities as associated with a political commitment. The reason they reached this conclusion is stated simply: "The implementation of the goal through groups such as Parent Advisory Boards often gives little actual power to the parents."[4] The fact remains, however, that the programs offered alternatives to the parents involved.

Choosing Alternatives

Several innovators in parent education programs have traced the beginnings of political awareness to programs originally concerned with parents as educators of young children. Tuck (1971) describes how fathers floundered through their first parent meetings. As they became aware of alternative techniques and methods, they implemented their decision after choosing a new method. (The "new" method might have been an

---

[1]B. D. Goodson and R. D. Hess, *Parents as Teachers of Young Children: An Evaluative Review of Some Contemporary Concepts and Programs* (Palo Alto, Calif.: Stanford University Press, 1975), p. 1.

[2]Ibid., p. 2.

[3]Ibid.

[4]Ibid., p. 3.

extension of the old or a combination of practices.) As they implemented their choices, they usually met with small success with their children. With success they gained recognition of their role as teachers of their children. They increased their ability to implement those choices by planning new activities so that they could be with their children. The activities had a snowball effect. The fathers wrote proposals for funds and eventually undertook business ventures in their community (e.g., one group bought an ice cream truck as a source of funds, while others established a credit union for the entire neighborhood). Berlin (1971) supports Tuck's conclusion in his description of a group of professionals who became involved in the community and "saw uninvolved hostile or helpless parents become more effective human beings."[5]

Implementing Choices

Additional studies have reported the success of parents as modifiers of various physical, cognitive, and affective behaviors of their children. Johnson and Katz (1973) have reviewed the procedures and results of researchers who have assisted parents to change children's antisocial, disobedient, and immature behaviors. Their analysis of the methodological approach of forty-five studies which used parents as change agents for their children suggests that many of the researchers took shortcuts in describing their studies. As a result, future researchers and program developers will have problems in estimating how much time is needed as well as having an adequate source of descriptions of parent training operations to share with the public. To fill that gap Appendix B includes a selected list of parent education programs available from ERIC.

In order to evaluate the programs selected for review the following simple checklist may be used.

1. What provisions are made for increasing awareness of alternatives?
2. What provisions are made for increasing the ability to choose among the alternatives?
3. What provisions are made for increasing the ability of parents to implement those choices?

For example, the parent education program described by Willis (ED 051 897) includes the program's provisions for making two career develop-

---

[5]I. N. Berlin, "Professionals' Participation in Community Activities: Is It Part of the Job?" *American Journal of Orthopsychiatry* 41 (1971): 496.

ment paths available to women (i.e., awareness of alternatives). A second aspect of the program (ED 051 892) suggests various learning experiences which allow both the child and the mothers to choose (i.e., awareness of alternatives, ability to choose among alternatives). Programs listed also describe how parents are helped to implement their choices. Champagne and Goldman (ED 048 945) have reported that role-playing simulation activities included in their program helped parents and teachers to choose the specific teaching skills they desired to learn (increasing awareness of alternatives, increasing ability to choose among them, and increasing ability to implement their choices).

The Link between Parents as Decision Makers and Implementing the Goal of a Capable Society

In chapter 2 we suggested that frustration is often the result of facing apparently unresolvable social problems plus overexpectations regarding what we can do about them. Table 6-1 reduces those apparently unresolvable social problems into three steps toward solution. Each of the steps recognizes parents as contributors to decision making.

The first three steps outlined above have been suggested by Gardner (1965) as the characteristics of a capable society. It seems to us that the three steps of improving internal communication, providing positive leadership, and enhancing pluralism are, in essence, the same characteristics of what could result from parent involvement. We will not fulfill the characteristics of a capable society unless we share the decision-making process with parents.

Before jumping ahead into chapter 7 to discuss how teachers may share the decision-making process with parents, we might add that the items outlined in table 6-1 reduce what might seem to be an impossible job into handling each problem as it comes up. To handle each problem we must have communication between the home and the school. For example, the first characteristic in both columns on the chart is concerned with awareness of alternatives. How many schools have taken the time to find out just what effect their curriculum has on the family? How much distance in communication between the home and school do we create by not helping parents become aware of what's going on? If you were always in the position of having to ask, "What did you do in school today?" rather than saying, "Next week looks exciting for your class," then your feelings of frustration could easily be channeled into thinking of problems as unresolvable. The second comparison of characteristics of a capable society and parent involvement is concerned with choosing among alternatives. We know from the section on community development studies that, in order to succeed, development programs must attend to presentation of alternatives in a way that allows the community to interpret any change as compatible with their way of life. The last points on the chart, enhancing pluralism and participatory democracy, point out that parents cannot contribute to decision making without having the opportunity to implement their choices.

TABLE 6–1. Comparisons of Home/School/Community and National Objectives

Expectations of Parent Involvement	Characteristics of a Capable Society
Institutional reform: Parents represent not only resources for program development but the extra-institutional force for change without which educational services will continue to bureaucratize and atrophy.	*Improving internal communication:* Aware of implications of the curriculum and can point out alternatives.
Educational viability: Parents become better informed through their involvement and complement the educational process, contributing to their children's growth and achievement.	*Providing positive leadership:* Keeping hope alive; educating future leaders.
Participatory democracy: Parent involvement is essential as a basic right of citizens in a democratic society.	*Enhancing Pluralism:* Bring together as many as possible in order to contribute to society's renewal.
SOURCE: Daniel Safran, *State Education Agencies and Parent Involvement* (Oakland, Calif.: Center for the Study of Parent Involvement, 1974).	SOURCE: John W. Gardner, *Self-Renewal: The Individual and the Innovative Society* (New York: Harper & Row, 1965).

Cynthia: *Perhaps we professionals are the problem. We suggest in this chapter a type of participatory democracy with which those of us with B.A.s, M.A.s, and Ph.D.s are uncomfortable. "What do they (parents) know about it? They haven't had the specialized training that we have received." What effect do you think the training of the professionals in education has on their behaviors?*

Richard: *Good question. I think that our readers who are professional educators should critique their training. How were* the issues of parental involvement, advocacy for parents and children, and participatory democracy dealt with?

Cynthia: After they complete this critique, I suggest that the readers continue their reading with chapter 7, "Teachers as Social Technologists." They may find some additional information about what occurred and did not occur in their (our) training.

Teachers As Social 7
Technologists

If one accepts the position that members of a society are engaged in interaction behavior and that the context of society can be viewed as an ecological system, then the most critical responsibility of the teacher is

an ability to play off the roles that go beyond the classroom and involve the teacher with everyone effecting educational enterprise—fellow teachers, parents, administrators, the school psychologist, the Board of Education —and to influence these people for the good of children.[1]

The purpose of this chapter is not to add to the volumes of pronouncements concerning teachers' tasks. The intent is to look at what is available to help the teacher enact the critical responsibility described above. Again admonitions that "we need each other" will not be as effective as exploring how Americans can build a capable society. Discussions of improving internal communication, providing positive leadership, and enhancing pluralism must give recognition to the absolute necessity of involving parents in the process.

---

[1]Thomas Lickona et al., *Project Change* (Cortland, N.Y.: State University of New York, 1972). ERIC File ED 083 140.

Toward a Definition

A brief explanation of the term *technology* as applied to the teacher's role may avoid confusion about how its definition as well as the social technologist role relates to parents.

> Technology refers broadly to linkages between means and ends . . . it is most important at this point to establish the idea that technology pertains to the means of getting a job done . . . identifying problems and analyzing their causes does not automatically insure appropriate solutions.[2]

Since *technology* refers to linkages between means and ends, the term *social technologist* has been adopted to describe the teacher's professional role in developing school/community communication. As we have seen earlier, there is no hope of change unless we involve the target population. The target of school/community relations is, simply, the home and the school. We need to attend to both the role of the parent and the role of the teacher. Just as we proposed in the chapters on parents as educators and parents as contributors to decision making, it would negate the purpose of this book if this chapter were to address a particular population. Acceptance of new roles is dependent on developing expectations of the appropriateness of those roles by the members of society involved. The review of community development studies in chapter 3 provided some ideas of what mechanisms or links could be established to implement communication between the school and community. We have also reviewed in the section on role conflict in chapter 2 that if society does not recognize the usefulness or value of a role, the parental or teacher role will receive little public support. One only needs to consider the role of poets and philosophers in this country to grasp this aspect of role theory. Poets and philosophers are not considered very useful in our technologically minded society; hence, they receive little recognition. If a poet said such and such an amount of our taxes should be set aside to support poets s/he probably wouldn't receive any space in the mass media. Along the same lines, one wonders how much space parents and teachers would get if they called for funds to insure that future educators would be prepared as

> highly skilled professionals who, through training and consequent internalization of a professional code of conduct, are able to collaborate in regulating

---

[2]A. Pomfret, "Involving Parents in Schools: Towards Developing a Social Intervention Technology," *Interchange* 3(1972): 115.

their own and colleagues' activities (and) participate in an analysis of their own professional work.[3]

Development of Roles as a Political Process

Whether enactment of professional roles will ever become commonplace is not assured. Each of the university preparation programs described in Appendix C is attempting to build various aspects of professional development. One of the reasons that the picture is not complete in any one program is because role expectations involve value judgments. Just as passage of legislative measures affecting various aspects of medical services have to be negotiated among interest groups, any change in teacher preparation courses will involve negotiations among interest groups on particular campuses. The negotiation of preservice courses does not have to be negative. It could mean that university professors, administrators, classroom teachers, school psychologists, and parents would be involved in evaluating professional development not only regarding the teacher's instructor role but also the role of a social technologist.

Social technologists are involved in questions such as who identifies, formulates, chooses, legitimatizes, communicates, implements, and evaluates the plans and strategies concerning what to teach (what books), how to teach, whom to teach, as well as who should teach. All these competencies require awareness of community development, parents as educators, and parents as contributors to decision making. Several years ago Kilpatrick (1932) described the "new task" of teachers as social technologists.

> To undertake this new task a wider conception of the profession of education is needed. We need to accept social responsibility for studying all significant educative effects . . . the new view demands a new social emphasis . . . the chief returns will be social attitudes built from the acceptance of social responsibility and the development of social intelligence.[4]

Although the words are no longer new, Kilpatrick's description is still up-to-date:

It is of course true—humiliatingly true—that the historic beginnings of the

---

[3]J. Lynch and H. D. Plunkett, *Teacher Education and Cultural Change* (London: Allen and Unwin, Ltd., 1973), p. 87.

[4]William H. Kilpatrick, *Education and the Social Order* (New York: Liveright Publishing, 1932), pp. 83–85.

profession did not carry the significance sketched above . . . our teachers have thought not in terms of social responsibility but rather of subject-matter and mere school keeping . . . we must then openly assume our social responsibility . . . in two directions must we work, the one to build up the profession from the point of view of organization, and the other to build up the individual members.[5]

We cannot build up either the organization or individual members unless we involve the public. Individuals will not attend to new duties or responsibilities without recognition of their value by society. The first task appears to be considering the appropriateness of the tasks which have been described implicitly or explicitly throughout this book. The conclusion to an overview of school/community relations cannot be written until we know whether the process is considered valuable by members of the educational community.

Past Attempts at Developing Competencies

There have been attempts to set down the competencies necessary to carry out the responsibilities of social technologists (Donegan and Gorman 1974). In 1952 Adams presented a review of 200 books and 400 articles that had been concerned with the principles of human relations in curriculum improvement. His summary of the research in this area was presented to 154 educators. (The educators had been selected by a "jury" of their colleagues as authorities in the field of curriculum.) The jury was asked to identify principles of human relations they thought school staff members had to attend to if they were concerned with influencing group values and attitudes. Twenty-five principles received unanimous support. Two of the human relations principles that the educators thought professionals must attend to were: creation of a community persuasion and identifying social and psychological factors working for or against improvement (Adams 1952). The original intent of these directions was to train teachers as change agents. We can see, however, that in order to be effective these directions for closing the distance between the home and school may be used by either parents or teachers. Indeed, they apply to all individuals who are working toward the solution of apparently unresolvable problems in our society.

1. Persuade the person that he is obligated to make the change because it is consistent with his publicly announced value sys-

---

[5]Ibid., pp. 44–49.

tem. The proposed change may be, for example, what is best for the children.

2. Present hard data to the person who attempts to make rational decisions.

3. Carefully explain the proposed program and provide the information necessary to carry out the change. Some innovations are opposed because they are not understood.

4. Appeal to some basic need—peer acceptance, esteem, power, security, etc.

5. Allude to the influential people who are in agreement with him, or prestigious systems which have made the adoption.[6]

McNally (1974) suggests that strategies such as these are not a panacea. He has written that the reasons for the failure of change agents in the schools is "ridiculously evident." In addition to the situations in which the wrong individuals have assumed responsibility and have gone about attempting to change conditions in various sites the wrong way, the conditions of successful change are more complicated and time-consuming than usually taken into account. He has overviewed conditions that affect change. Most of the conditions he describes have been dealt with in previous chapters. In order to build a climate of acceptance and support on the part of school/community, we must attend to keeping up with what we know, why we don't know more, and what's going on. McNally uses the following phrases to describe his position:

1. The staff realizes the role models, instructional techniques, behavior and strategies they will have to perform are congruent with their aims.

2. Financial, time, and equipment support are forthcoming in order to help develop a climate of acceptance and support on the part of parents, community, pupils and administrative-supervisory personnel.

3. Failure to attend to development of community support over time has resulted in abandonment of innovation, or so watered down as to be unrecognizable.

4. Building support and learning new roles usually takes from two to five years.

---

[6]Charles Hill, "Teachers as Change Agents," *The Clearinghouse* 45 (1971): 424–28.

5. Changes in original plan depend on making provisions for continuous feedback.[7]

Sarbin and Allen (1968) have examined another aspect of building a climate of acceptance. They suggest that an individual integrates himself in a social system, such as the community, through a cognitive process. The decision on how and when to act involves "the ability to analyze a social situation and accurately infer the role of the other."[8] The cognitions within the community (i.e., rights, privileges, duties, and obligations) offer cues of appropriate conduct for individuals occupying a particular position. These cognitions, generally called *role expectations,* are not always rigid or specific directives. "Most role expectations require only that some end result be accomplished within some limits."[9]

The conceptualization of climate building has been interpreted on a more personal dimension. Chall (1975) suggested that recognition of rights, duties, and obligations of those concerned with current practices in education are not always specific because we have failed to include the teacher category in our recognition of who is an educational leader. We would like to add to the quote from Chall's article that we have also failed to recognize parents.

> [Parents' and] teachers' dignity and self-worth could be enhanced appreciably if the distinguished among them were honored along with the distinguished among education—scholars, writers, and administrators. . . . If they suffer from a diminished sense of self-worth and dignity, we might well look to the education profession itself—to the manner in which it recognizes its leaders.[10]

Rossi (1957) has described the concept of role behavior in his discussion of contemporary communities. After reviewing forty studies on community decision making, he suggested an approach to understanding a decision-making role. An individual may act differently when placed in different roles. The research can't look only at an individual's socioeconomic background and/or personal characteristics to predict this behavior. Past studies of teachers' and parents' characteristics have not touched the decision-making role of the expectations we have presented

---

[7]Harold J. McNally, *Who's Changing What, and Why?* Speech presented at National Association of Elementary Principals, April 1974. ERIC File ED 094 453.

[8]Theodore Sarbin and Vernon Allen, "Role Theory," in *Handbook of Social Psychology,* ed. Gardner Lindsey and Eliot Aronson (Reading, Mass.: Addison-Wesley, 1968), p. 498.

[9]Ibid., p. 503.

[10]J. Chall, "Restoring Dignity and Self-Worth to the Teacher," *Phi Delta Kappan* 57(1975): 174.

below under the term *social technologists*. Most adults, be they parents or teachers, have not been placed in the position to implement decisions concerning educational issues. Teachers, for the most part, have been trained to be technicians rather than social technologists. Parents who have been through the educational system described by Litt (1965) have not been prepared to enact their citizenship role. Browdy (1972) has observed that

> the almost farcical attempts to evade the task of (implementation) is the prime cause of most of the ills from which the schools of America suffer.[11]

Toward the Enactment of Roles

One approach to the analysis of the teacher's role in school/community relations is to consider, first, the objective of the situation and, second, the expectations in that situation. In the following outline of the teacher's school/community role, the objective is described in the definition of the *social technologist role*. The expectations in your particular situation have to be determined by comparing the extent of agreement between a sample of parents, teachers, school board members, and administrators. It is only after you have a publicly announced system of activities that the school and community value that you can persuade additional parents, teachers, school board members, and administrators to make a change because it is consistent with hard data. Without awareness of what type of involvement is considered appropriate, we cannot build the mechanisms to implement decision making. It is only after we have a starting point that we can offset another "ridiculously evident" failure.

The social technologist role is based on the recognition that the venturesome are professionals. We have learned that preparation for our professional role as social technologists rests on recognition that implementation of school/community relations is a matter of persuasion and a matter of taking a stand rather than dictating.

Social Technologist Role

A. Definition: The collection of responsibilities associated with the professional role of the teacher in implementing school/community interaction.
B. Cognitions
   1. Developing public expectations of education services

---

[11]H. S. Browdy, *The Real World of the Public School* (New York: Harcourt Brace Jovanovich, 1972), p. 67.

  a. Contribute to the decision-making process relating to educational services.

  b. Cooperate with other groups in examining and bringing about changes in educational services.

  c. Seek out community resources for support of solutions to local educational problems.

  d. Organize community support for examination of services parents and teachers have identified as beneficial.

  e. Plan and organize the means of influencing passage of educational referendums.

  f. Lobby for legislation affecting the quality of educational services.

  g. Lobby for legislation to insure involvement in control of certification requirements.

  h. Lobby for legislation to ensure participation in establishing criteria for appointments.

  i. Exercise the right to present partisan positions concerning educational issues that develop in the community.

  j. Use membership in social organizations to influence others regarding the status of teachers who have accepted responsibility in implementing school/community interaction.

  k. Use membership in political organizations to influence others regarding the quality of educational services.

  l. Promote membership in professional organizations that have taken a positive stand on school/community relations.

2. Establishing the nature of professional services and criteria for performance.

  a. Participate in the determination of what obligations are related to the teacher's role in school.

  b. Support community studies pertaining to career requirements.

  c. Establish committees concerned with identification of behavior prescriptions which reflect a code of school/community communication.

  d. Be involved in establishing minimum criteria for teacher preparation programs.

  e. Be involved in determining criteria for tenure and/or continuance in the field.

  f. Be involved in developing accountability systems.

  g. Be involved in establishing in-service systems.

  h. Be involved in establishing mechanisms for the evaluation of performance.

  i. Participate in selection of administrators.

j. Participate in setting minimum criteria for all contracts relative to conditions of employment.

k. Be involved in interviewing candidates for teaching positions and presenting recommendations to the school administrators.

l. Set up bodies to resolve areas of conflict within the profession.

> Richard: What a beautiful checklist.
> Cynthia: I've already evaluated my behavior using the checklist criteria. I am quite strong in the areas of. . . .
> Richard: Wait. Let's allow our readers to evaluate their behaviors. After this initial analysis, each reader may want to select the one or two areas on which they will concentrate during the next few months.

As an aid in evaluating your accomplishments in the area of school/community relations, we would like to share with you a rating scale used by a superintendent. The superintendent was asked how he evaluated his teachers. The answer:

Teachers about whom I hear bad things from parents, I rate as poor. Teachers about whom I hear fine things from all quarters, I rate as C. If they get into the newspapers I get really worried. "Who, then," he was asked, "are the teachers who rate an A or B?" "Why," he answered, "the teachers about whom I hear nothing."[12]

The above quote can be added to the sections on the victims, the vacuum, the venue, and the verdict as another answer to "Why We Don't Know More." However, a far more positive summary of the venturesome has been offered by the Director of the Center for the Study of Parent Involvement. Safran (1974) has suggested the following ventures as a means of developing the competencies we have described under the term *social technologist*.

How Can Teachers Achieve These Competencies?

The college or university which includes in its teacher preparation program a component on parent development will have to start by helping their students *unlearn* some major conceptions of what a teacher is and what a teacher does. Few other occupations are so clearly conceived in the minds of

---

[12]Ibid., p. 40.

its novices as is the job of "teacher." From the moment that students identify with the image of teacher, the training they receive will be influenced by the experiences they've had throughout their own school years. A new role model must be established immediately and vividly. Students should be encouraged to scrutinize "classroom" and "community" models of "teacher" (as well as any other concepts of the role of educator) in order to discern the openness any concept has for interpretation. Students must be helped to refer to their feelings about becoming a teacher, drawing upon both the fears and the promises.

A more difficult "unlearning" which must take place is the alteration of existing conceptions of "professional status." Students must learn that professionalism can be a liability in that it sets the teacher apart from ordinary people, particularly the parents of the children they will teach. Teacher education has the task of assisting student teachers to realize the dangers of professionalization as well as its benefits. It is essential that teachers who work with parents have a value orientation which is non-elitist and which accepts and respects the parents and community of the children they teach.

Schools of education must continue the progress they've made in treating their students like adults. Professional elitism pales next to *professorial* elitism!

There are three techniques familiar to teacher education which could be extended to the new objective of preparing teachers to work with parents:
  a. role playing to simulate teacher-parent interactions and enable students to experience some of the emotional dynamics
  b. supervised fieldwork with parent and community groups
  c. working with "master teachers," not necessarily as role models to be emulated but as representatives of existing professional values to be challenged.

Role playing is described by Matthew Miles as:

essentially an action, *doing* technique. . . . Role playing members react to each other spontaneously within the framework of a defined situation which is provisional, or "not for keeps." In this way, behaviors of people can be examined with a minimum of threat, and their approach to the problem can be improved after discussion and analysis (1959).

At a minimum, teacher preparation should include the following role playing situations in preparing teachers for the competencies proposed above:
  a. a parent-teacher conference
  b. encountering an angry parent
  c. encountering a passive parent
  d. encouraging parents to participate as classroom observers
  e. encouraging parents to perform specific "educational" tasks with children at home and in school

f. encouraging parents to participate with other parents in existing school or community organizations

g. assisting a parent chairperson in planning a meeting

h. maximizing the value of chance meetings with parents

These experiences, while simulated, should enable the students to appreciate the multiple human relations factors in teacher-parent transactions. Moreover, many of the subtle dynamics of these interactions can be addressed during the analyses succeeding each role playing experience.

Supervised fieldwork with parent and community groups should combine students' observation and participation in "other" groups with increasing their sensitivity to their participation in their *own* groups. Prospective teachers should be encouraged to reexamine their own group experiences —in social clubs, professional associations, church groups, etc.—in any formal settings. Student-teachers should have the opportunity to work with parents on "real" community issues. Moreover, students and parents should be helped to meet together to share their perspectives of school activities.

The technique of working with "master teachers" is a little more complicated than obtaining guidance from an experienced professional. In this case, the professional is less the guide than the participant in a dialogue. Many of the suggestions made in this paper have been criticized for "leading the lamb to slaughter." Or, to quote a colleague, "Do you realize that the minute your parent involvement teachers get to their schools the old 'warhorses' will cut them to ribbons?"

Student teachers need to be prepared for encounters with the old warhorses. They need to be strengthened for the culture of the school, particularly the debilitating and depressing aspects of institutional behavior which tend to dampen the ardor of new teachers, especially those with "innovative" approaches. One exercise, which has provided support to new teachers in inservice training, I call "The Teachers' Lunchroom Experience."

"The Teachers' Lunchroom Experience" places a new teacher in the midst of Anyschool's teachers' room during his/her first week. In the exercise, the student is encouraged to engage other teachers in conversation about a "serious" educational issue such as irrelevant textbooks, inadequate services, incessant demands for records, insufficient parent involvement. The student is urged to make some recommendations rather than to simply gripe about the problems. The "other teachers" (usually fellow trainees or training staff) have been preprogrammed to respond in a number of "typical" (usually mildly exaggerated) ways. Most of these responses are thus "tedium," "impatience," "don't bother me," "silence." Finally, one of the "teachers" will come over to the "new teacher" and, placing a hand gently, but firmly, on one shoulder will say: "I used to be enthusiastic like you are, honey, but you'll learn; just stay here awhile and you'll learn!"

Can the student teacher be prepared for this kind of encounter? Or should new teachers be permitted to "cut their teeth" on reality when they arrive at their first job?

The culture of the schools can be made an overt subject of teacher education. "Master teachers" can be engaged in discussions not as supervisors having evaluative control over student teachers' freedom of speech, but as professionals whose views are sought and whose perceptions are accepted as interpretations rather than truth. The simulation described above can be made a part of students' experiences *before* they leave teacher education. Value conflicts can be exposed rather than glossed over.

But, perhaps the best preparation student teachers can have for contending with experienced teachers is to establish links with parents from the outset. Such links can demystify the gobbledegook which student teachers get as part of their indoctrination. A concept of accountability can be created based upon mutual trust between teachers and parents so that new teachers have someone other than old teachers to whom to turn.

My final proposal is to place the burden, once again, on parents. Parents can ask some amazing questions of the right person in the right place. Perhaps they should begin to attend meetings of teacher educators, maybe even a faculty meeting. After all, the teachers being produced this year will be teaching their children in the years to come. It is very possible that the restructuring of teacher education so that teachers are prepared to work with parents will begin like this:

(Spokesperson for thirty parents assembled peacefully in the hall outside the office of Dean Strumpht of the School of Education of Happy Valley State): "Good morning, Dean Strumpht. We had a discussion at our meeting last night and decided to talk to you about teacher education."

(Dean Strumpht) "But . . . What . . .? Who . . .?"

(Spokesperson) "Yes, I realize that you are a busy person, but everyone thought that if anyone knew the answers to our questions it would be you. Some of us have been getting tired of the same old hassles at the school every year. In fact, several of our parents said that they have had the same kind of hassles at the other schools their children went to before moving here."

(Dean Strumpht) "What . . .? Where. . .?"

(Spokesperson) "We don't want to bore you with the details, but we do want to know how teachers are being trained here at Happy Valley. After all, some of your students may be teaching at Kinder Hollow Elementary School next year or the year after and we want to know whether you're preparing them for what they're going to face."

(Dean Strumpht) "Kinder Hollow . . .? Is that far from here?"

(Spokesperson) "Now, Dean Strumpht, let's not get off the subject. We want *you* to tell *us* what you do here. Isn't that right, parents?"

(Thirty Parents) "Right." "Sure." "Right on." "Let's hear it, Deano!" "Tell us what you do here!"

(Dean Strumpht) "Well, you see, that's a very complicated question. First, there are philosophical, psychological, sociological, methodological, geographical considerations to be considered."

(Spokesperson) "Dean Strumpht, we just came from the Dean's Office at the University; they ran the same stuff on us and even said 'phenomenological'; now are you going to talk with us or at us?"

(Dean Strumpht) "Uh . . . Ummm . . . Nothing like this has ever happened here before. Would you like to visit some of our classrooms and talk to our students and faculty members?"

(Spokesperson and Thirty Parents) "Hey-hey, Deano, you're okay! The Dean is together; we're finally getting inside to see what they do. Far out!"

Such a scenario is unlikely because so few parents see the school of education as the most immediate cause of woe. Their problem is their children's teachers and the local school. However, I predict that parents will soon be taking on the places where teachers are trained—not because training results in "bad" teachers but because parents need strong teachers with whom to ally in fighting the educational inadequacies and inequities in their communities.[13]

Cynthia: I like Safran's suggestions. Here is another one to add to his list. A parent (or small group of parents) adopt a teacher from her child's school. The "adoption" could include the following ideas:
1. Invite the teacher to the home to discuss school-related issues. Often a change in environment—from the formal school to the informal home—will allow discussants to relax;
2. Take the teacher(s) on a walking tour of the neighborhood—community center, churches, children's "hangouts," police, offices of politicians, cultural centers;
3. Ask the teacher to attend a meeting of the education committee of the neighborhood.

Richard: Why not suggest to the parents to meet with the dean of the

[13]D. Safran, *Preparing Teachers for Parent Involvement* (Oakland, Calif.: Center for the Study of Parent Involvement, 1974), pp. 16–25. Entire text available from the Center for the Study of Parent Involvement, 5240 Boyd Street, Oakland, California 94610 ($2.50) or ERIC File ED 104 543. Used with permission.

School of Education? A focus of the discussion will be on including the activities you just mentioned as part of a teacher education program.

Cynthia: If parents need additional specific examples of competencies to support their case they can also go through the university preparation program descriptions in Appendix C. Some might want to get in touch with the individuals listed from the geographical area closest to their home.

What's Next? PART III

Where Do We Go From Here?

Richard: Well, Cynthia, we've said just about all that we want to say—where do we go from here?

Cynthia: I think that you and I and each one of our readers need to decide this. The readers now have a framework, a map that will help them to make the decisions as they try to improve school/community relationships. My desire is that each reader realize that the building of these positive relationships requires planning, effort, caring . . .

Richard: The "planning, effort, caring" were the main messages of the narrative we gave to the readers. Why don't we share with our readers the "planning, effort, caring" that our students/colleagues/friends in the community have used to design programs to improve school/community relationships. Each program will include a summary and a description of how the principles we presented in this book were used to build the program.

Cynthia: Good idea. The program summaries should give our readers the expectations that change can occur in school systems similar to their own.

Richard: One additional suggestion. I would like our readers to mail us written summaries of their school/community programs and the principles they have used. These summaries will be included in future editions of this book.

Cynthia: The intent of your request sounds fine. If our readers did send us summaries of what is going on in their schools to foster school/community communication, we could begin to break the vicious cycle of blame the parents/blame the schools. But one of the multiple roles you described when we introduced ourselves on page 4 is showing. Your request for principles sounds just like a prof! We'll have people thinking that if they don't include an elaborate discussion of principles they have failed some kind of test. This is not the case. When I read over the descriptions as they came in, my first impression was that all of the programs had reached the heart of the matter in school/community communication. The programs can be evaluated as successful because of commitment to one general principle—PEOPLE.

All the programs and projects described in part III have attended to a variety of specific principles when enacting each level of their commitment to **PEOPLE.** As you spell out the general principle at each decision point the specifics become clearer.

P ersonal level
  E laboration level
    O rganization level
      P articipation level
        L aunching level
          E ffects level

The **P**ersonal level is concerned with awareness of values and attitudes. In order to determine possible areas of agreement in school/community expectations, a great deal of time is spent at the personal level throughout the program. The focus of your time is spent on continuous climate building, feedback, and support. Attitudes, values, and expectations have a great deal to do with the issues raised in chapter 2. To accomplish specific goals, we have to be aware of attitudes of those involved in school/community activities. This aspect of attitude formation has been elaborated in the Model of Human Ecology (see pp. 126–27). Attitudes and values also include an individual's belief as to whether or not s/he can be an influence both on one's children's lives and the life of the community. Many individuals are not convinced that participation is appropriate. Society's definition of political activity has become associated more with something that is "dirty" rather than as a human, personal activity.

Elaboration level is a fancy term for problem identification. Principles at this level involve data collection to determine the effectiveness of present services and to identify potential linking mechanisms between school and community. Some of the questions to keep in mind are: What programs are presently operating? What are possible competing organizations (competing in time)? Who can benefit from a program or project? What training is needed for participants?

The **O**rganizational level is concerned with past results from community development studies (see chapter 3). Effective programs can spread from school to school starting at the local level. Since organizational charts often omit **P**ersonal levels, we cannot depend on someone else's blueprint being a perfect fit. At each phase of the **O**rganization level, roles and functions must be specified. The checklist for the social technologist role (see pp. 141–43) and characteristics of parent involvement (see pp. 54–56) can help you in identifying specific principles. One way to approach the organization level is to develop a time schedule, or building blocks, and long-range goals.

Taking the time to develop your program step-by-step will help to clarify the **P**articipation level. Once the **O**rganization level of the Family Life Program was established, the directors went back through the description and identified participation resources (pp. 171–72).

Enactment of the **L**aunching level will depend on how much time you consider necessary for preparing the resource people you have identified. We heard a harrowing tale about an individual who spent a great deal of time on climate building for recruitment and organization. After convincing approximately 100 mothers that they should be involved in the social technologist role of lobbying for legislation and funding of day care, a plan was launched for evaluating day care facilities in northeastern Ohio. With *no* attention given to educating the group about evaluation criteria, subgroups were sent to visit day care centers to determine whether they were good or bad. This incident points out that the **E**ffect level may be hampered by getting so caught up in specifics that you lose sight of the general principle **PEOPLE.** If this group had gone into preschools unprepared, the effect could have been an additional case of "blame the schools." We can't "throw out the baby with the bath water." The day care facilities that are available need support for staying open. A more effective strategy would be to ask preschool directors to meet with the parents. Directors could explain their programs, answer questions, and add suggestions to an effective evaluation plan such as the Lafayette Plan described on page 44.

In addition to evaluating with teachers the effects of a school program, the **E**ffect level is concerned with weighing costs, time, and effort. Sharing of "budget" books among school districts would save all new programs and projects from recreating the wheel. As mentioned by Goodson and Hess (1975), most projects have not reached the public's attention because they have not been documented. The sharing of program information helps other people to replicate parts of a program to fit local needs. School/community communication is not a one-shot undertaking. Hopefully, you will keep up to date on the progress of NETWORK to establish an ERIC system for parents (see p. 182). Some of the questions to keep in mind are (1) How many individuals now know about your project activities? (2) How important do they believe the purposes of your program are? (3) What changes do they believe have taken place in their attitudes? behavior? and relationships between the school and community?

The Effects level is not only outwardly directed. Personal evaluation includes the questions we asked at the beginning of this book. Have I taken into consideration how change will be perceived? How long do I expect people to remain interested? Will change appear threatening to community members, teachers, parents, and administrators? Have I attended to developing expectations about educational services? Have I attended to developing support systems? Have I arranged to keep up-to-date on publications of inexpensive source books and publications in ERIC?

Each program described below was designed to fit specific needs of its school/community. As you study each program, keep in mind the **PEOPLE** principles described in this section.

Parent Involvement Program (Robinson School, Akron, Ohio)

RATIONALE

The intent of this program is to help parents acquire formal and informal teaching skills that they can use with their children in their homes.

PROGRAM DESCRIPTION

The parents complete a multiphase training program in the school. They learn teaching skills such as use of positive reinforcement, how to use the home as an informal learning environment, and how to make inexpensive materials.

A major outcome of this program is the incidental (unplanned) learning of the parents. By being in the school on a regular basis, the parents are able to evaluate the various components of the school. A major concern of the parents was the problem faced by substitute teachers in the program. The substitutes did not understand the operation of the complex individualized curricula used in this school (the parents did!); therefore, these substitutes did not use the methods needed for this program to operate effectively. The parents, with the support of the teachers and director of the program, met with the assistant superintendent. During this meet-

154

ing they presented the reasons for training substitutes in the methods needed for the individualized curriculum. The assistant superintendent agreed to the parents' proposal. All groups involved—parents, teachers, administrators—worked together for the benefit of the children.

PRINCIPLES INVOLVED IN PROGRAM

Personal—"I" can be an effective influence in children's lives
Elaboration—What to do is not always determined in advance
Organization—Awareness of need for evaluation criteria
Participation—Familiarizing parents with content of program
Launching—Takes only a few people
Effects—Identification of parents as positive change agents

Designing Schools: A Cooperative Effort Among Parents, Students, Teachers, Architects (Urban Design Associates, Pittsburgh, Pennsylvania)

RATIONALE

An architectural firm has developed a planning design which includes all those involved in the conceptualization of a school. These architects feel that buildings are for people who use and live in them and that their purpose is not to serve as monuments for future generations.

PROGRAM DESCRIPTION

The architects of Urban Design Associates have evolved a plan that involves all those who work/learn/care about the schools. For example, they interview parents and teachers about the needs they have. Children are asked for their impressions of what their new school should be through discussions and designs produced by the children. The architects have concluded that the involvement of all concerned in the project during the planning stage is productive for numerous reasons. These reasons include:
   a. More efficient use of time. It is easier to tear down or put up a wall during the planning stage than after the building is complete;
   b. All parties feel an ownership of the program if they are involved in the planning. This involvement must be a real involvement, i.e., the ideas of the people are actually used in the final design.

PRINCIPLE INVOLVED IN PROGRAM

Personal—Awareness of the effect of negotiation process
Elaboration—Awareness of community education concepts
Organization—Awareness of variables associated with change

155

Participation—Awareness of concepts of viability
Launching—Provide positive leadership
Effects—Encourage participatory democracy

School/Community Cooperation (University School, Kent, Ohio)

RATIONALE

Herbert Goldsmith, the principal of the University School, feels that the place for learning should not be limited to the perimeter of the school and that the role of teacher should not be limited to those who have the proper certification. Therefore, he designed a program which utilizes the resources of the total school/community.

PROGRAM DESCRIPTION

The University School, located within the campus of Kent State University, has numerous resources that can be tapped on the university campus. After identifying resources on the campus (biology laboratory, computer center, student newspaper, etc.), the principal and the University School faculty designed mini-courses which last from a day to two weeks. The pupils involved in these courses spend time each day completing an individualized plan of study which was developed jointly by the pupil, teacher, and a university faculty member.

The second major resource in this program includes the use of community people as instructors within the University School. For example, a Kent State University journalism student assisted with the development of the University School student newspaper. Parents lead ongoing groups in ballet, drama, and photography, and architecture students work with early childhood faculty in designing space and equipment based on current knowledge in child development.

PRINCIPLES INVOLVED IN PROGRAM

Personal—Discuss together how to help each other and children
Elaboration—Identify mechanisms of cooperation
Organization—Attention to fragmented services in the community
Participation—Parents as educators
Launching—Change does not require an elaborate new curriculum
Effects—School/community politics are not "dirty" but involve human
        activities

Project-Teach-Along (Janice Rushin, Cleveland Public Schools, Division of Continuing Adult Education, 1380 East Sixth Street, Cleveland, Ohio 44114)

Rationale

If parents don't know what their children are doing, they can't be meaningfully involved.

Program Description

Parent Education, or Project-Teach-Along, is an innovative Adult Basic Education Program offered in elementary schools throughout the city of Cleveland. In Project-Teach-Along, the parents are taught a variety of instructional methods involving language arts, mathematics, child development, and parent-child-school relationships, which they will later use to enrich the learning experiences of their children.

Parents learn the importance of play, academic skills, child growth patterns, better communication, and effective discipline. They are taught how to be creative with their children in the areas of art and music, and how to use inexpensive materials found in the home to make creative educational crafts and games while playing with their children. Parents learn about libraries, museums, and other points of interest in the city.

A major goal of Project-Teach-Along is to develop parent understanding of curricula, methods, and materials used to teach reading and math skills in the elementary schools. This program equips parents with the necessary tools to reinforce the child's learning experiences and to develop an educational setting in the home. As the parents study child growth and development, emphasis is placed on normal behavior and characteristics of children at various developmental stages—their learning rate, personality, health, and individual differences. Parents are enlightened as to the necessity of building the child's self-image through praise and encouragement. They are also taught the value of proper rest, food, and medical and dental care. Stressing the importance of open communication between parents and school personnel encourages parents to become involved in school activities and to react to school reports in meaningful ways. Parents learn to discipline their children effectively through positive educational methods.

The children whose parents have participated in this parenting program develop more positive attitudes toward school and become more successful in educational endeavors. Project-Teach-Along's unique design enables parents to pursue their individual educational goals while participating in the parenting process. Greater facility in reading, writing, spelling, and math is offered through the composite Adult Basic Education learning program.

Individualized instruction allows the parents to develop skills at various levels including grades 1 through 8 and G.E.D. (the General Education Development Test) for the High School Equivalency Certificate. Project-

Teach-Along parents who need to learn English spend a portion of their time in an English-As-A-Second-Language class, learning to speak, read, and write English. Project-Teach-Along classes are usually offered five hours a week including at least a one-hour Parent Education lesson. The parent-student may attend only the Parent Education session, but most parents find it helpful and rewarding to be involved in all sessions.

The staff of Project-Teach-Along includes certified elementary teachers, teacher assistants, and child-care aides. These professionals and para-professionals participate in intense in-service training tailored to develop skills for this specific program. Competent child-care aides create learning experiences for preschool children through educational activities while their parents are engaged in adult classroom learning. The project manager, Janice Rushin, involves the elementary school principals in program planning. Cooperation and support from the respective elementary schools is evidenced through the provision of attractive classroom space and elementary curriculum guides and materials.

Project-Teach-Along assists the elementary school in acquainting parents with the Parent Resource Center. This center makes it possible for parents to borrow educational materials and games to use with their children at home. Elementary school principals, curriculum specialists, teachers, community liaisons, and parent resource aides along with the teachers function as a team in curriculum development and recruitment. The open enrollment policy allows the student to enroll at any time from October through May. At the beginning of each school year every student in approximately a half dozen elementary schools where the program is offered is asked to deliver the brochure reproduced below to his/her parent(s).

GENERAL INFORMATION

Enrollment:
You may enroll in Basic Education and Parent Education day and evening classes anytime during the school semester.

AGE Requirements:
You must be 16 years of age or older to register and attend.

Learn how *reading* is taught in school.

Learn how *math* is taught in school.

Learn how to help the teacher help your child.

PARENT EDUCATION CLASSES ARE OFFERED AT:

1. **Elementary Schools**—For parents of children 5 to 12 years of age.
2. **Family Life Centers**—in cooperation with the Parent-Child-Training Program of Family Life Education. For parents of children 1 to 3 years old.
3. **Community Agencies**—For parents of children 1 to 3 years of age.

YOU CAN

Learn how to help your child in school through FREE *Project-Teach-Along* Parent Education classes.

Learn how your child develops.

Learn how to stimulate development of your child's intellect and creativity.

COST: There is no fee. Classes are **FREE** to all adults.

Individualized Instruction:
Classes are tailored to meet the individual need of the student.

Counseling:
FREE counseling and testing services are available to all.

Child Care:
Child care is offered FREE in some locations while mothers attend the classes.

Activities:
Classroom instruction is enriched with the use of films & filmstrips, teaching machines, fieldtrips, guest speakers, and various related materials.

Free babysitting services are available at most locations.

Project-Teach-Along

Call 229-9636 for details

PRINCIPLES INVOLVED IN PROGRAM

Personal—Developing public expectations of education services

Elaboration—Translating the goal of aiding individuals in analysis and examination of societal values and institutions

159

Organization—Members of the profession legitimize their own concerns for effective education

Participation—Attention is given to the basic question of who is responsible for sifting through all the advice to help parents become effective

Launching—Development programs attend to presentation of alternatives

Effects—Disseminating an awareness of the arguments for community involvement

Styles and Techniques in Administration (Nancy Jacobs, Director, Jewish Day Nursery, Cleveland, Ohio)

RATIONALE

The Jewish Day Nursery is the Day Care Center of the Jewish Children's Bureau of Cleveland, Ohio. It serves children, ages three to six, needing full-day care because parents are working, in career training, or need to be away from home. The staff consists of professionally trained teachers, caseworkers, and child development consultants. Any family, regardless of race, religion, or income, can be served by the Jewish Day Nursery, which is supported by parent fees, the Jewish Community Federation of Cleveland, and the United Torch.

PROGRAM DESCRIPTION

The preschool is often the first opportunity outside of the home for the parent and the child to enter into long-term relationships. It's a place for growth, certainly for enjoyment, and sometimes, pleasantly or painfully, for evaluation. In our school we refer to our program as one with a special dimension—that of parent participation. Our parents participate in the classroom on at least a once-a-month basis. Their duties range from helping a child scrub after finger painting, to storytelling, or help with game play, dramatic play, or art experiences. They may spend time listening, sympathizing, loving, or observing.

The teacher and the parent work as a team in the classroom. The parent is a second pair of eyes, ears, and hands. Recently, one of our former teachers became a consultant for a federal program in which parents had never been a part of the classroom. She was helping her staff to prepare to satisfy a new directive calling for parent participation, and she told me that her staff were all quite worried because they would be "under the scrutiny" of parents. She told them not to worry because at the J.C.C. (Jewish Community Center) in Cleveland the only time the staff ever gets agitated and worried is when parents *DON'T* come to class.

The obvious advantages of parent participation are

1. The parent sees other children at the same stage of development as his/her own child and thereby develops realistic expectations for the child's progress. Often a parent will leave a classroom saying, "You know, I have been expecting my child to do something I thought *I* could do when I was four, but now that I think about it—I don't think I did it until I was seven or eight. I realize I was asking him to be too grown up." This type of learning is a bonus for the parent *and* the child.

2. Parent participation is also an opportunity for parents to see their child as a member of a group—to know the child's peers and to share in the child's world without the everyday interruptions of home and responsibility.

3. Parent participation offers the advantage that children learn to trust other adults, thereby broadening their relationships and increasing their flexibility.

For the school, parent participation offers us the opportunity to see the child with his/her parent for furthering our understanding of the child's experiences as well as have the talents of the parent to enhance our program. Furthermore our staff-parent relationships are professional but informal, and it is good for two people to work side by side. We somehow feel closer, more humorous, and less in awe of each other as we work together on behalf of each child.

In our midyear conferences we are ready to present our observations to each parent. We tell the parent how we see the child and then we ask, "How do you see *your* child at home? At school? Are we seeing the same child?" If not—perhaps the discrepancy tells us that something is keeping that child from feeling comfortable at school and suggests that together we should take a closer look at the child's behavior.

As parents and staff we are partners. We explore together, we learn together. The child's successful development and good self-image are our mutual interest. The question "What do you think?" is an important part of our relationship. It is almost a temporary marriage on behalf of the children's interests.

This philosophy of respect and mutuality is a part of our program right from the moment of intake when the parent comes to hear about our program and to visit in the classroom so that s/he can evaluate whether our school will meet the child's needs. We may have two or three parents together to hear each other's questions because it is always good to meet others who are making similar decisions. Each parent has an opportunity to have a private time with me to discuss his/her individual child as well.

When the child is formally registered we make a second appointment for the parent and the child to come together with five or six other new children and their parents for a play time with me. We do not bring the new children into an ongoing class because we believe it is hard to feel comfortable when you are the only one who is new. It is easier to have everyone be new and explore the school together. Friendships seem to develop quickly, and feelings of adequacy and "school is a nice place to be" have a chance to grow.

Sometimes at these group interviews, I observe a child who I feel may not be able to succeed in our program. The child's behavior may not be appropriate for his age, or physically there may be an impairment which might interfere with his successful management of the program. The parents may appear to be unaware of this, and it is here that I become involved in the referral process.

I ask the parent to return alone so that we can speak further and I share my concerns. I suggest that s/he might want to speak with a physician about our talk, and perhaps the physician would want to recommend an evaluation of the child to determine how school or another agency might serve him/her best. I give the parent the names of three agencies and three private child therapists who do child evaluations, and I offer to speak with the doctor or to make the contact with the agency or therapist if preferred. I assure the parents that, if possible, we will be interested in serving them in any way that the evaluation suggests. I know that I've given the parents great concern, but for many parents a referral gives them the direction they need if they suspected a problem but could not identify it.

Sometimes a child will be in our program for several months and display behavior that we do not understand. This is portrayed by the child who cannot comfortably separate from a parent or the child who appears worried or anxious and displays it through aggressive behavior or passive, inappropriate, infantile behavior. We request a conference—and the teacher and I and the parents begin to evaluate what we are observing. We describe the behavior and explain how we are trying to help the child to manage in the class. We find out if the behavior exists at home and how the behavior is managed in the home. If the behavior continues or increases, we discuss it with our school consultant.

Our school is very fortunate to have the services of a psychiatric consultant through a special program sponsored by the Cleveland Psychoanalytic Foundation and the Cleveland Association for Education of Young Children. I meet bimonthly in 1½ hour sessions with the consultant and two other directors of similar parent participation nurseries. We discuss the special problems pertaining to children in our schools, and by discussing a particular child's behavior with the consultant, I receive a better understanding of how we can be more helpful to the child and the family.

If a referral seems appropriate, a conference is once again arranged and, depending upon the situation, we might suggest referral to the Child

Psychiatry Clinic of University Hospital, private child therapists, or the Mental Development Center associated with Western Reserve University. The contact names and telephone numbers are supplied for the parents, and I offer to make the initial contact if they wish it.

Occasionally a child with very special needs will come to our school. For example, in the past four years we have had some children in our classes with limited vision, cerebral palsy, hearing and speech difficulties, epilepsy, a missing limb, congenital heart involvement, or minimal retardation.

At the time of intake, after my initial interview with the parent, I explore in great detail all the possibilities in our city to serve this special situation in order to insure that we are the ones who can be of maximum help. Depending on the child's needs, I speak with the worker at the special agency—this might be the Society for Crippled Children, the Society for the Blind, the Cerebral Palsy Foundation, or the Cleveland Hearing and Speech Institute.

If the child is currently enrolled in a special class, I try to observe the child in this environment. I also may talk with the child's physician, and, if the child isn't in school, I ask the parents to explore the special agencies which have schools which might more specifically fit their child's needs.

Many times I have found that our school *can* serve a special child very well with support from an agency or a physician with special knowledge of the child's condition. We work together to give the child maximum opportunities for growth. My responsibilities in this process, however, have just begun at the point of acceptance—and it is here that I want to return to our philosophy about relationships with parents.

There are two aspects of our philosophy which deal with responding to children with special needs. The first is to let our attitude of acceptance set the tone and hope that parents and other children will respond positively when seeing our model. The second involves a preparation of parents and children to increase their understanding of the special child's needs and to shortcut their feelings of worry or fantasies regarding the special child's handicap. When a new child with a special problem comes to our school, I take the time to contact parents and discuss the news that a new child will be in the classroom. Often parents need time to understand that the special child will not be "taking the teacher's time away from the others" and reassurance that their own child can accept the other child's condition comfortably. I explain the condition and help parents to encourage and anticipate their children's questions. Later I follow up and make sure that the parents have felt supported and comfortable with their children's questions.

I believe that real friendships result faster with this approach because from our staff and from the home the child receives similar messages and

163

explanations. The result is that our children see the special child as a person not to be feared but to be befriended.

Through our parent-education programs, we work to reinforce and increase parents' understanding of normal child development and we try to reinforce and improve our staff-parent communication. This year we presented four programs which were very successful on both these counts.

In the fall our first program was entitled "What Should Your Child Be Learning in Preschool?" After a short presentation on our curriculum, the parents became their children for the evening and visited specially prepared activity tables. We had eleven tables each staffed by a preschool teacher who demonstrated in a ten minute presentation how we use the materials in the classroom and what our goal and methodology are in particular areas of learning. Parents could attend the demonstrations of interest to them—art, music, science, waterplay, numbers, literature, etc. This meeting answered many parents' questions and prepared them for what they were seeing in the classroom.

In early February we had a readiness meeting which took the form of a panel discussion. The panel included a preschool teacher, a parent, a kindergarten teacher, and an education specialist. Questions involved in the discussion included "What is Readiness?" "How do we know that a child is ready for the next step?" "How do we prepare children for the next step?" Our parents' committee conducted a survey of how the area schools oriented children into school and what was expected of them. This survey was available in written form for all interested parents. This readiness meeting was very helpful for parents whose children were about to go to school in fall and helpful to those who were in the process of evaluating whether to request early entrance to school.

In March our psychiatric consultant offered two evening discussions entitled "Things That Are Hard for Parents to Talk About with Their Children." Parents were sent the topic title a few weeks beforehand and were asked to return a checklist of topics they wished discussed. As a result of the checklist, the two evenings included discussion of adoption, divorce, death, aggression, differences, and handicaps.

The last of our parent education series was a discussion entitled "Sex and the Young Child." It was led by a J.C.C. worker with training in family health. The interchange proceeded from a dialogue about our own hesitancies to talk about these matters, dependent upon our own upbringing and backgrounds, to real insight into how often children act out their questions about sexuality through such fantasies as doctor play.

In addition to our parent education meetings, a second reinforcement technique has been the establishment of a Parent Lending Library where parents can obtain preschool books on special subjects to read to their children at times of stress or special need. The topics available include child's or parent's hospitalization, handicaps, death, jealousy, night fears, and pregnancy. A special book list is available for parents so that they can find their books by topics.

During the past few years, I have noted some significant results of the participation of staff and parents in our school programs. From my observations and experiences in early childhood centers, I have become convinced that parents who have had the opportunity to learn to recognize attributes of a good school program during their child's preschool years will continue to be effective child advocates when their children enter the public school system.

For example, in one situation, it came to my attention that some parents of children who had previously been in our program were the most outspoken in their expression of concern over a teacher in their school system who had become unable to do her job. They were sympathetic to the teacher and understanding of the administration's problems, but steadfast in their insistence for protection of their children. As a result, they provided daily volunteer help in the classroom and worked constructively with the school board toward the attainment of a paid aide, with teacher certification, to "assist" the teacher until the year was up and the teacher could leave the system.

Another example occurred when a child was ready for kindergarten and she and her parent left our program to soon become involved in the kindergarten orientation program at her local school. The parent told me that she had realized from our "Readiness Programs" the importance of the gradual induction to school. She used her knowledge to assure her child's participation in an orientation program for successful gradual adjustment.

A third example of the effects of our parent involvement program after the preschool years was that of parents who involved themselves as public relations chairpeople for their school parent-teacher association and worked to better the communications between their integrated neighborhood and the school. They said it was admittedly a "hot potato," but they moved comfortably in their role. They did not dwell on the differences but saw the similarities of goals and shared this knowledge with others.

For the most part, parents who have participated in a preschool program which encouraged their involvement felt ready to undertake responsibilities on behalf of their children as they progressed through the public school system.

PRINCIPLES INVOLVED IN PROGRAM

Personal—Awareness of issues of recruitment
Elaboration—The essential prerequisite for child development requires

165

continued feedback between program personnel and parents

Organization—Establishing the nature of professional service and criteria for performance

Participation—Work through community agencies already established

Launching—Providing for direct involvement in problem identification

Effects—Awareness of criteria for evaluating a school's success

Leisure Time Activities for Pupils: An Example of Teacher/Parent Cooperation (Richard Goldman, U.S. Armed Services School, France)

RATIONALE

One of the authors was a teacher at an American Army Dependent School in Europe. The school and army base were located in an isolated, rural part of France. The parents of the pupils and I were concerned that the children lacked leisure time activities which would encourage healthy activity and group cohesion. Together we designed and built our indoor roller skating rink.

PROGRAM DESCRIPTION

The parents of my pupils requested a meeting with me to discuss the lack of leisure time activities for their children. After a few minutes of discussion, the parents agreed that many of the children missed the neighborhood roller skating rinks that they had in the United States. As we evaluated the leisure time resources in the neighboring towns, few activities existed and nothing approaching a roller rink could be found. We then toured our army base which contained many empty barracks. We entered a dark, dusty barracks and were surprised at its large area and concrete floor. We realized that we had found our roller rink. With a community effort which included the parents, children, and teachers, the barracks were cleaned and windows covered with wood. The children had a new roller rink!

PRINCIPLES INVOLVED IN PROGRAM

Personal—Support for parental role

Elaboration—Data collection on what is available for parents and children

Organization—Agreement on common objective

Participation—Community effort

Launching—Evaluate existing facilities

Effects—Support parent/child interaction

The Share Program (Shaker Heights Public Schools, Shaker Heights, Ohio)

RATIONALE

The Share Program was initiated by a small group of parents who felt that their "community contains a wealth of untapped resources which could serve to enrich the educational programs of the schools. It is hoped that the program will continue to be an aid to the teachers and an important contribution to the youth of Shaker Heights."

PROGRAM DESCRIPTION

The parent organizers of the program attended numerous school/community activities with the intent of informing the community of Share's goals and recruiting resources for the program. This recruitment effort led to the accumulation of over 500 possible resources. As stated in the Share brochure, the topics of these experts vary from Accounting to Zaire with numerous topics in between: backpacking, scuba diving, Indian music, women and law, gun control.

A description of the resources and their areas of competencies are compiled in a resource book. Copies of the book are located at each school in the district. When a teacher identifies a resource, s/he completes a short form which is sent to the Share office. This office, which was staffed by volunteers and now has a part-time paid director, makes all arrangements between the resource and the teacher. At the completion of the resource's presentation, both the teacher and the resource evaluate the interactions between the resource and pupils.

PRINCIPLES INVOLVED IN PROGRAM

Personal—Developing expectations of the public
Elaboration—Improving internal communication data
Organization—Descriptions of resources specified
Participation—Target people identified in public
Launching—Use of membership in social organizations
Effects—Resource support is forthcoming to continue climate of support

Involving Families in the Kindergarten (Susan Marx, University School, Kent, Ohio)

RATIONALE

It has always been my belief that the classroom should be a natural extension of the child's world. Growth and learning by the young child are a result of his total life experiences. For this reason, I have created methods

167

of connecting the child's school and home environment through welcoming parent involvement in my classroom.

PROGRAM DESCRIPTION

I invited parents, colleagues, and members of the College of Education to meet during the first week of school in order to give their input for making a decision about the length of our kindergarten day. Twenty-eight parents of the twenty-five children in my class discussed the pros and cons of extending the kindergarten day. The decision to end early the first two weeks of school was based on the parents' belief that their children were not physically able to keep the extended day schedule of 9 to 3. The parents decided that the extended day schedule would go into effect the third week of school. An agreement was reached that the teacher and parents would decide on an individual basis if any child needed more than two weeks to get used to the extended day schedule.

The shared decision-making process concerning kindergarten scheduling and use of resources was the beginning step for parent involvement which continued throughout the year. The specifics of the kindergarten program and the parent involvement process are outlined in figure 8-1.

During the orientation meeting, twelve parents volunteered to serve on the Parent Advisory Board. Our Parent Advisory Board meets once a month at the homes of various board members or at my home. The purpose of this group is two-fold. It helps to monitor the effectiveness of the parent involvement process as well as encourages the Parent Advisory Board to participate in decision making that is relevant to the total learning program. When parents expressed an interest in learning more about the daily activities in the classroom, we scheduled a Parent-Child Exploration meeting. Parents accompanied their children to school one evening and shared together a "mini-day" in the classroom.

In addition to parent-teacher conferences scheduled for specific times during the year, parents are welcome to take part in day-to-day activities. A parent's resource file was developed. So far this year parents have taught clay modeling techniques, wood sculpture techniques, cookie recipes, and music and rhythm lessons. We have adopted the term *Parent Interest Stations* for our parents' creative additions to the curriculum.

PRINCIPLES INVOLVED IN PROGRAM

Personal —	A	Community studies
	W	
Elaboration —	A	Parents as educators
	R	
Organization —	E	Parents as contributors to decision making

Process of Integration

Integration Graph

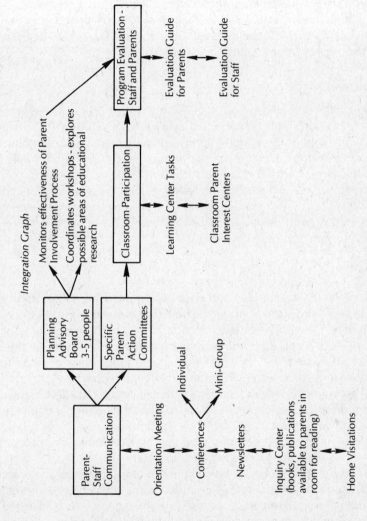

FIGURE 8–1. The kindergarten program and the parent involvement process

169

Participation — N Teachers as social technologists
  E
Launching — S The Venue
  S
Effects — OF The Venturesome

Family Life Education Program (Connie Garcia, Early Childhood Education Specialist and School Psychologist; Dorothea Snyder, Principal, Evamere Elementary School, Hudson, Ohio; Kay Bayless, Hudson Cares Coordinating Committee)

RATIONALE

Through the combined efforts of the community of Hudson and personnel of the Hudson public schools, a Family Life Development Program has been developed. The major emphasis of this program is a commitment to human development and positive mental health within families. Since schools alone cannot adequately cope with the multiplicity of concerns and the vast number of children needing help, the program concentrates on prevention over remediation, early intervention over crisis response, and the program should be based on human development rather than individual responses to failures.

PROGRAM DESCRIPTION

In June of 1974 the clergy and educators of Hudson, Ohio, published a "Statement of Concern" about the behavior of some of the Hudson young people and the apparent lack of communication between some parents and their children. After the people were made more aware of the problems that existed, they became motivated and indicated a desire to take positive and constructive action to remedy the problems.

The community's concern resulted in an organized effort to develop a community-wide program designed to meet the present and future needs of both young people and adults in Hudson. Because it was felt that the people within the community cared about each other, the program became known as the "Hudson Cares" program.

The Community Service Association of Hudson agreed to serve as the organizational sponsor of this unique community venture. A community coordinating committee, composed of eight people, was charged with these responsibilities: to develop and implement programs and projects that would utilize the resources of the community in human relations, to assist parents in their efforts to improve family communications, to provide needed facilities and programs for youth, adults, and families, and to meet the needs of both adults and youth in the field of drug use and abuse.

In the late fall of 1974 the Hudson Cares Coordinating Committee named three task study forces: (1) Human Relations and Communications, (2) Drug Education and Crisis Counseling, and (3) Community Resources and Facilities. One of the most unique and prime recommendations submitted by the Task Force on Human Relations and Communications was that increased attention should be devoted to the early years of family life and preschool child development. It was felt that a program of assistance to parents and children prior to school entry could eliminate or reduce many problems before children reach the teenage years. Such a program would concentrate on detecting and working out problems within families and on providing family life education programs. Specifically, it was recommended that the preschool program that had only recently been initiated within the Hudson community should be continued and expanded. The school and community would provide a support system for the children and their families. This team approach encourages all those who work with the child and the family to provide an environment conducive to the optimal growth of the youngster in order to insure his/her eventual meaningful integration into the larger society.

FAMILY LIFE EDUCATION SERVICES

A. Long-range plans
  1. *Parent education*
     a. Prenatal—emphasis will be placed on specific areas of importance for parents during the prenatal period
        (1) Resources—specialists, audio-visual materials, and literature
        (2) Discussion topics—nutrition, exercise, childbirth classes, breast-feeding, mother/infant bonding
     b. Child development—neonatal, infant through preschool. Programs to be established in specific areas of child development
        (1) Contact the family of the newborn
        (2) Expand the area of parenting discussion groups
        (3) Consultation service for parents and children (hot-line and drop-in centers)
        (4) Home visitation
        (5) Diagnostic center for preschool children (screening of preschooler and establishment of parent implemented intervention)
        (6) Home base for the Parent Preschool Organization
        (7) Child care service (available to parents during times of counseling, discussion groups, etc.)
        (8) Parent-teacher programs
     c. Curriculum development for parent-child in the home

171

2. *Training center*
   a. Teenagers—Implementation of Exploring Childhood Curriculum in Hudson High School. This curriculum was developed through the U.S. Office of Education.
   b. Interns—Kent State University school psychology program which trains specialists in early childhood through the Department of Early Childhood Education
   c. Nursery school-kindergarten teachers—objectives
      (1) Consistency between parent-teacher handling of children
      (2) Continuity between preschool and formal education
3. *Auxiliary services*
   a. Establishment of a lending library of resource materials for parents
   b. Parent workshops for the construction of educational toys
   c. Summer parent-child programs utilizing the facilities of the primary school library

B. Personnel
   1. *Director—Early Childhood Specialist*—Specialist in early education, employed half-time
   2. *Consultants*
      a. Physicians (pediatrician, ophthalmologist, otologist)
      b. Speech and hearing therapist
      c. University consultants in Early Childhood and Psychology
      d. Nutrition experts
      e. Teachers
   3. *Volunteers—paraprofessionals*
      a. Senior citizens
      b. Community volunteers
      c. High school students
   4. *Trainees*
      a. Kent State University Early Childhood School Psychologists
      b. High school students

The transition from home to school at the time of beginning kindergarten is smoother because of several support systems at Evamere. The support systems are specifically concerned with teacher-child, teacher-teacher, teacher-staff, and home-school. Children who will be entering kindergarten in September have their first introduction to their new school in the spring. They are "adopted" by members of the kindergarten in session that year and spend a morning or afternoon with the "old" kindergarteners who introduce them to the space, materials, and activities in the kindergarten.

During the time the children planning to enter kindergarten are becoming acquainted with the activities, physical environment, and role relationships in kindergarten, the new parents meet with the principal and early childhood school psychologist. The parents introduction to Evamere is smooth because of the support system between teachers. The Evamere faculty have taken the time to clarify their curriculum goals and child development objectives at each grade level. In this way communication between teacher and staff remain open. The kindergarten teachers are concerned with what is going on in the other grades, and the primary grade teachers have a clear picture of what the kindergarten objectives are.

One of the support systems for home/school communication in addition to the long-range plans presented earlier is the availability of a parent handbook. The sample pages reproduced below demonstrate the awareness of faculty, staff, and parents of children at Evamere that in order to communicate effectively parents and teachers need a shared context. Parents need to be aware of what the school hopes to accomplish (i.e., the philosophy) so that they can see how the techniques and strategies used by the teachers are consistent with that philosophy. The question of consistency between goals and methods employed provide one means for evaluating their children's work on a day-by-day basis. Parents will also be able to discuss how each day's work fits into the overall goals of the program. The target populations of child, teacher, staff, and home can only work together if the schools goals are clearly stated. The purpose of the *Evamere Parents Handbook* is to identify the areas of shared context in the home and school. The sample pages reproduced below offer a clear statement of the five Rs as well as offer an overview of specific daily activities that parents can ask their children about rather than having to rely on the vague question "What did you do in school today?" The program called CARES as well as the silent reading program can be a focus and an opener in communication.

The VIP (Vitally Interested People) program is an effective means to give community members recognition as well as to provide opportunities for teachers, children, and parents to interact in the school setting.

Evamere Parents Handbook

Preface

Since the elementary school is the child's initial contact with formal education, it is important that his experience be pleasant and profitable during the primary years. Effective instruction, combined with sympathetic, understanding consideration, is essential to the future progress and success of all students. The 3 R's receive the basic emphasis of our academic program. In addition to the 3 R's of reading, 'riting and 'rithmetic, we would add the 2 R's of respect and responsibility as basic to the education of our children.

There must be close cooperation between the home and the school. Every effort must be exerted to promote mutual understanding and assistance in helping children develop into well adjusted, academically capable citizens who will constructively participate in our democratic society.

This handbook deals with the curriculum, procedures and practices relative to Evamere Elementary School. This information is provided to assist you and your children in planning for a successful school experience.

Dorothea Snyder
Principal, Evamere School

Evamere Elementary School Philosophy

THIS WE BELIEVE . . .

—That education in the primary grades should be designed to meet the unique needs of the young child and be compatible with what we know of his physical, mental, social and emotional patterns of growth.

—That the child as an individual should be the paramount concern of every teacher.

—That the educational environment should furnish continual challenge and excitement without undue tension or pressure.

—That, in order to build a strong self-image, each child should have the opportunity to meet with continuing success and to move at his best possible rate of progress through the expected levels of achievement.

—That maximum educational achievement is best accomplished in a relaxed environment which provides well-defined guidelines of behavior.

—That discipline should be consistently enforced through the cooperative efforts of teacher, child, parent, and principal.

—Finally, that the total program should help the child understand his world and aid in his development of good human relationships.

Special Programs

EVAMERE CARES PROGRAM (E.C.)

Citizenship, respect and concern for individual rights of children as well as adults within Evamere School are encouraged through the Evamere Cares Program (E.C.). The significance of the "CARES" is derived from the words which are associated with each letter: .

C—cooperation
A—appreciation
R—responsibility
E—effort
S—sharing

This program was initiated because we had concerns regarding some of the behavior which we observed in our children. We feel that the children have grown in their awareness of the goals of Evamere Cares. We feel a need to continue our efforts on a daily basis in order to maintain the gains that have occurred and to bring about even further improvement. We are setting high expectations for behavior, but we feel that these expectations are realistic in terms of the developmental age of the children. We are trying to be fair, firm and consistent in the enforcement of our expectations.

We encourage you to work closely with us because your support is really what makes the difference. Consistency of expectations between home and school provides security for children. It also conveys to the children that what they do is really important to all of us. Please feel free to ask your child's teacher how the Evamere Cares program functions in that classroom since it varies by grade levels. What is meaningful for a kindergarten child may not be appropriate for a second grader. However, the basic concepts of Evamere Cares are consistent throughout the building.

Perhaps an ideal for which to strive is to view discipline as what we have so that punishment is unnecessary.

EVAMERE'S SUSTAINED SILENT READING PROGRAM (ESSR)

Reading is an area that we all view as extremely important. Not only do children need to develop the ability to read, but they also need to experience the pleasure of reading and to feel that reading is important. Children need to see adults reading and to have time to read for the sheer joy of reading. In order to provide this opportunity, first and second graders have a ten-minute silent reading period every day from 3:05–3:15 p.m. All adults in the building will also participate.

The only exceptions will be kindergarten and special subject areas (art, music, physical education). From 3:15–3:25 p.m. the children and their teacher will chat informally about their books, events of the day or whatever may interest them. We hope this time block will serve as a "wind-down" time, so that the children leave school in a more relaxed manner.

We would encourage our families to have a time set aside each day as "family time" during which the television set is turned off. This family time would provide an opportunity for children and parents to be involved

175

together in activities such as reading aloud or silently, talking and listening to each other, working on a project or playing together. The concern with television is perhaps not as much the behavior it may create as much as the behavior it prevents—that is, the opportunity for families to communicate with each other in an active manner.

Parent Programs

VIP PROGRAM (*Vitally Interested People*)

Many parents volunteers work in the Hudson Schools through the VIP Program. We know that, if we become involved in a project, our own lives are enriched. What better way to become involved than in something that concerns our own children? The VIP Program not only helps to enrich the educational experiences of the children, but can give you an opportunity to become involved in a rewarding experience and obtain considerable personal satisfaction.

Volunteers are involved in the following activities:

1. Typing and clerical work in the office.
2. Registered nurses assisting in the clinic at noon.
3. Assisting in the lunchroom.
4. Assisting individual classroom teachers.
5. Assisting in the library.
6. *Skyrockets*—This catchy name belongs to a program in large and/or small muscle development and improved coordination skills. A child will meet each week individually with his volunteer to participate in a variety of physical activities.
7. *Perceptual Skills Development*—Some children write letters or numbers backwards or read words in reverse such as saw for was or confuse similar words such as house for horse. They may benefit from activities which help their eyes and hands to work together in a left-right direction. On a one-to-one basis a volunteer can help with these activities.
8. *Phonics Games Program*—A games approach may help a child to improve his phonic skills. A volunteer will work with the child through the use of learning game packets at the child's own pace. The volunteer will also administer a check test as each packet of games is completed before proceeding to the next packet.
9. *Math Tutoring*—Some children need extra help with math facts or concepts. Volunteers will help to make needed drill fun for individual

children or small groups of children. They will also use concrete
materials to develop math concepts.

10. *Auditory Memory—Listening*—Some children have difficulty recall-
ing directions or repeating what they have heard. The volunteer will
use activities which develop listening skills and recall of information
as she works with small groups of children.

PRINCIPLES INVOLVED IN PROGRAM:

Personal —	A	Community studies
	W	
Elaboration —	A	Parents as educators
	R	
Organization —	E	Parents as decision makers
	N	
Participation —	E	Teachers as social technologists
	S	
Launching —	S	The Venue
Effects —	OF	The Venturesome

Richard: This is the first book I've worked on that ended at the
beginning.

Cynthia: Your invitation to parents and educators to share their
program descriptions does seem an appropriate place to
begin. The venturesome may write to the following
addresses:

Dr. Cynthia Wallat
College of Education
Kent State University
Kent, Ohio   44242

Dr. Richard Goldman
Behavioral Science Center
Nova University
Fort Lauderdale, Florida   33314

APPENDIX A

Inexpensive Source Books

A Matter of Service: How to Monitor Agencies That Serve Children.
>Harold D. Holder et al. Durham, N.C.: Learning Institute of North Carolina, 1974, ERIC File ED 104 565 or $3.80 ERIC Document Reproduction Service.

A Parent Involvement Conference Model.
>Oakland, Calif.: Center for the Study of Parent Involvement, 5240 Boyd Street, Oakland, California 94618. A Do-It-Yourself Guide to planning, implementing, and evaluating a parent involvement conference; sample of effective conference announcements, objectives, registration forms; suggestions on process, creating a conference planning committee, finding conference facilities, developing an atmosphere conducive to sharing and learning. ($5.00)

A Primer for Publicity.
>Public Relations Bookshelf #6. NEA Publications Order Department, The Academic Building, Saw Mill Road, West Haven, Connecticut 06516.

A Selected Bibliography on Planned Change and Community Planning Practice: Making Things Happen.
>Charles K. Bolton and Donald W. Lenz. Council of Planning Librarians, P.O. Box 229, Monticello, Illinois 61856 ($2.50) or ERIC File ED 106 953 or $1.97 ERIC Document Reproduction Service.

Be Honest with Yourself.
>Doreen Croft. Belmont, Calif.: Wadsworth Publishing Co. A self-evaluation handbook designed for teachers, student teachers, parents, and volunteers.

Incidents are grouped into four categories (teacher-child, teacher-children, teacher-parent, and teacher-colleague). Accompanying each incident are possible reactions for the reader to check, space to write in reactions, and possible questions. Available from Wadsworth Publishing Co., Inc., Belmont, California 94002. ($5.95)

Citizen Action in Education.
This source of exchange of ideas for citizen involvement in decision making is published 4 times a year. Institute for Responsive Education, 704 Commonwealth Avenue, Boston, Massachusetts 02215. ($5.00 a year)

Community Decision Making for Education Associations
(Selecting the "Knowledgeable" Cross-Section of the Community: Business, Education, Government Politics, Religion, Chamber of Commerce, Public Agency heads, News Media Editors). Public Relations Bookshelf #10. NEA Publications Order Department, The Academic Building, Saw Mill Road, West Haven, Connecticut 06516.

Developing Citizens Committees.
Public Relations Bookshelf #8. NEA Publications Order Department, The Academic Building, Saw Mill Road, West Haven, Connecticut 06516.

Early Childhood Education: How to Organize Volunteers; How & Where to Find Volunteers.
Los Angeles, Calif.: Los Angeles City Unified School District, Volunteer and Tutorial Programs, 450 N. Grant Ave., Rm. G-114, Los Angeles, California 90051, Fall 1973, Sarah A. Davis, Director. ERIC File ED 104 560 or $1.97 ERIC Document Reproduction Service.

Encouraging Institutional Change.
R. Sherman, L. Schwartz, H. Morris. New York: Queens College and Relationship Development Center, 1974. ERIC File ED 090 464 or $1.97 ERIC Document Reproduction Service.

Don't know where to start? This reports a module for evaluating and formulating a plan; assessing strengths and weaknesses; practicing through videotaping; evaluating a community participation session.

Facts & Figures: A Layman's Guide to Conducting Surveys ($3.50) and *Facts for a Change: Citizen Action Research for Better Schools* ($5.00)
Both guides were written by Bill Burges and are available from Institute for Responsive Education, 704 Commonwealth Avenue, Boston, Massachusetts 02215.

Handbook for a Parent-School-Community Involvement Program.
Austin, Texas: Southwest Education Development Lab, 1974. ERIC File ED 118 709 or $7.76 ERIC Document Reproduction Service.

Well done—even "lesson" plans for parent involvement and guides for parent classroom observation Anytown Independent School District, Anytown, U.S.A. "Lesson" Plans for parent involvement
a) objectives of parent involvement/separate lesson plans—suggestions for each month, e.g., acquainting parents to activities—business meetings

179

b) procedures outlined step-by-step
c) summary
d) analysis

Home-School-Community Project Simformation Series.
B. Dean Bowles and Marvin J. Fruth, Faculty Associates. Wisconsin Research and Development Center for Cognitive Learning, The University of Wisconsin, Madison, Wisconsin.

The series of technical, practical materials includes:

Simformation 1: Introducing Parents to the Wisconsin Design for Reading Skill Development
Simformation 2. A Guide to organizing a Volunteer Program in IGE Schools
Simformation 3. Home-School Visits
Simformation 4. School Administrator's Interview Handbook
Simformation 5. Reporting Pupil Progress
Simformation 6. Parent-Teacher Conferences

Set of 6 w/binder sells @ $15.00 or individually @ $3.00. Available from CCL Document Service, 1025 West Johnson Street, Madison, Wisconsin 53706.

How to Research the Power Structure of Your Secondary School System.
David Rosen, Bert Marian, David Osborne. Study Commission on Undergraduate Education and the Education of Teachers, Lincoln, Nebraska, October 1973. Sponsored by Office of Education, Department of Health, Education and Welfare, Washington, D.C. ERIC File ED 087 749 or $6.42 ERIC Document Reproduction Service.

How Well Do They Represent You? A Handbook on Local School Boards for Parents and Other Citizens.
ERIC File ED 096 077 or $1.97 ERIC Document Reproduction Service.

How does your school board rate? Very low 0, Low 3, Average 5, High 7, Very high 10
a) How many meetings are open to the public?
b) Is the school board dominated by one person? One family? One racial or occupational group? One political party? One faction of the community?
c) What are the agenda items—mostly money or quality of education?
d) Do students have contact with the board?
e) Are the board's policies available in a written statement?

Keys to Community Involvement.
A series of booklets including:
1. Community Groups Keeping Them Alive and Well
2. Group Decision Making: Styles and Suggestions
3. Problem Solving: A Five-Step Approach
4. Planning for Change: Three Critical Elements
5. Personal and Professional Development
6. Governing Boards and Community Councils: Building Successful Partnerships
7. Innovative Projects: Making Them Standard Practice
8. Successful Projects: Examining the Research

9. Effective Groups: Guidelines for Participants
10. Group Progress: Recognizing and Removing Barriers
11. Measuring and Improving Group Effectiveness
12. Finding the "Right" Information: A Search Strategy
13. Community Surveys: Grassroots Approaches
14. Using Consultants: Getting What You Want
15. Group Leadership: Understanding, Guiding, and Sharing

Available from The Office of Marketing and Dissemination, Northwest Regional Educational Laboratory, 710 S.W. 2nd Avenue, Portland, Oregon 97204. Each title can be ordered (by number) for $2.00. All 15 titles are available for $24.00. Five copies of the same title are $9.00.

101 Activities for More Effective School-Community Involvement.
Available from Home and School Institute Trinity College, Washington, D.C. 20017. ($4.75—bulk prices on request)

Publishing a Newsletter.
Public Relations Bookshelf #5, NEA Publications Order Department, The Academic Building, Saw Mill Road, West Haven, Connecticut 06516.

RX for School-Community Relations.
C. R. Utermohlen, Editor. 219 Dillon Ave., Mankato, Minnesota 56001. The 528 practices suggested in the 109-page source can be obtained for $5.95.

School Finance Campaign.
Public Relations Bookshelf #1, NEA Publications Order Department, The Academic Building, Saw Mill Road, West Haven, Connecticut 06516.

Schools Where Parents Make a Difference.
Don Davies, Editor. Order from The Institute for Responsive Education, 704 Commonwealth Avenue, Boston, Massachusetts 02215. ($3.95)

TIP: Theory Into Practice 16 (1977).
The entire issue of *TIP* is devoted to discussion of home/school/community relations. Available from The Ohio State University, 242 W. 18th Avenue, Columbus, Ohio 42310. Reprints are $2 an issue (50 or more copies— $1.50 each).

Tips for PR Chairman.
Public Relations Bookshelf #2, NEA Publications Order Department, The Academic Building, Saw Mill Road, West Haven, Connecticut 06516.

Washington Report on Federal Legislation for Children Newsletter.
Provides information on federal legislation and voting records of members of Congress. Available from American Parents Committee, Inc., 1346 Connecticut Avenue, N.W., Washington, D.C. 20036.

APPENDIX B

Parent Education Programs—ERIC*

The programs listed in this appendix were selected from monthly indexes called *Resources in Education*.[1] Articles, speeches, and parent education program descriptions are collected in clearinghouses such as the National Laboratory on Early Childhood Education in Urbana, Illinois, and then sent to a central office for listing in *Resources in Education*. Abstracts of the articles and/or documents are given an ED number and listed with their titles under main headings such as Parent Education, Parent Participation, Parent-School Relationship, Home Community, and Home Instruction. If you want to obtain the full document of the sources listed below you may view the document on microfiche machines in the library or order a Xerox hard copy through the ERIC Document Reproduction Service.

The ERIC Document Reproduction Service (EDRS) is the central facility for ordering ERIC microfiche copies and Xerox hard copies. This public service from NIE (National Institute of Education) is now under contract by Computer Microfilm International Corporation. The ordering address is

> ERIC Document Reproduction Service
> P.O. Box 190
> Arlington, Virginia 22210

---

*ERIC is an acronym for Educational Resources Information Center initiated by the Office of Education in 1965.

[1]The selected list was generated from a search of ten years (1967–1977) of citations in *Resources in Education*.

The prices for Xerox hard copies of ED # articles are presented below. All orders, including postage, must be paid in advance. Materials are sent at book rate for the first pound (one pound equals 100 hard copy pages) and at a fraction of that rate per pound after that. If you want it sent first class or air mail, indicate that on your order; the extra amount needed for postage will be billed to you. Postage for foreign mail is extra.

EDRS Hard Copy Price Listing

Number of Pages in Document	Price
1-25	$1.67
26-50	2.06
51-75	3.50
76-100	4.67
101-125	6.01

Add $1.27 for each additional 25-page increment or fraction thereof.

The possibilities for using the information from ERIC are practically limitless. We have given some ideas in the text as well as in the dialogues in this book. At this point, we would like to share with you some ideas on how the list of titles and reference numbers can be used. Since our readers have different information needs as well as different ways of problem solving, we will give two possible approaches for using the ERIC list.

The Wholistic Approach

Some individuals like to get a feel for what's available before they make up their mind about what activities they will use. For example, one of our students wanted to find out what activities were available to share with parents so that she could choose among the alternatives methods that matched her ontology (i.e., her belief that children and adults develop through interaction with each other). The student was convinced that parents are educators. She was also convinced that the academic success of her students could be fostered if she involved their parents. Succinctly stated, she wanted to find experiences that parents could share from school. However, she didn't want to have to spend a great deal of money buying materials. To solve the problem, the student read through a list of 200 ERIC sources. As she read through the list of titles, she wrote notes about the titles that she picked out. Since her concern was to find programs that seemed to be concerned with parent involvement in academic matters, and to find activities, the list looked like this after she read the titles.

Sources for Family-oriented Programs			Sources for Family-oriented Activities		
ED	134 306	Guide for Establishing	ED	088 609	Guiding Your Child
	086 317	Guide for Readiness		105 989	Home Learning activities

Sources for Family-oriented Programs			Sources for Family-oriented Activities		
105	691	Guide for Instruction	105	999	Home Learning activities
120	993	Units	086	316	Ideas for kits
082	833	Guidelines	058	954	Skill Learning
115	382	Handbook	085	211	Handbook of Activities
129	710	Sources of Information	120	994	Play Ideas
122	565	Sources of Information	107	344	Package of Material

After the student made the list, she went to the ERIC section in the library and read the sources she had picked. Then she put together a booklet entitled *Experiences Parents Can Share* for parents based on the activities she found and on the program she had developed for her class. Teachers, parents, administrators, and students from fields other than education can use the list in the same way as *Experiences Parents Can Share* was put together. Individuals interested in the areas of child development, bilingual programs, parent activities, and group processes, such as interviewing, can go through the list for reference. The list is also a source for finding an idea for a team paper or a speech to a group.

Readers can also use the list of ERIC sources as an introduction to what's going on, what is known, and what authorities in the field are calling for in needed directions. You will have a good grasp of the topics of current interest in the field of home/school/community interaction if you read the titles and write down one, two, or three words from each title. For example, we went through the 200 item list together in a half hour and wrote down the key word from the first forty-five titles. We soon found out that there were many different ways of saying the same thing so we just wrote all the words that seemed to go together around each other and drew lines every time the key words were repeated.

The following is a reproduction of the list. We are sharing the list as an example of how we used the title references. We are both convinced that if ten different people used the list there would be ten different sets of key words. There is no one right answer to this wholistic approach.

FIGURE B-1. Sample worksheet for ERIC

Family oriented programs/centers/workshops	‖‖‖ ‖‖‖
Toys	
toy-lending	‖‖
Home learning	‖‖‖ ‖‖‖ ‖‖‖ ‖‖‖
programs/guides/	‖‖‖ ‖‖‖ ‖‖‖ ‖‖‖
manuals/activities	‖
Assumptions	
low income/disadvantaged	
class differences/compensatory	‖‖‖ ‖‖‖ ‖‖‖
Health Care	
doctor/nutrition/health info.	‖

Birth to three
    early stimulation/infant   卌 卌 卌 |||
    early intervention program

Special Education
    mentally ill/retarded
    mental health/blind   卌 卌 |
    exceptional/deviant
    oppositional/high risk
    autistic/emotional reaction

Parents
    narrative/interviews   卌 卌 卌
    communication/ed. team
    involvement/discussion   卌
    partners/sharing
    participation/home-school

Preschool
    school readiness |||||
    Head Start age

Reading |

Programs
    day care/child care   卌 ||

Parent-child centers   卌 ||||

Issues
    needs/policy/finance   卌 卌
    advocacy/recommendations/   卌 卌 |
    revenues of field
    prevention of incompetence

General topics of parent education   卌 卌 卌
    conferences/evaluation   卌 卌 卌
    child development theories   卌
    adaptation/child rearing
    competence

Television ||

Mother's language style |

After making the above list, we rewrote and reordered the sixteen topics we found according to frequency counts and then, after running for the calculator, added percentages.

TABLE B–1. Content Analysis of 200 ERIC Sources

Topics	Frequency	Percentage
Home Learning Programs	42	21 %
General Reviews of Parent Education and Child Development	35	17.5
Statements of Need Policy, Recommendations	21	10.5

TABLE B–1.—Continued

Topics	Frequency	Percentage
Statements Concerning Parent Involvement and Communication	20	10
Early Intervention	18	9
Low Income/Disadvantaged	15	7.5
Special Education Topics	11	5.5
Parent-Child centers	9	4.5
Family-oriented Programs	9	4.5
Day Care/Child Care Programs	7	3.5
School Readiness & Head Start Age	5	2.5
Toy-lending	3	1
Doctor, Nutrition, Health	2	1
Television	2	0.5
Mother's Language Style	1	0.5
Total	100	100 %

After reading the above list, you can get a clear, wholistic idea of what's going on in home/school/community interaction. Remember that the above were chosen from *Resources in Education* because they included the words *parent education* in the description in the index. One could for example, find hundreds of citations for mother's language style or television if one were interested in what we know and why we don't know more about the marriage of theory and practice in mother's language style. But for our purposes in this book, if you compare the above content analysis of 200 parent education programs to the Model of Human Ecology presented earlier, you can see that little attention has been given to supporting the dimensions of the immediate setting. While it is true that the creation and delivery of home learning programs tops the list and as such there is concern for roles and relationships, the dimensions of biological development, human activities, and design of physical space and materials have been neglected. Although we know that poor health and nutrition is one of the primary causes of learning and personality problems in later life,* only 1 percent of a total of 200 references to parent education programs included this topic. We also know that toys and inanimate objects available to children have a great deal to do with early cognitive and motivational development (Yarrow, Rubenstein, and Pedersen

---

*Note: An excellent and free source of information on this topic is available from the U.S. General Accounting Office, 441 G Street, N.W., Washington, D.C. 20548. Write for *Preventing Mental Retardation—More Can Be Done*. H R D 77–37 October 3, 1977. Report to the Congress.

1975); yet from the initial list of topics it seems as though this aspect did not receive enough attention in the years 1967–77. You might want to compare the listings in *Resources in Education* for the years 1978–79, 1979–80, etc.

Although the wholistic approach is an effective way of getting a general idea of what's going on, as well as an effective way of finding specific references, you will need criteria to judge the material. As such, you will need an itemized approach.

The Itemized Approach

In chapters 4 and 5 we introduced two itemized approaches to building home/school/community interaction. Chapter 4 included an outline of specific steps toward implementing and communicating school curriculum among colleagues, children, and parents. In chapter 5 we presented criteria for evaluating potential program effectiveness. The primary purpose of sharing this information was to provide the means of implementing what we know. We know, for example, that substantial change will not occur unless the target audience is involved in the action. Rather than add to the multiple criticisms that exist, we can strengthen what is currently available. The ERIC sources which follow include descriptions of a sample of what is currently available in programs for parents. As you go through the programs you have identified through a wholistic approach, use the following checklist to determine whether it has the potential for being effective or whether it is merely a one-time, "shotgun" approach.

Criteria for Determining Potential Success
of Programs Concerned with
Parents as Educators

Does the program provide time for modeling, rehearsal, and comparing pre- and post-program behavior?	Yes	No
Does the program provide for direct involvement in problem identification and goal setting?	Yes	No
Does the program provide for continued communication and feedback between the program personnel and parents?	Yes	No

---

You might want to make a list of how various programs listed in ERIC accomplish the above steps or, more immediately, read through the following three sources and keep all the ideas for supporting communication on 3 x 5 index cards.

Adult Involvement in Child Development
for Staff and Parents   ED 077 562

Inclusion of Parents in Supportive
Educational Experience   ED 081 468

Parent and Teacher Strategies for
Working Together   ED 124 293

An easy and efficient way of keeping track of the dozens of ideas for modeling, problem identification, goal setting, and feedback is to type up a sheet similar to the following before you go to the library.

ERIC #_____

Title_____

Modeling

Rehearsal

Pre-& Post-Behavior Record-keeping Techniques

Problem Identification

Goal Setting

Feedback Mechanisms for Program Personnel & Parents

The Weston Approach Applied To ERIC

In chapter 4 we introduced the steps taken by the Weston faculty to implement their articulation and implementation framework. The framework presented in chapter 4 can be used for reviewing the 200 sources from ERIC. Students in our class have found the framework invaluable for organizing their reports. We ask our students to use 5 x 8 cards so they will have a file of resource ideas to use after graduation. Parents and teachers will also find the system useful for meeting immediate solutions.

   The following description of a program available in the ERIC files is offered as an example of how what we know about successful programs can be replicated on a wide scale.

MOTHER-TODDLER GROUPS AS NEW SOURCE FOR PARENT EDUCATION

Author—Madeline Lieber

Source—ED 124 294

FRAMEWORK

Awareness/	**Step 1**	Distinguish between what can be taught and what can
Identify		be fostered

The author believes that parenting is not instinctive; therefore, it involves skills that can be taught.

The means suggested for fostering the learning of new parenting skills is to provide an atmosphere of support for becoming aware of alternative methods of child rearing. This atmosphere is defined as one which provides contact with others who have young children and one which provides contact with a resource leader who has been trained in child development.

The author's rationale for providing contact with other parents of young children is based on her belief that urban environments may result in feelings of isolation rather than feelings of involvement. Apparently she is convinced that individuals have the ability to control their development of feelings of isolation through the alternative development of feelings of involvement.

Communicate/ Inform **Step 2** A clear statement of expectations according to the child's level

What model will be available to emulate?
   Other children in the group
What new roles will he learn?
   This point is not considered
When and where will interaction with peers and adults take place?
   The structural techniques employed in setting up the mother-toddler groups are as follows:
   a. *Group size* Ten mothers with toddlers
   b. *Time* One morning a week for two hour session
   c. *Physical setting* Nursery school with basic nursery school equipment and adjoining play yard
   d. *Interaction* Parent/Child: During the first hour the mothers and children used the equipment together. The only direction was to have the mother and child have a time to relax and enjoy the setting and equipment together.
      Parent/Group: Group sessions began the second hour. The leader's assistant worked with the children as the leader directed discussions that centered on the concerns of the group.
Who will be the audience for sharing and sounding out ideas?
   The purpose of this program was to provide a structured atmosphere for mothers of young children so that the group became a support system for each other. The leader's role was to serve as a resource for ideas concerning child development for the group.

Involvement/   **Step 3**   Elaboration of techniques to diagnose and teach
Verify   specific skills

This step was not articulated in this program. The following
sample of what could be done at this step appeared in the
Weston Language Arts Handbook.

Step 3   Elaboration of Techniques to
Diagnose and Teach Specific Skills

Sample Problem: Processing of Information

Observe and diagnose	Teaching techniques
Attention fluctuates?	Break input into small steps.
Needs time to process info?	Provide an activity at each step.
Afraid of new tasks?	Mediate task verbally to provide fedback.
Has difficulty sequencing?	Provide structure and repetition.

Sample Teaching Techniques for Processing of Information

Give rhythm and structure to what is being learned—
    chant the alphabet
    tap out words
    reproduce rhythmic patterns
    teach words in a visual series
    allow child to detour around the missing word
    copy sequences of blocks
    read words aloud as he is writing them
    give visual cues, use chalkboard, use gestures
    give child a written question or picture to think about before requiring an
       answer
    provide specific check points
    provide support at each check point
    write child's dictated ideas down in outline

Refinement/   **Step 4**   Parent and Teacher's Joint Assessment of Activities
Resolve   from Step 3

Assessment procedures in this program were concerned with
parental attitudes. The surveys reported indicated that after 6 or
7 sessions the mothers generally developed more confidence in
themselves as parents and were not as concerned about their
child's behavior or his ability to function in a group.

It would be interesting to have notes on the sessions that were
held during the second half hour. We would be able to have a
frequency count on the types of questions asked and could
make an assessment of what was actually involved in this group
in reference to "change in attitude." With field notes the author
would also have been able to share the number of times she did

not have to answer a question concerning child development, i.e., in what areas of child development were the parents relying on each other for answers and in what areas did they rely on the discussion leader. With more specific information of this type we could have a clearer idea of what areas parents need further help in assessing their child's growth and could plan specific points to cover in parent and teacher joint assessment.

Since the program was concerned primarily with providing an atmosphere of support we can not be critical of the results, i.e., the author articulated her goal beforehand and therefore set the criteria open to scrutiny. We would like to point out, however, that sources are available for ideas for joint assessment. The following sources are useful for parents and teachers for collecting ideas for joint assessment.

Step 4: Refinement/Resolve

Clinchey, B., and Rosenthal, K. "Analysis of Children's Errors." In *Psychology and Educational Practice,* edited by G. S. Lesser. Glenview, Ill.: Scott, Foresman, 1971, pp. 90–129.

Darnell, Diane. *A Parent–Teacher Joint Assessment of the Entering and Exiting Preschool Child 1976.* ERIC Document File ED 129 446.

Farnham-Diggory, Sylvia. *Study Guide for Cognitive Processes in Education: A Psychological Preparation for Teachers and Curriculum Development.* New York: Harper and Row, 1972.

Kagan, Jerome. *Understanding Children.* Chicago: Harcourt, Brace, 1971. (Observable behaviors of young children and implications for teachers)

Kogan, Nathan. *Cognitive Styles in Infancy and Early Childhood.* New York: Wiley, Halstead Division, 1976.

Newell, A., and Siman, A. *Human Problem Solving.* Englewood Cliffs, N.J.: Prentice-Hall, 1972.

Van Nagel, Clint. *Cooperative Diagnosis and Prescription between Parent, Teacher and Other Professionals: An Eclectic Model.* ERIC Document File ED 135 151.

ERIC Sources

A Doctor Discusses the Preschool Child's Learning Process & How Parents Can Help	ED 078 961
A Guide to Establishing and Directing a Family Oriented Structured Preschool Activity	ED 134 306
A Guide to Securing & Installing the Parent/Child Toy-Lending Library	ED 078 893
A Home Learning Center Approach to Early Stimulation	ED 056 750

Parent Education Programs—ERIC

192

Educating Parents about Education: A Review of Some Issues,
Methods and Sources of Information   ED 129 710

Education of Children Aged One to Three:
A Curriculum Manual   ED 072 872

Education for Parenting   ED 103 093

Education Preparenthood and the Schools   ED 084 022

Effect of the Parent Involvement Program on Reading
Readiness Scores   ED 104 527

Effectiveness of 4-C Manpower Training Program for
Entry Participants   ED 076 505

Family Learning Center Workshops   ED 132 514

Family and School Centers of Learning for Young Children   ED 077 572

Focus on Parent Education as a Means of Altering the
Child's Environment   ED 033 758

Focus on Parents: The Parenting Materials Information Center   ED 122 565

Fostering the Mother's Role in the Cognitive Growth of Low
Income Preschoolers: A New Family Agency Function   ED 059 789

From Birth to One Year: The Nova University Play &
Learn Program   ED 111 489

Future Directions in Parent Education Research   ED 114 171

Guiding Your Child to a More Creative Life   ED 088 601

Home as a Learning Center   ED 120 033

Home Instruction Programs for Exceptional Student Ages 0–5.
Florida State Department of Education, Tallahassee Education
for Exceptional Children Section   ED 089 528

Home Learning Activities Designed to Provide Educational
Experiences for Children and Parents. Part I, Part II   ED 105 989
     ED 105 990

Home-Oriented Preschool Education   ED 122 564

Home-Oriented Preschool Education: Curriculum
Planning Guide   ED 082 848

Home-Oriented Preschool Education: Evaluation of the
Prototype Home Visitor Training Package   ED 093 358

Home-Oriented Preschool Education: Field Director's Manual   ED 082 844

Home-Oriented Preschool Education: Materials
Preparation Guide   ED 082 849

Home-School-Community Systems for Children
Development. Final Report   ED 085 610

Home Start: School for Parents   ED 080 185

Home Teaching with Mothers and Infants   ED 113 030

Houston Parent Child Development Center ED 135 459

How Deviant is the Normal Child? A Behavioral Analysis of the
Preschool Child and his Family ED 069 356

How Much Do Mothers Love Their Children? ED 081 485

Ideas for Parent-Teacher Made Home Learning Kits ED 086 316

Implementation of the Toy Lending Library in the State of Utah.
Summary Report ED 076 255

In-Home Early Childhood Project ED 111 401

In the Beginning: A Parent Guide of Activities and Experiences
for Infants from Birth to Six Months. Book I. New Orleans
Parent Child Development Center's Infant Program ED 081 484

Inclusion of Parents in Supportive Educational Experiences ED 081 468

Infant Day Care: Hazard or Mental Health Resource? ED 054 851

Infant Education Research Project: Implementation and
Implications of a Home Tutoring Program ED 054 865

Infant Toddler Curriculum of the Brookline Early
Education Project ED 135 475

Instruction Pamphlet for Parents of Oppositional Children ED 070 220

Instructional Strategies in Infant Stimulation ED 056 751

Intellectual Skill Learning in the Home Environment. Interim
Research Report ED 058 954

Investigation of the Effects of Parent Participation in Head Start ED 080 215
ED 080 216
ED 080 217
ED 080 218

Kedman (Parent-Teacher Discussion Groups) ED 103 112

Kramer School Something for Everybody ED 069 437

Language Experiences for Your Preschools Part I. Activities
at Home ED 095 987

Living & Learning with Children: A Handbook of Activities for
Children from Three to Six ED 085 08 211

Living Room School Project. Final Evaluation Report, 1972–73 ED 082 850

Manual for Replication of the Mother-Child Home Program.
(Preliminary Version, for Field-Testing) ED 059 790

Maternal Behavior and the Development of Reading
Readiness in Urban Negro Children ED 031 309

Mother-Toddler Groups as a New Source for Parent Education ED 124 294

Mother Training as a Means of Accelerating Childhood
Development in a High Risk Population ED 104 522

Mothers as Early Cognitive Trainers: Guiding Low-Income
Mothers to Work with Their Prepreschoolers ED 059 786

APPENDIX C

University Preparation Programs

In *The Art of Schoolmanship,* Haberman has suggested that

> behavioral competencies are developed by practice. The behaviors selected
> for practice . . . must be clear and specific and in addition, supported by
> theoretical explanation of human development and compatible with the
> ethics of providing education in a free society.[1]

The chapters you have just completed have attempted to cover these points. For
those who feel discouraged by the observation that redefinition of roles takes from
two to five years, we offer the following selected review of what is going on in
some universities as testimony to the fact "something can be done."

The descriptions of these venturesome preparation programs are arranged
alphabetically by the name of the college or university for easy reference. The
authors who wrote the descriptions of their programs have all given presentations
on various aspects of home/school/community interaction at national conferences
such as NAEYC (National Association for the Education of Young Children).
Although we have provided parents with information such as the NETWORK toll
free number and information about how to get in touch with The Center for Parent

---

[1] Martin Haberman, *The Art of Schoolmanship* (St. Louis, Mo.: Warren H. Green, 1970),
pp. 146–47.

Involvement, there are no formally established networks for identifying individuals concerned with home/school/interaction at the university level.

In order to provide a mechanism for keeping in touch with new developments around the country we asked professors from Arizona, Colorado, Florida, New York, Washington, and Washington, D.C. to outline the purposes of their programs in terms of preparation for home/school/community interaction. The ERIC reference to teacher preparation at Nasson College, Maine, was included as an example of a university program which reinforces the discussion of the teacher as social technologist in chapter 7. The reader may wish to add these points to the checklist included in that chapter or use the ERIC source as a follow-up on Safran's discussion of competencies needed by teachers (see chapter 7).

Arapahoe Community College
A Two-Year Early Childhood Education Program to Meet Community Needs

Rationale: The two-fold goal of our program is

1. To provide early childhood education information to all students that stresses the importance of the parent as the primary educator of the child;

2. To provide early childhood education information and services to the community and provide information to students about community resources available for young children.

Program:

1. Course content provides information on the developmental needs of the young child and different methods of providing for these;

2. Students analyze existing early learning programs to select and develop appropriate teaching philosophies;

3. Students learn to evaluate early learning environments to more accurately match program and child;

4. Students develop ways to involve themselves in their own children's education as well as ways to promote the involvement of other parents;

5. Community people are invited to inform students about agencies, programs, and facilities that are available to young children, their families, and other educators;

6. Student volunteers are placed in community early learning programs to gain experience and to provide service to the community;

7. The early childhood education program recognizes different learning styles of students; therefore it provides alternatives to traditional campus offerings through off-campus courses, on-the-job course work, cooperative education opportunities, and individualized course work.

SOURCE: Suzanna Bramlet, Coordinator/Instructor Early Childhood Education, Arapahoe Community College, 5900 S. Santa Fe Drive, Littleton, Colorado 80120

Arizona State University

Teacher Preparation: The Vehicle for Enhancing Parent Involvement

Rationale: The major purpose of this program is to prepare teachers of young children to work effectively with parents.

During the seventies, investigations revealed that when parents are involved in school programs, child success is more often achieved. We realize that parents have the possibility of becoming better teachers of children and schools have the responsibility to prepare them to do this job effectively.

However, just as effective parenting skills are not instinctive, nor is teacher ability to work with parents.

Program: Preservice/Inservice Training Program for Teachers

The major goal is accomplished through a variety of well-planned experiences that provide opportunities for teachers to:

a. Clarify and if necessary modify their attitude and understanding about the importance of parental involvement in the teaching-learning process.

b. Clarify and if necessary modify their perceptions of parental interest.

c. Develop effective communication skills.

d. Identify, develop, implement, and evaluate a variety of methods and activities that are intended to ensure parent involvement in meaningful successful experiences.

e. Identify and utilize formal and informal survey methods that will provide information about parents.

f. Establish realistic parent involvement program goals.

g. Identify and utilize a variety of evaluation methods that would provide information on the effectiveness of the parent involvement program.

SOURCE: Dr. Betty Greathouse, Assistant Chairperson, Department of Education, Arizona State University, Tempe, Arizona 85281

Trinity College
Home and School Institute

Rationale: The overall mission of the nonprofit Home and School Institute is to raise children's abilities as learners and adult competencies as teachers through specific, practical approaches to share educational accountability between the home, school, and related institutions. Research, including the more well-known works of Coleman and Jencks and the lesser known but significant early childhood "intervention" studies, has revealed that not even the best school can do the job alone, that the home is the critical make-or-break educational institution, that the early years are determiners of later academic achievement.

Program: Family Involvement is integral to all HSI programs.

1. The institute works with community adults to help them use ordinary resources around the home to help students learn.

2. HSI works with educators, prekindergarten through grade 12, to help them tap the educational gold mine outside the school walls.

3. HSI works with community adults, teenagers, and teachers together in joint training programs to bridge the school-community gap through group problem-solving strategies.

4. HSI is currently offering, with Trinity College, a complete concentration for the Masters of Arts in Teaching degree in School and Parent Involvement.

5. HSI has publications which put its training strategies to print. Among them are *101 Activities for More Effective School Community Involvement* and *A Family Affair: Education.*

SOURCE: Dr. Dorothy Rich, Director, Home and School Institute, Trinity College, Washington, D.C. 20017

Nasson College
Springvale, Maine

Rationale: The teacher preparation program should be concerned with developing the expectation that a professional continually offers to carry higher levels of responsibility.

Program: The competencies listed below were adapted by the director of student teaching, Dr. Bartholomew Ciampa, from USOE (United States Office of Education) Teacher Education Models and program descriptions from Columbia University, Florida State, University of Massachusetts, Michigan State, North West Regional Educational Lab, University of Pittsburgh, and the University of Toledo.

The following competencies were described as indicative of positive evidence of intellectual and professional energy.

1. Occupies positions of leadership in several different groups or organizations.

2. Shows interest in many different community activities and projects for social betterment.

3. Exhibits the ability to contribute as a group member in cooperative planning and provides leadership in group situations whenever necessary.

4. Displays an ability to find and utilize resources, people, and materials in instructional improvement and professional development.

5. Is able to communicate effectively with other staff members, administrators, consultants, resource people, parents, and laypeople.

203

6. Is aware of professional organizations and the role of these in the instructional improvement and development of the profession.

7. Assumes a responsibility for the development of education as a profession outside of classroom or instructional duties.

The following competencies are related to general instructional competencies which are relative to local conditions.

1. Is aware of local factors which influence educational conditions in the school, local school district, community, county, and state.

2. Is conscious of cause-effect relationships between local factors and school conditions.

3. Employs evaluative techniques for assessing the extent of influence which local factors have on school conditions.

4. Examines strategies for effecting change in local environments.

5. Examines patterns of action research as means of local solutions to problems.

6. Understands social and philosophical factors as they influence local conditions.

7. Seeks out community resources which apply toward the solution of problems relating to local conditions.

8. Is aware of local and state school policies, procedures and regulations.

9. Understands the importance of maintaining public relations.

Nova University
A Cooperative Learning Environment
for Involving Parents in the
Education of Their Children

Rationale: Parents have a need and desire to become involved in the education of their children. This is a valuable and essential asset to a school program. Parents who have an opportunity to become involved in the education of their children add a new dimension to the total school environment. As a result, there is improvement in communication among home, school, and community, increased understanding of school philosophy, policies, and programs, and more effective public relations. Essentially, the school is providing education for both parents and children. Their continued growth and development should be the aim of every school. Research has shown that children achieve better academically when their parents are involved in their education.

Program: The University School of Nova University houses a preschool and kindergarten unit (mainstreamed Head Start, visually limited children, and tuition-paying youngsters); a primary and middle grade unit; and a high school-middle college unit. Some of the parent activities follow.

1. The school maintains constant communications with parents, bringing home and school closer together.

2. The school recruits, trains, develops programs for and supervises volunteers who work closely with educators as paraprofessionals. They work individually with children on a prescriptive basis to improve basic skills.

3. Parents and children participate in a toy-lending library where educational toys and games are explained and readily available. The goal is to improve parent/child communications and interaction and to involve parents more directly in their own children's educational growth and development at home as well as at school.

4. Parents assist parents in providing for the needs of the total school population. Parents work cooperatively so that all youngsters have the opportunity to attend the local circus or enjoy a "turkey" Thanksgiving.

5. Parents enrich the curriculum by sharing their ethnic customs with small groups of children.

6. Parents serve as models for involving high school students in school projects.

7. Parents are encouraged to become involved in curriculum decision making as members of the Sex Education Committee.

8. Parents achieve greater understanding of their role as a parent. Planned parenting sessions as well as informal discussions provide parents with the opportunity to share ideas and common problems and explore whether their personal goals for their children are realistic.

9. Through their involvement parents learn more about the school, its philosophy, its methods, policies, and programs, and about children's needs and how they learn.

10. Parents, children, and educators achieve greater understanding, communications, and interaction. They learn to value each other more.

11. Parents are recognized and utilized as one of our greatest natural resources of talent and free services. They are also valued as one of the greatest sources of information about their own children.

SOURCE: Joan A. Gelormino, Ed.D., The University School of Nova University, 7500 S.W. 36 Street, Fort Lauderdale, Florida 33314; Tobene Rosenthal, The University School of Nova University, 7500 S.W. 36 Street, Fort Lauderdale, Florida 33314

SUNY-Geneseo, New York
Early Childhood Center of the Holcomb Learning Center
Division of Education
Social Competency Research and Development Project

Rationale: The overall mission of the Early Childhood Center is to provide experiences for all participants—children, their families, and staff—which maximize the opportunities for the development of those skills and knowledges which are prerequisites for the development of social competency.

Program: The objectives of the research and demonstration project are

1. To develop a theoretical definition of social competence in young children, ages 3-5.

2. To derive an assessment format for evaluating social competence, in both summative and formative modes.

3. To design feedback routes to convey assessment information to teachers and families.

4. To design classroom and home-based experiences which will maximize social competency development in young children.

5. To develop a four-way interactive and ongoing communication network among child-family-teachers-researchers.

SOURCE: Dr. Marce Verzaro-Lawrence, Assistant Professor, SUNY-Geneseo, Geneseo, New York 14454; Dr. Jane Hogan, Director, Holcomb Learning Center, SUNY-Geneseo, Geneseo, New York 14454

University of Arizona
(TEEM)
Parent Involvement in Two Worlds

Rationale: The home environment exerts a powerful influence on the child. Parents are the first teachers a child encounters, and the formative years before a child enters school have an impact on how that child sees himself and help determine the school success a child will enjoy. Parents not only have a strong influence on the children who are in schools, but parents have a right to, and are demanding to, have an influence on these public institutions as well. Therefore, in order to develop this large body of stakeholders into an informed, organized, effective voice in the educational process, TEEM has developed a parent program which concentrates on educating parents as well as developing parents into more effective educators.

The parent program which has evolved emphasizes the complementary roles of school and home as centers of total child development. TEEM's ultimate goal is to prepare parents to become advocates for the best interests of their children.

From this broad outline TEEM has identified specific skills parents need to achieve these goals. Emphasis has been placed on the following five competency areas:

1. Knowledge and identification,
2. Development and planning,
3. Implementation procedures,
4. Recording and documenting,
5. Assessment and evaluation.

With these skills parents will have an understanding of the functioning of the local school system, be able to participate responsibly in community affairs, and have the knowledge necessary for utilization of resources in order to meet the economic and social demands of the society.

206

SOURCE: Mrs. Alice Paul, Coordinator of Educational Development, Mr. Jerry Maulson, Coordinator of Parent Involvement, Arizona Center for Educational Research and Development, TEEM Follow Through Program, College of Education, University of Arizona, Tucson, Arizona 85721

Western Washington University
IT TAKES MORE THAN ONE

In the early 1970s, a group of in-service teachers participated in an *Early Childhood Project,* sponsored by Western Washington State College, Bellingham, Washington. The teachers developed programs whereby other adults might share in helping young learners.

One teacher combined her sensitivity to herself and others to plan an innovative approach that increased more effective educational experiences for Indian parents and their children. Both the VIP (Very Important Person) program and her Diary of Community Involvement demonstrate the unique sincerity, patience, and resourcefulness of a committed teacher.

Another teacher reinforced the goal of parental involvement by making sure that groups of parents exchanged experiences. She designed an activities workshop where the parents were encouraged to develop and carry through their own projects for summer activities for their children.

These and other examples of parent involvement are described and reported by teachers in the booklet entitled *It Takes More Than One—A Collection of Articles by Teachers of Young Children.*

SOURCE: Dr. Roberta Bouverat, School of Education, Western Washington University, Bellingham, Washington 98225

APPENDIX D

Oral Language Components*
Weston Public Schools

INTRODUCTION

Children come to school with considerable listening and speaking ability, an extensive vocabulary, and much to talk about. As teachers, we have to build on this base in order to have an effective oral language program. The school day abounds with natural situations for oral language development since oral language is basic to teaching and learning in every subject area.

These natural situations should be the basis for much of the instruction in oral expression. Focus should not be restricted to blocks of time earmarked for oral language. However, the teacher must not only plan activities and opportunities that connect with and capitalize on these natural situations but also must figure out new strategies that provoke a wider range of output.

HOW TO USE THIS SECTION

The following pages contain:

    1. Explanations of each oral language component

---

*Reprinted courtesy of Weston Public Schools.

208

2. Suggestions for exploration within the classroom

3. Resource materials for additional strategies

Keeping in mind that oral language activities will occur throughout the day, our hope is that you will look for ways to make these suggestions suit the needs of your students and the intent of your units. We have included examples of specific activities to serve as illustrations. The looseleaf format is intentional; you are encouraged to make this book your own by adding pages during the year.

A. *Conversing*

Casual conversation takes place among students, with and without the teacher present. Those conversations involving the teacher usually occur at the beginning of the day, at snack time, before lunch break, and at dismissal time. It is crucial that teachers realize the importance of conversation that occurs during these brief moments. It is during these individual and less structured times that we show a child just how important his words are to us. Case in point: Ellen returns to school on Monday morning with a giant conch shell to show you. You look; the children crowd around and look. But—what if Ellen merely came up to the desk to *tell* you about the shell? Would you be willing to put down your bulletin, or pencil, or lunch list, and give her your full attention? Or, would you listen with one ear, and continue with your writing or reading? Soon, Ellen will begin to get the idea that words do not deserve or demand attention. If this attitude, this lack of respect for communication which is solely oral, is allowed to develop, all the other expertly planned oral language activities will fail.

It is up to you to show the children that what they SAY does COUNT.

B. *Describing*

Describing things is an important skill that should be developed by the teacher. Description of places, objects, and people takes place throughout the day and cannot be isolated in one little block of time. The teacher should encourage accurate description of things and people so that better communication can take place.

Suggested Activities

Describing a familiar place is one way of getting at this important skill. A teacher can take two children and ask them to describe a certain part of the room. The place being described may be the area where the sink exists. If one child gives some erroneous information and the other child gives accurate details, the teacher should point out the difference between the two descriptions. In this way it will be brought to everyone's attention that describing a place is important, and in order to describe it, accurate information is needed.

The same thing may be done with objects. Describing such a mundane object as a pencil sharpener may turn out to be a very revealing experience. Some children may have a great deal of difficulty giving information orally to others. Charts on the board may help such children. Attributes such as color, texture or size can help children organize their information. In this way the teacher is helping the child to systematically organize his or her thoughts.

209

Password, a familiar game, is an excellent way to increase descriptive ability. The teacher picks two children to go to the front of the room. These two children face the blackboard so that they are not facing the other children. Another child is selected to write a word on the opposite blackboard or on a card. The word should be large enough to be seen by the children in their seats. The two children at the board are then allowed to turn around and face the others. Children at their seats may only give the players one-word (descriptive) clues.

The teacher may use other games or vary the *Password* game in order to get at describing things accurately. The teacher should encourage students to consider *all* their senses in formulating a full description. Children tend to respond to visual information, neglecting how an object or place feels, smells, tastes or sounds. Gather several different restaurant menus and have the children look at the variety of ways the menus appeal to the senses.

C. *Explaining*

The classroom provides many occasions for children to share what they know with others through the giving of oral explanations and/or directions.

Able students can help each other learn how to work A-V equipment, design a mobile, use a microscope, play a game, or use an index.

Directions serve as a "mirror" for the sender because once they are delivered, there is immediate feedback showing whether or not the communication was effective. A possible beginning activity that illustrates this point is the Back-to-Back game:

Give each of two players the same number of paper shapes or attribute blocks. Give the children the following directions:

1. Sit back-to-back with your materials in front of you. One of you is the sender, the other the receiver. No assistance may be given by friends or onlookers.

2. If you are the sender, assemble the pieces in a specific pattern, telling the person behind you what you are doing.

3. If you are the receiver, listen to the other person and assemble your pieces in the same pattern. Of course, you may not turn around or ask questions.

4. Compare what you have done. Ask the observers what you might have done to make the directions clearer.

Note to teacher: Use your own variations on this, i.e., players may be separated by a wall, the entire game may be taped for replay of what was said, etc. There are also other activities that are suitable for back-to-back games such as drawing, origami (paper folding), tying a half-hitch knot. Gear your choice of task to the pair of children selected.

Most classroom activities are introduced through directions. Children should be allowed and encouraged to engage in direction-giving themselves. One possibility is setting up an "I'll Show You" program for skill sharing. Children pick a skill or talent they feel able to share with others and prepare an oral presentation with or without demonstration. Materials may be brought from home as needed. Possible samples include playing checkers, bathing a dog, preparing fudge, loom weaving. This special form of "Show and Tell" is an excellent way to make children aware of the need for order and clarity in direction-giving. As the "respondents" show confusion and ask questions, the "show-er" becomes more aware of how to improve his own skill.

Certain activities lend themselves to whole-class exploration. You might try giving each child an unlined piece of paper, asking them to fold the paper into eight boxes, and give an oral direction to follow for each box.

Simple Example:
> In box 1, draw 2 circles.

More Complicated: (2 or 3 step)
> In box 1, draw 2 circles. Now put a dot in the first circle and a cross in the second.

When doing this, children must be aware that papers should be "covered" and will *not* be collected, thus taking off the pressure of a "test" situation. When all directions are given, the class should compare results and discuss their varying interpretations of your oral instructions.

Another appropriate activity is the Blindfold Obstacle Walk. One child is blindfolded and given oral instructions to walk through an obstacle course you have prepared in one part of the room. The object is to safely reach the end without bumping into anything. The children's mistakes will reveal the direction-giving ability of both the "instructor" and the "follower."

D. *Questioning*

Far too many teachers rely on questions requiring students only to *remember* ideas rather than to *use* them.

The following categories are from Benjamin Bloom's *Taxonomy of Educational Objectives*. When applied to questions (see Norris M. Sanders, *Classroom Questions What Kinds?*), these categories help a teacher to improve his questioning techniques, and in turn, will provide a model for students to follow.

1. *Memory*
   To which animal group do frogs belong?

2. *Translation*
   What does "being a paper tiger" mean?

3. *Interpretation*
   How did the invention of barbed wire help the cattle farmer?

4. *Application*
   How do you think we should decide who gets the playground ball each day?

5. *Analysis*
   Why do you think Prokofiev used the bassoon to represent the grandfather in "Peter and the Wolf"?

6. *Synthesis*
   How could you use a paper plate to make a hand puppet?

211

7. *Evaluation*

Which character in *The Last of the Really Great Whangdoodles* did you find most entertaining? Why?

A teacher's conscious effort to include all types of questions exposes the listeners to useful models. In addition, there are many ways to assist the students in refining their own skills of questioning.

You might try a variation on Twenty Questions which stresses guessing with as *few* questions as possible. Children will ultimately recognize that certain questions are wasteful, whereas others produce a great deal of information. For instance, children may be helped to see that if the answer to "Is the object in the right half of the room?" is "No," then obviously the object is in the left half of the room. This involves the use of inference, and not all children are ready for this skill. However, they *can* be exposed to it, and internalization will occur at a later stage.

Children should also be guided to use questions in a purposeful setting. One such possibility is the interview. This can be used, especially at the beginning of the year, in a get-acquainted situation. Students interview each other, and then present their partner to the class, thereby restating what was learned in the interview, telling as much as they remember. Interviewing can also progress to more complicated areas, as in interviews of people who are not class members. Emphasis should be placed on questions that go beyond name, date of birth, education, etc. Tape recorders are a valuable memory tool for some and also help those who wish to later transcribe the interview into written form.

Another technique for encouraging use of oral questioning is taking polls. Student pollsters may use the school or class population, or include outsiders, as appropriate. Polls can be taken on many topics, such as:

—What is your favorite school lunch?

—Who are you voting for in the upcoming election?

—Would you participate in a school cribbage tournament?

Results may be reported in a variety of ways, including the use of graphs, charts, etc., with accompanying oral explanations.

E. *Discussing*

Proper use of classroom discussion will lead to development of critical thinking, reasoning, problem solving and organized presentation. Children need to be helped to discover what needs discussing, define the topic, and explore viewpoints. The teacher's role is to foster a discussion that sharpens skills as well as retains interest. The general Moffett approach indicates that true discussion only evolves in a *small* group situation. He says, "The sheer size of a classroom of students precludes enough attention, participation and interaction—3 essentials for authentic discussion. The teacher invariably talks too much to maintain continuity" (p. 74).

Classroom discussions fall into these four basic categories:

1. *Simple Recitation*—serves similar function as testing; allows teacher to find out what the student knows; based mainly on factual knowledge.

2. *Inductive Questioning*—helps child develop a concept; leads him or her to draw new conclusions from present information.

3. *Open-Ended*—doesn't necessarily teach a concept; focus is on thinking, sharing ideas, and valuing contributions of others.

4. *Solving a Problem*—a goal is to be attained; students attempt to reach a consensus.

In thinking about the above categories, bear in mind that not all discussions are "one-method," and a particular discussion may include a combination of purposes: to solve problems, air opinions, find out what others think, vent feelings, clarify viewpoints, reevaluate one's own opinions. A quality discussion will result when students are skilled in discussion techniques. Simply listing "Steps for Good Discussion" will not accomplish this. Children need to participate in activities and games which focus on skills of discussion.

The following developmental sequence of discussion skills may help you to assist your class in becoming better discussion participants. These have been identified by Gene Stanford and Barbara D. Stanford, *Learning Discussion Skills Through Games*. Actual game suggestions are found in their book, pp. 18–49.

Skill 1.   Getting Acquainted
Skill 2.   Organizing for Action
Skill 3.   Recognizing the Value of All Contributions
Skill 4.   Taking Responsibility to Contribute
Skill 5.   Responding to Other Contributions
Skill 6.   Careful Listening to Perceive Differences
Skill 7.   Careful Listening to Perceive Agreement
Skill 8.   Encouraging Contribution Rather than Argument
Skill 9.   Learning New Roles
Skill 10.   Arriving at a Consensus

In examining the activities suggested by the authors, we felt the Murder Mystery Clue Game, aimed at developing skill 3, was particularly useful. Clues may be used as given in the book or rewritten as you see fit.

As teacher, there are several discussion problems to be aware of. These may occur, regardless of how well your group is progressing in mastering the discussion skills. Be aware of the possibility of dealing with these difficulties:

1. Students not listening to each other

2. Disgression from the topic

3. Repetitions and *Non Sequiturs*

4. Impulsive Interruptions

5. Non-participation

There is no one method which works best to effectively eliminate the above difficulties. The teacher must determine if the digressing student (a) doesn't understand the topic, (b) isn't interested in the subject matter, (c) is incapable of patiently waiting until his point fits in, (d) is unaware that he has strayed from the topic, (e) is seeking attention for personal reasons.

As soon as possible, a small discussion group should meet without you, while you observe unobtrusively. You want the children to learn to talk to each other, not to you. A major reason youngsters may not listen to each other is that they assume that they can learn only from adults, not from other children. This is a fallacy. The teacher should let them do most of the talking. The teacher's role is to guide, not to dominate.

An excellent model for evaluating discussion appears in Moffett (p. 402). It should also be pointed out that tape-recording initial discussions can help students become aware of how they interact. Let the recorder run as they talk, then play back and go over the discussion with them, stopping the tape whenever they (or you) wish to note something.

Small group discussion may evolve into panel discussion, which is discussion held before an audience, unplanned except for the designation of a topic. Panels are one of the options open to students who have had small-group discussion experience and are comfortable in front of an audience. There are three basic types of panel discussion.

1. *Scribe Approach*—A panel is formed from scribes who are reporting to a class from their respective small groups. As each reports, the others can question him; then they can proceed to full discussion.

2. *Inner-Outer Circle Approach*—Participants sit facing each other in a circle with the audience in a larger concentric circle around the outside. One way to arrange this is to have the two circles nearly equal in number. The outer circle can observe the quality of the interaction of the inner circle, noting who contributes, who seems to want to contribute but does not, etc. Then the inner circle and outer circle can exchange places, and the others watch. After participants have shared their notes, evaluation of the procedure can take place.

3. *Mock Panel Approach*—Students play roles, pretending to be certain people or kinds of people engaged in discussing an issue. They can play roles from an imagined situation or those of characters of fiction, improvising a discussion of an issue according to how they think the characters would have talked about it.

F. *Reporting*

The type of reporting we are dealing with here is *not* oral reading of written research reports. This constitutes "rehearsed reading" and is discussed later. Rather, oral reports are given with a minimum of written notation. Among the various types of oral presentations children can try are the following:

1. *Sharing*—The child should begin oral reporting with simple sharing, centering on topics about which he or she feels comfortable communicating. The subject should be well-defined: Caring for a Horse; My Rock and Mineral Collection.

2. *Reporting from Research*—The child will use either note cards or an outline, but the majority of the presentation is not in written form. Students must be helped to understand the value of rehearsing their talk before giving it to the group.

3. *Reporting with Accompanying Audio-Visual Aids*—The child speaks about something he has made—a science project, animal scene, etc. The

object itself is a reference point for the presentation. Information will probably include how the project was designed, and what has been learned in the process. The child may also speak while using a chart or poster.

4. *Book Reports*—The child shares his selection with the group by any one of a variety of means—straight narrative, dressing up as a character; acting as a salesperson "selling" the book.

With all forms of oral reporting, children need to be made aware of diction, rate of speech, voice tone, pitch, and eye contact. They should be encouraged to critique each other on these points as well as respond to the information a classmate has presented.

Some activities or topics lend themselves to group reports, in which a broader category is divided among several children. As a committee, they prepare a cohesive series of talks, each one on a particular aspect of the major theme. This is suitable only for children who have become proficient at oral reporting, because it requires coordination of ideas to avoid overlapping information.

G. *Persuading*

Children can be taught to recognize the difference between fact and opinion. Persuasive language may be explored by having the students listen to all types of oral situations in which persuasive talk plays a part.

One of the most enjoyable activities is the use of radio and television commercials. Children will have great fun noting slogans, jingles, and claims which stretch the truth. They can discuss what they hear, compare approaches, and possibly organize a real situation of evaluation, e.g., a Taste Test—which company makes the best chocolate milk? The idea of what "best" means can then be pursued, and the children can branch into reviewing the language of advertising—"greatest," "biggest," "newest." An entire class project on evaluation, validity, and propaganda may evolve from this, with children testing, comparing, reporting, and formulating their own ads, and in the process discovering how oral language can be used to best advantage.

Another possibility for working with persuasive language is exploring the use of the political speech. This can be done in conjunction with school, local, or national elections. Students may listen to and evaluate speeches presented by classmates, deciding how each used persuasive language to gather potential votes.

Children could also discuss how *they* use persuasive language in everyday life, for example: asking parents for higher allowance or later bedtime; obtaining permission to see a special movie; convincing a friend to loan his bicycle, etc.

A more formalized approach to using persuasive language is the use of debate. Although this is appropriate only at advanced levels, it is discussed in section H.

H. *Debating*

Debating is a very difficult skill to incorporate in the elementary classroom. Despite this fact, debating can provide an excellent opportunity for good oral language to emerge. In both debate and discussion, opposing ideas are presented

215

in an attempt to persuade people. The two differ, however, in the kinds of ideas that can be argued and in the method of argument.

In a debate the subject, usually stated as a declarative sentence, is one to which you can say, "I agree" or "I disagree." In a true debate the side that agrees with the resolution is called the affirmative, the side that disagrees is called the negative. The subject in a debate is usually stated as a question and may have a wide variety of solutions. A framework and time period must be set by the teacher in order to have the debate work.

In *formal* debates judges decide which team has presented the best arguments. They choose a winner. A teacher may select just two children to oppose each other instead of two teams. He or she may also want to incorporate a variation on the above mentioned model. In elementary school, having a winner need not be that important. Here the teacher must use his or her own discretion.

Debating is only effective when in-depth research has been carried out by the child. He or she must organize notes in order to be ready for the debate. The teacher may help the child gather information on the topic, but should leave a lot of the responsibility to the child.

The debate itself consists of two main parts: the presentation and the rebuttal. In *formal* debates the speaker is usually given six or seven minutes to present his argument. A speaker from the opposing team is given equal time to present his or her position. After this the original speaker is again given the opportunity to speak, elaborating on his or her points. The teacher need not be tied to a set time. (If teams are being used, the amount of time will definitely be limited.) The teacher may also let the audience become involved by asking the debators questions. The teacher may use any given situation that arises during the course of the week for debate material. For example, a special rule for the recess period may be debated by the children.

Whatever format is used by the teacher, these four suggestions may be helpful in setting up a debate.

1. The child must decide on the topic.
2. The child should study the history of the problem to be argued.
3. Research is done by the child (adult assistance may be used).
4. Notes are brought to the debate by the child.

Fictional Language

A. *Rehearsed Readings*

Reading aloud—whether by child or adult—demands rehearsal. In preparing students for effective oral reading, teachers should emphasize certain skills.

1. Clear and Distinct Enunciation
   Use words that end in *d, t, b, p, k* and hard *g* for practice in speaking distinctly.
   Enjoyable practice materials for achieving clear and distinct reading of alliterative passages are found in tongue twisters.

2. Rate of Reading

A competent reader varies his rate of oral reading to suit the action and mood of the situation which the words depict. Use passages that portray strong emotion for practice.

3. Phrasing

Words within sentences should be read in meaningful groups. Pauses for breath should not interrupt the thought.

One exercise that may be helpful is to place sentences on the board or overhead and use slashes to divide them into thought units.

4. Emphasis and Intonation

Typically our voices use four levels or pitches. Most words are spoken at level two, but at key words in a sentence the voice rises to level three for emphasis.

Ask students to listen to tapes of their conversations to note differences and have children listen to commercial taped stories read by experts.

Try a sentence like this for practice:

A YOUNG RABBIT GOT INTO THE GARDEN AND ATE THE LETTUCE.

a. Read the sentence as you normally would.
b. Make it clear that a *rabbit* got into the garden.
c. Show that it was a *young* rabbit.
d. Stress that it was the *garden* he entered.
e. Make it clear it was *lettuce* he ate.

Oral readers are made, not born. Constant practice is the only way children will gain confidence. Prose, poetry, and plays should all be part of the child's experiences in oral language. Reading aloud is the base from which performing a text is a natural extension.

B. *Choral Speaking*

Choral speaking is oral group interpretation of a text. It is a social yet unthreatening way for beginners to participate without fear of embarrassment. Support and correction comes from the blend of voices, with the more able speakers helping those who are less able.

The choice of a text requires careful selection. There are many excellent poems and songs which are suitable for choral reading. There should be a strong rhythm in the phrases, and the chosen piece must retain the children's interest throughout the many necessary repetitions.

In preparing a selection, the class should discuss the ways to interpret the piece. The words themselves may be put on a large chart or dittoed. Examine the text for different voice parts—characters, moods, themes, etc. Steps to follow are presented in Moffett (p. 111). Choral Speaking selections fall into four major categories.

1. *Refrain*—Soloist reads the narrative and others join the refrain.
   "The Wind"   Robert Louis Stevenson
   "The Mysterious Cat"   Vachel Lindsay

217

"The Lamb"   William Blake
"Wynken, Blynken and Nod"   Eugene Field

2. *Antiphonal*—contrasts light voices with heavier ones.
   "Who Has Seen the Wind?"   Christina Rossetti
   "Night"   Sara Teasdale
   "Father William"   Lewis Carroll
   "Choosing Shoes"   Frida Wolfe

3. *Line-a-Child*—small groups of two to four, or a single child, speaks a line or couplet. Selection continued by next speaker. The text should have lines or couplets forming natural separations.
   "Jump or Jiggle"   Evelyn Beyer
   "Mice"   Rose Fyleman
   "The Night Before Christmas"   C. C. Moore

4. *Unison*—Considered to be the *most* difficult of all choral work. Elementary children will have trouble coordinating their voices. Begin with *short*, familiar poems; limericks are a good way to start.

There are other possibilities to consider for choral speaking. Fritz Bell (*Let's Create*, pp. 19–20) presents a useful, sound-effects technique to accompany the tale, "King with the Terrible Temper." Each character in the story has a phrase repeated by the group whenever that character's name is heard (In this tale, children responded "grr" every time they hear "the king"). This technique may be modified for many tales, including ones written by the children.

Songs are also very effective for choral work. They can be used with or without the music. Children might enjoy comparing various singers' interpretations of one song.

For selections that are suitable for choral interpretation, use any poetry anthology or book you have; appropriate selections may be found in almost all collections.

Dramatic Inventing

A. *Rhythm and Movement*

One of the first steps toward a sequential development of skills in creative dramatics comes through work with rhythm and movement.

Guided exploration is a way of introducing movement. Ask children to move their bodies in isolation in as many ways as possible. Hands, feet, knees, elbows and in combination. They soon become aware of the different elements of movement by focusing on space, time, and force or combinations of two or more.

Movement also provides children with an opportunity to express and explore their inner feelings and their reactions to stimuli from outside their immediate environment. They can use both the impressive (arousing emotion) and expressive (responding to feeling) properties of movement.

They can also use their senses to explore and create movement. Visual, auditory, touch, taste and smell, provide many ideas and reactions leading to movement.

218

Imagery may also be used. This imagery may be taken from literature without actually using the literary piece. Creating movement is a major aspect of how many children will interpret literature. It is worthwhile to spend initial time with movement so that when literature is introduced, this prior experience provides the foundation for combining movement with literature.

In movement, children have virtually the same basic equipment. Although some differences appear, children are more equal than in most other skills. A child may have success in movement expression even though he has done poorly in other areas. Movement permits the child to develop his powers of non-verbal expression, allows him to run up against the limitations, and thus encourages the child to see the need for verbal expression.

B. *Improvisation*

Improvising is making up the particulars as one goes along. This creative process is at the heart of oral language development, for any speaker plays the options of the language and makes up new sentences he has never heard before. Whatever their age, improvising helps people respond to others relevantly and spontaneously.

Characterization and *role playing* are directly tied in with improvisation. Characterization, as defined in *Improvisation for the Theater*, is the ability to spontaneously select physical qualities of a chosen character while improvising. *Role playing* is defined as imposing a character, as opposed to creating a role out of the problem.

Implementation

When does a teacher use improvisation, role playing or characterization? Improvisation may be used effectively during short or long periods. Improvisation may be used with large or small groups. One child may improvise in front of a large class. Groups consisting of two, three or four people may improvise in front of an audience or by themselves. Here the children may improvise by imagining they are doing different things in a specified setting.

Small Groups

In small groups the children act out the main actions of the story in their own way, ad-libbing if necessary, making up some of the details and dialogue, and using some details and dialogue that they remember. They improvise their parts. They need not refer back to the source at this point, for they can change and add things to extend and expand the original material. They should feel free to enlarge or eliminate the role of any character or add a character if they like. They can change events in the plot or make up different endings to a given story.

When a small group has decided on one particular version of a story they like, they may decide to put on a performance for a small or large group of people. The children involved will have to listen to each other's dialogue and respond spontaneously to what's been said. This demand for relevant response makes improvised drama a particularly valuable stimulus to language development.

Crowd Scene Improvisation

Large group improvisation attunes children to the presence and actions of many people at once and lets individuals experience the collective energy of large numbers.

Large group improvisations are best done in a group of fifteen to thirty students, which is large enough for each person to feel comfortable in the crowd, yet not so large that the teacher cannot be aware of individual performance. There must be a lot of room in order for the child to express himself or herself freely.

Suggested Crowd Scenes (Props not needed)
—Market place
—Museum
—Carnival
—Airport Terminal

(For further information on both small and large group improvisational settings please consult Moffett—pages 95 & 96)

It is suggested that teachers consult the following major sources for improvisation:

1. ideas presented on activity cards
2. actions to be elaborated from previous reading selections
3. situations abstracted from plays
4. original student ideas from their own direct experiences or *imagined* ones
5. situations that involve issues raised in group discussions

(For further elaboration please see pages 95–100 in Moffett)

C. *Pantomime*

Pantomime is the individual interpretation of an idea, feeling or role through bodily movement without sound. The child invents a series of bodily movements to express a recognizable action, emotion, story or object related to a general idea or concept.

In the child's early school experience, pantomime might begin as a whole-class experience and then become more sophisticated in the higher grades. However, students without a background in pantomiming should not be plunged into advanced activities. It is best to start by forming groups and giving students a list of actions from which each could select an action to perform for the group.

Pantomime Activities
For one student:

1. A teacher in a classroom
2. A yo-yo
3. A mechanical toy
4. A tube of toothpaste
5. A skier going off a jump
6. Getting gum off your shoe
7. Walking in the snow

220

8. Eating a peanut butter sandwich
9. Having an itchy foot, and not being able to take off your shoe

For more than one student:

1. Nails being pounded into a board
2. Children who broke a window
3. Being a baseball team
4. Being a pinball machine
5. Being a rock music group
6. Having a snowball fight
7. Working on an assembly line
8. Acting out a hockey game.

These ideas are just starters. Further suggestions will be found in Gary L. Gerbrandt's *Idea Book for Acting Out and Writing Language*.

Also see *Pantomimes, Charades and Skits* by Vernon Howard for other possibilities.

Guessing Games

Guessing games are activities in which a prescribed situation, scene or set of written directions is enacted with an audience on hand to interpret the action. Guessing should not be held until the act is over.

For One Student

1. Practice a musical instrument.
2. Trim a Christmas tree.
3. Blow a bubble and have it pop in your face; try to get it off.
4. Go grocery shopping; have a list, check off items, put them in basket, go through checkout counter, put groceries in car.

For More Than One Student

1. Eat your lunch, which contains raw celery, and annoy your neighbors with the crunch.
2. Give your parents your report card.
3. Strike out in an important game and the crowd gets nasty.

Charades

Charades is the nonverbal acting out of phrases, titles or quotations before the audience. The audience verbally feeds back the word or phrase that it guesses as a result of the actor's clues. The actor communicates to the audience whether or not its guess is correct.

Success in charades depends upon the use of an agreed upon list of symbolic actions. The teacher should go over each word and its action.

See Gerbrandt's *Idea Book* for a sample list of accepted actions.

D. *Puppetry*

Puppetry is another way of encouraging dramatic play. The puppets themselves serve as an additional stimulus to evoke oral language. For some children, especially the young or shy child, the use of puppets makes speaking seem less threatening. Those who are unwilling to participate may be helped by the cover of anonymity which the puppets provide. If the puppetry experience proves to be positive, these children may be more willing to experiment with other forms of dramatic inventing.

Planning a puppet show stimulates a lot of talk centering on group decisions. Children must decide on which puppets to use, how to make them, who will do the various parts, what type of scenery is needed, etc. This type of communication occurs even before the players are actually dealing with the script.

Puppets may be used informally, without a planned script. These "impromptu" puppet plays are much like improvisation. Puppets may also be used for planned puppet shows, involving use of scripts and rehearsal.

Bibliography

Ainsworth, M. D.; Bell, S. M.; and Stayton, D. J. "Infant-Mother Attachment and Social Development: Socialization as a Product of Reciprocal Responsiveness to Signals." In *The Integration of a Child into a Social World,* edited by M. P. Richards. London: Cambridge University Press, 1974.

Adams, Raymond. "Observational Studies of the Teacher Role." *International Review of Education* 18(1972): 440–59.

Adkins, D. C. *Programs of Head Start Parent Involvement in Hawaii.* A section of the Final Report for 1969–70. ERIC File ED 048 935, 1971.

Almy, Millie. *The Early Childhood Educator at Work.* New York: McGraw-Hill, 1975.

Badger, E. D. *Mothers' Training Program: The Group Process.* ERIC File ED 032 926, 1969.

Barbee, David E., and Bouck, A. J. *Accountability in Education.* New York: Petrocelli Books, 1974.

Barr, Robert D. *The Growth of Alternative Schools: The 1975 ICOPE Report.* Bloomington, Ind.: School of Education, International Consortium for Options in Public Education, 1975. ERIC File ED 106 898.

Becker, Howard S. "Some Problems of Professionalization." *Adult Education* 6(1956): 101–5.

Becker, W. et al. "Factors in Parental Behavior and Personality as Related to Problem Behavior in Children." *Journal of Consulting Psychiatry* 23(1959): 107–18.

Berkowitz, L. *The Development of Motives and Values in the Young Child.* New York: Basic Books, 1964.

Berlin, Irving N. "Professionals' Participation in Community Activities: Is It Part of the Job?" *American Journal of Orthopsychiatry* 41(1971): 494–500.

223

Bibliography

Berlin, R., and Berlin, I. N. "Parent's Role in Education as Primary Prevention." *World Journal of Psychosynthesis* 6(1974): 8–12.

Bernard, Jesse. "Some Psychological Aspects of Community Study." *British Journal of Sociology* 2(1951): 12–30.

Bernier, N. R., and Williams, J. E. *Beyond Belief: Ideological Foundations of American Education.* Englewood Cliffs, N.J.: Prentice-Hall, 1973.

Berthoft, Rowland. *An Unsettled People: Social Order and Disorder in American History.* New York: Harper and Row, 1971.

Biddle, Bruce J. "Role Conflicts Perceived by Teachers in Four English-Speaking Countries." *Comparative Education Review* 14(1970): 30–44.

Biddle, Bruce J., and Thomas, Edwin J. *Role Theory: Concepts and Research.* New York: John Wiley and Sons, 1966.

Braun, Robert J. *Teachers and Power.* New York: Simon and Schuster, 1972.

Braun, S. J., and Edwards, E. P. *History and Theory of Early Childhood Education.* Worthington, Ohio: Charles A. Jones, 1972.

Bromwich, R. M. "Focus on Maternal Behavior in Infant Intervention." *American Journal of Orthopsychiatry* 46(1976): 439–46.

Bronfenbrenner, Urie. "Developmental Research, Public Policy and the Ecology of Childhood." *Child Development* 45(1974): 1–5.

———. *The Experimental Ecology of Human Development.* Ithaca, N.Y.: Cornell University, Department of Human Development and Family Services, 1976.

Broudy, H. S. *The Real World of the Public School.* New York: Harcourt, Brace, Jovanovich, 1972.

Bucher, Rue, and Strauss, Anselm. "Professions in Process." *American Journal of Sociology* 66(1961): 325–35.

Buskin, Martin. *Parent Power.* New York: Walker and Co., 1975.

Butler, A. L. *Current Research in Early Childhood Education.* Washington, D.C.: American Association of Elementary, Kindergarten, Nursery Educators, 1970.

Caldwell, B. M. "A Decade of Early Intervention Programs: What We Have Learned." *American Journal of Orthopsychiatry* 44(1974): 491–96.

———. "Infant Day Care—The Outcast Gains Respectability." In *Child Care—Who Cares,* edited by P. Roby. New York: Basic Books, 1975.

Carson, R. B.; Goldhammer, K.; and Pellegrin, R. J. *Teacher Participation in the Community.* Eugene, Ore.: Center for the Advanced Study of Educational Administration, University of Oregon Press, 1967.

Cazden, C. *Language Research Conference Keynote.* Speech presented at the Department of Learning, Development, and Social Foundations. Cincinnati, Ohio: University of Cincinnati, 20 May 1977.

Chall, J. "Restoring Dignity and Self-Worth to the Teacher." *Phi Delta Kappan* 57(1975): 170–74.

Champagne, D. W., and Goldman, R. M. *Simulation Activities for Training Parents and Teachers as Educational Partners: A Report and Evaluation.* ERIC File ED 048 945, 1971.

Chess, Stella, and Whitbread, Jane. *How to Help Your Child Get the Most Out of School.* New York: Doubleday, 1974.

Christy, Nils. "Relativity in Development." In *Agents of Change: Professionals in Developing Countries,* edited by G. Benveniste and F. Illchman. New York: Praeger, 1969.

Cibulka, James G. *Suburban and Urban Models of Control.* Paper presented at the Annual Meeting of the American Educational Research Association, Washington, D.C., April 1975. ERIC File ED 105 030.

Clark, M. L. et al. *The Responsive Parent Training Manual.* Lawrence, Kansas: H & H Enterprises, 1976.

Clark, W. W. *An Analytic Review of a School-Community Commission.* ERIC File ED 114 918, 1975.

Clausen, John A. *Socialization and Society.* Boston: Little, Brown, 1968.

Clausen, John A., and Williams, Judith R. "Sociological Correlates of Child Behavior." In *Child Psychology, 62nd Yearbook of the National Society of the Study of Education,* edited by H. W. Stevenson. Part 4. Chicago: NSSE, 1963.

Contrell, Donald P., ed. *Teacher Education for a Free People.* Oneonta, N.Y.: Association of Colleges for Teacher Education, 1956.

Datta, Lois E. *Parent Involvement in ECE: A Perspective from the United States.* Paper presented at the Centre for Educational Research Innovation Conference on ECE, Paris, October 1973. ERIC File ED 088 587, 1973.

Donegan, D. I., and Gorman, C. J. *Proposal for Specialist Diploma for Experienced Teachers.* Pittsburgh: University of Pittsburgh, Division of Teacher Development, 1974.

Dreikurs, Rudolph. *Children—The Challenge.* New York: Hawthorne Books, 1964.

Dunkin, M. J., and Biddle, B. J. *The Study of Teaching.* New York: Holt, Rinehart & Winston, 1974.

Edman, Marion. *A Self-Image of Primary School Teachers.* Detroit: Wayne University Press, 1968.

Emelen, Arthur C. et al. "The Myth of Day Care Need." *American Journal of Orthopsychiatry* 43(1973): 35.

Fallon, Berlie J., ed. *40 Innovative Programs in Early Childhood Education.* Belmont, Calif.: Fearon, 1973.

Friedenberg, Edgar. "Critique of Current Practice." In *New Perspectives on Teacher Education,* edited by D. McCarthy. San Francisco: Jossey-Bass, 1973.

Friedman, Robert, ed. *Family Roots of School Learning and Behavior Disorders.* Springfield, Ill.: Charles C Thomas, 1973.

Gallup, G. "Eighth Annual Gallup Poll on Public Attitudes Towards the Public Schools." *Phi Delta Kappan* 58(1976): 187–201.

Garbarino, James. "A Preliminary Study of Some Ecological Correlates of Child Abuse: The Impact of Socioeconomic Stress on Mothers." *Child Development* 47(1976): 178–85.

Gardner, D. B. *The Influence of Theoretical Conceptions of Human Development on the Practice of Early Childhood Education.* ERIC File ED 033 766, 1970.

Gardner, John W. *Self-Renewal: The Individual and the Innovative Society.* New York: Harper and Row, 1965.

Gildea, M. C. L. et al. "Maternal Attitudes and General Adjustment." In *Parent Attitudes and Child Behavior: Proceedings,* edited by J. Glidewell. Springfield, Ill.: Charles C. Thomas, 1973.

Glasser, William. *Schools Without Failure.* New York: Harper and Row, 1969.

————. *The Identity Society.* New York: Harper and Row, 1975.

Goode, W. J. *The Family.* Englewood Cliffs, N.J.: Prentice-Hall, 1964.

Goodlad, John I. *The Dynamics of Educational Change: Toward Responsive Schools.* New York: McGraw-Hill, 1975.

Goodrich, Burton E. *But How Do You Know Their Opinions Count: The Influence of Knowledge about Community Opinions on School Board Opinion.* ERIC File ED 117 813, 1976.

Goodrich, D. W. "Recent Research in Early Family Development and Child Personality." In *Recent Research Looking Toward Preventive Intervention,* edited by R. H. Ojemann. Iowa City: State University of Iowa, 1961.

Goodson, B. D., and Hess, R. D. *Parents as Teachers of Young Children: An Evaluative Review of Some Contemporary Concepts and Programs.* Stanford, Calif.: Stanford University, 1975.

Gordon, Ira J. *Parent Involvement in Compensatory Education.* Urbana, Ill.: University of Illinois Press, 1971.

Gordon, Ira J., and Breivogel, W. F. *Building Effective Home-School Relationships.* Boston: Allyn and Bacon, 1976.

Gordon, Thomas. *Parent Effectiveness Training.* New York: Prenctice-Hall, 1970.

Gray, S. "Home Visiting Programs for Parents of Young Children." Paper presented at the meeting of the National Association for the Education of Young Children, Boston, 1970.

Grodner, B., and Grodner, A. "Children, Parents and Community: The Peanut Butter and Jelly Pre-School." *American Journal of Orthopsychiatry* 45(1975): 251–52.

Groth, N. J. "Mothers of Gifted Children." *The Gifted Child* no. 3, 19(1975): 217–22.

Gump, Paul V. "What's Happening in the Elementary Classroom." In *Research into Classroom Processes: Recent Developments and Next Steps,* edited by J. Westbury and E. Bellack. New York: Teacher's College Press, 1971.

Guskin, Alan E., and Ross, Robert. "Advocacy and Democracy." *American Journal of Orthopsychiatry* 41(1971): 43–57.

Gutek, G. *A History of the Western Educational Experience.* New York: Random House, 1972.

Guthrie, James W., and Craig, P. A. *Teachers and Politics.* Bloomington, Ind.: Phi Delta Kappa Educational Foundation, 1973.

Haberman, Martin. *The Art of Schoolmanship.* St. Louis, Mo.: Warren H. Green, 1970.

Hadley, E. E. "Unrecognized Antagonisms Complicating Business Enterprise." *Psychiatry* 1(1938): 13–31.

Hess, R. D. et al. *The Cognitive Environment of Urban Preschool Children.* Chicago: University of Chicago Press, 1969.

Hill, Charles H. "Teachers as Change Agents." *Clearing House* 45(1971): 424-28.

Holleman, I. T. *The Use of Power Structure in the Attainment of Educational Goals.* ERIC File ED 116 266, 1975.

Holzman, M. "The Verbal Environment Provided by Mothers for Their Children." *Merrill-Palmer Quarterly* 20(1974): 31–42.

Hunt, J. McVicker. *Intelligence and Experience.* New York: Ronald Press, 1961.

————. "Parent and Child Centers: Their Bases in the Sciences." *American Journal of Orthopsychiatry* 41(1971): 13–42.

Illuzzi, S. J., and Milstein, M. M. "Are Teachers and Policy Makers in Conflict Concerning Citizenship Education?" *Phi Delta Kappan* 57(1975): 714–15.

James, Howard. *The Little Victims: How America Treats Its Children.* New York: David McKay, 1975.

Jarvik, L. F.; Eisdorfer, C.; and Blum, J. E., eds. *Intellectual Functioning in Adults: Psychological and Biological Influences.* New York: Springer, 1973.

Jennings, M. K., and Niemi, R. G. "The Transmission of Political Values from Parent to Child." In *Socialization to Politics,* edited by Jack Dennis. New York: John Wiley, 1973.

Johnson, Claudia A., and Katz, Roger. "Using Parents as Change Agents for Their Children: A Review." *Journal of Child Psychology and Psychiatry* 143(1973): 181–200.

Kagan, J. *Birth to Maturity.* New York: John Wiley, 1962.

Kanun, Clara. *Patterns of Response: Faculty Community Service Survey.* Minneapolis: University Continuing Education and Extension Research Department. ERIC File ED 107 882, 1975.

Katz, Fred E. "The School as a Complex Social Organization." *Harvard Educational Review* 34(1964): 428–55.

Kay, A. W. *Moral Development.* New York: Schocken, 1969.

Kerr, Norman D. "The School Board as an Agency of Legitimation." In *The School in Society: Studies in the Sociology of Education,* edited by S. D. Sieber and D. E. Wilder. New York: The Free Press, 1973.

Kilpatrick, W. H. *Education and the Social Order.* New York: Liveright, 1932.

Bibliography

Kimball, Solon T. *Culture and the Educative Process: An Anthropological Perspective.* New York: Teacher's College Press, 1974.

King, B. F. *Inclusion of Parents in Supportive Educational Experiences.* Fort Worth, Tex.: Royal Enterprises, 1972.

Kohl, H. "Community Control. Failed or Undermined?" *Phi Delta Kappan* 57(1976): 370–429.

Landis, J. "A Reexamination of the Role of the Father as an Index of Family Integration." *Marriage and Family Living* 24(1962): 122–28.

Leibowitz, A. "Home Investments in Children." *Journal of Political Economy* 82(1974): 111–31.

Levenstein, P.; Kochman, A.; and Roth, H. "From Laboratory to Real World: Service Delivery of the Mother Child Home Program." *American Journal of Orthopsychiatry* 43(1973): 72–78.

Lickona, Thomas et al. *Project Change.* Cortland, N.Y.: State University of New York, 1972. ERIC File ED 083 140, 1972.

Lille, D. L. *Early Childhood Education.* Chicago: Science Research Associates, 1975.

Litt, Edgar. "Education and Political Enlightenment." *Annals of the American Academy of Political and Social Sciences* 361(1965): 32–39.

Litwak, Eugene, and Meyer, H. J. *School, Family and Neighborhood: The Theory and Practice of School-Community Relations.* New York: Columbia University Press, 1974.

Lurie, Ellen. *How to Change the Schools: A Parents' Action Handbook on How to Fight the System.* New York: Random House, 1970.

Lynch, James, and Pennkett, W. D. *Teacher Education and Cultural Change.* London: Allen & Unwin, 1973.

Lynn, N. B., and Flora, C. B. "Motherhood and Political Participation: The Changing Sense of Self." *Journal of Political and Military Sociology* 1(1973): 91–93.

Macfarlane, J. W. "From Infancy to Adulthood." In *Early Childhood: Crucial Years for Learning,* edited by M. Rasmussen. Washington, D. C.: Association for Childhood Education International, 1966.

McNally, Harold J. *Who's Changing What, and Why?* Speech presented at the National Association of Elementary Principals, April 1974. ERIC File ED 094 453, 1974.

Mattox, B., and Rich, D. "Community Involvement Activities: Research into Action." *Theory into Practice* 14(1977): 29–34.

Mesa, Pete. *Community Involvement and In-Service Teacher Education: The Urban/Rural Approach.* SCIP No. 4. ERIC File ED 117 034, 1976.

Miller, B. "What Parents Can Do for the School." In *Parents and Reading,* edited by Carl B. Smith. Newark, Del.: International Reading Association, 1971, pp. 107–111.

Mok, Paul P. *Pushbutton Parents and the Schools*. New York: Dell, 1964.

Morris, A. G., and Glick, J. "The Pediatric Clinic Playroom: A Classroom for Parents of Preschoolers." *American Journal of Orthopsychiatry* 45(1975): 256–57.

Mosher, D., and Scodel, A. "Relationship Between Ethnocentrism in Child and the Ethnocentrism and Authoritarian Rearing Practices of Their Mothers." *Child Development* 31(1960): 369–76.

Mussen, P. H.; Conger, J. J.; and Kagan, J. *Child Development and Personality*. New York: Harper and Row, 1969.

Newman, Fred M. *Education for Citizen Action*. Berkeley, Calif.: McCutchan, 1975.

Newsweek. "What Parents Can Do to Help." 22 May 1972.

Nolte, M. Chester. "And How Hard Is It to Oust a Bad 'Professional' Teacher." *American School Board Journal* 159(1972): 21–22.

Olim, E. G.; Hess, R. D.; and Shipman, V. D. "Role of Mother's Language Style in Mediating Their Preschool Children's Cognitive Development." *The School Review* 75(1967): 414–24.

Ornstein, Allan C. *Race and Politics in School/Community Relations*. Pacific Palisades, Calif.: Goodyear, 1974.

Parker, Ronald K. *The Preschool in Action: Exploring Early Childhood Programs*. Boston: Allyn and Bacon, 1972.

Pomfret, A. "Involving Parents in Schools: Toward Developing a Social-Intervention Technology." *Interchange* 3(1972): 114–29.

Pungle, Katherine. "1909–1960: A Half Century of the White House Conference." *Child Study* 37(1959–60): 3–8.

Resnik, Henry. *Turning on the System: War in the Philadelphia Public Schools*. New York: Pantheon, 1970.

Ressing, C. "Education's Bad Press." *Phi Delta Kappan* 57(1975): 272–73.

Rheingold, Harriet L. "The Contents of Boys' and Girls' Rooms as an Index of Parent's Behavior." *Child Development* 46(1975): 459–63.

Robinson, D. W. "Citizen Education and the Revolution at the Department of HEW." *Phi Delta Kappan* 58(1976): 355–56.

Roby, P. *Child Care—Who Cares? Foreign and Domestic Infant and Early Childhood Development Policies*. New York: Basic Books, 1973.

Rosen, B. C. "Family Structure and Value Transmission." *Merrill-Palmer Quarterly* 10(1964): 59–76.

Rosencranz, W. A., and Biddle, B. J. "The Role Approach to Teacher Competence." In *Contemporary Research on Teacher Effectiveness*, edited by B. J. Biddle and W. J. Ellena. New York: Holt, Rinehart & Winston, 1964.

Rossi, Peter N. "Community Decision Making." *Administrative Science Quarterly* 4(1957): 415–33.

Ryan, D. G. *Characteristics of Teachers.* Washington, D.C.: American Council on Education, 1960.

Ryan, Joanna. "Early Language Development: Towards a Communicational Analysis." In *The Integration of a Child into a Social World,* edited by M. P. Richards. London: Cambridge University Press, 1974.

Safran, Daniel, director. *State Education Agencies and Parent Involvement: A National Survey of State Legislation and the Policies and Perspectives of State Departments of Education.* Oakland, Calif.: Center for the Study of Parent Involvement, 1974.

Sarason, Seymour. *The Community at the Bargaining Table.* Boston: Institute for Responsive Education, 1975.

Sarbin, Theodore R., and Allen, Vernon L. "Role Theory." In *Handbook of Social Psychology,* edited by C. Lindsay and E. Aronson. Reading, Mass.: Addison-Wesley, 1968.

Schaeffer, Earl S. "Parents as Educators: Evidence from Cross-Sectional, Longitudinal and Intervention Research." In *The Young Child: Reviews of Research,* edited by W. W. Hartup. Vol. 2. Washington, D.C.: National Association for the Education of Young Children, 1972.

————. *Development of Inventories for Assessing Parent and Teacher Interaction and Involvement.* ERIC File ED 105 980, 1974.

Scheinfeld, David R. "On Developing Developmental Families." In *Critical Issues Related to Disadvantaged Children,* edited by E. Grotberg. Princeton, N.J.: Educational Testing Service, 1969.

Schuman, David. *A Preface to Politics.* Lexington, Mass.: D. C. Heath, 1973.

Scribner, Harvey B., and Stevens, Leonard B. *Make Your Schools Work.* New York: Simon and Schuster, 1975.

Seymour, F. J. C. "What Is Professionalism?" In *Professionalization,* edited by Howard M. Vollmer and Donald L. Mills. Englewood Cliffs, N.J.: Prentice-Hall, 1966.

Simon, Anita, and Boyer, E., eds. *Mirrors for Behavior: An Anthology of Classroom Observation Instruments.* Philadelphia: Research for Better Schools, Inc., 1970.

Smethurst, Wood. *Teaching Young Children to Read.* New York: McGraw-Hill, 1975.

Smith, Carol B., ed. *Parents and Reading.* Newark, Del.: International Reading Association, 1971.

Smith, P. G. *Philosophy of Education.* New York: Harper and Row, 1965.

Sparks, Richard K., and Strauss, Hermina. "The Naggingly Logical Question: How Soon Before Those 'Professional' Teachers of Yours Can Be Sued for Malpractice?" *American School Board Journal* 159(1972): 19–21.

Steinfels, M. *Who's Minding the Children? The History and Politics of Day Care in America.* New York: Simon and Schuster, 1973.

Stern, C. et al. *Increasing the Effectiveness of Parents-as-Teachers.* ERIC File ED 048 939, 1970.

Stevens, J. H. "Training Parents as Home Teachers: A Review of Research." Paper presented at the annual meeting of the National Association for the Education of Young Children, Anaheim, California, November 1976.

Streissguth, A. P., and Bee, H. L. "Mother-Child Interactions and Cognitive Development in Children." In *The Young Child: Reviews of Research,* edited by W. W. Hartup. Vol 2. Washington, D.C.: National Association for the Education of Young Children, 1972.

Talbot, Nathan B., ed. *Raising Children in Modern America, Vol. 2: What Parents and Society Should Be doing for Their Schools.* New York: Little, 1976.

Thelen, Herbert. "Profession Anyone?" In *New Perspectives on Teacher Education,* edited by D. McCarty et al. San Francisco: Jossey-Bass, 1973.

Thomas, Alexander et al. *Behavioral Individuality in Early Childhood.* New York: New York University Press, 1971.

Thomas, Alexander, and Chess, Stella. *Temperament and Development.* New York: Brunner/Mazel, 1977.

Thomas, C. T., and Harman, W. *Critical Issues in the Future of American Education.* Menlo Park, Calif.: Stanford Research Institute, Educational Policy Research Center, 1972.

Totten, W. Fred. *The Power of Community Education.* Midland, Mich.: Pendell, 1970.

Tuck, Samuel. "Working with Black Fathers." *American Journal of Orthopsychiatry* 41(1971): 465–72.

Tucker, C. "Language of Mothers and Children." In *A Study of Mothers' Practices and Children's Activities in a Cooperative Nursery School.* New York: Columbia Teachers College, 1940.

Van Meter, E. C. "Citizen Participation in Policy Management." *Public Administration Review* 35(1975): 804–11.

Walberg, H. J., and Marjoribanks, K. "Family Environment and Cognitive Development: 12 Analytical Models." *Review of Educational Research* 46(1976): 527–51.

Wallat, C. "Guidelines for Identifying Appropriate Professional Behavior." *Teacher Education Forum* 4(1976): Issue 18.

Walters, J., and Stinnett, N. "Parent-Child Relationships: A Decade Review of Research." *Journal of Marriage and the Family* 33(1971): 70–111.

Wandersman, L. P. "Stylistic Differences in Mother-Child Interaction: A Review and Reevaluation of the Social Class and Socialization Research." *Cornell Journal of Social Relations* 8(1973): 197–215.

White, Burton L. "Informal Education During the First Months of Life." In *Early Education: Current Theory, Research and Action,* edited by R. D. Hess and R. M. Bear. Chicago: Aldine, 1968.

Wilensky, Harold L. "Problems in Application of Social Science." In *Agents of Change: Professionals in Developing Countries,* edited by G. Benveniste and W. F. Illchman. New York: Praeger, 1969.

Bibliography

Williams, T. M. "Childrearing Practices of Young Mothers: What We Know, How It Matters, Why It's So Little." *American Journal of Orthopsychiatry* 44(1974): 70–75.

Willis, E. *A Study in Child Care (Case Study from Volume II-B): "I'm a New Woman Now."* Day Care Programs Reprint Series. ERIC File ED 051 897, 1970.

Wirt, Frederick, and Kirst, M. W. *The Political Web of American Schools.* Boston: Little, Brown, 1972.

Wittes, G., and Radin, N. "Two Approaches to Group Work with Parents in a Compensatory Preschool Program. *Social Work* 16(1971): 42–50.

Wittes, Simon. *People and Power: A Study of Crisis in Secondary Schools.* Ann Arbor, Mich.: University of Michigan, 1970.

Work, Henry H. "Parent-Child Centers: A Working Reappraisal." *American Journal of Orthopsychiatry* 42(1972): 582–95.

Yarrow, L. J.; Rubenstein, J. L.; and Pedersen, F. A. *Infant and Environment: Early Cognitive and Motivational Development.* New York: Wiley, 1975.

Ziegler, H. *The Political World of the High School Teacher.* Eugene, Ore.: Center for the Advanced Study of Educational Administration, University of Oregon Press, 1966.